DevOps for Web Development

Achieve the Continuous Integration and Continuous Delivery
of your web applications with ease

Mitesh Soni

BIRMINGHAM - MUMBAI

DevOps for Web Development

First published: October 2016

Production reference: 1171016

Published by Packt Publishing Ltd.
Livery Place
35 Livery Street
Birmingham
B3 2PB, UK.
ISBN 978-1-78646-570-2

www.packtpub.com

Credits

Author
Mitesh Soni

Reviewer
Allan Espinosa

Commissioning Editor
Pratik Shah

Acquisition Editor
Smeet Thakkar

Content Development Editor
Amedh Gemraram Pohad

Technical Editor
Vishal Kamal Mewada

Copy Editor
Madhusudan Uchil

Project Coordinator
Judie Jose

Proofreader
Safis Editing

Indexer
Pratik Shirodkar

Graphics
Kirk D'Penha

Production Coordinator
Deepika Naik

About the Author

Mitesh Soni is an avid learner with 9 years' experience in the IT industry. He is an SCJP, SCWCD, VCP, and IBM Urbancode certified professional. He loves DevOps and cloud computing, and also has an interest in programming in Java. He finds design patterns fascinating. He occasionally contributes to `http://etutorialsworld.com`. He loves to play with kids, fiddle with his camera, and capture photographs at Indroda Park. He is addicted to taking good pictures without knowing many technical details. He lives in the capital of Mahatma Gandhi's home state.

"I've missed more than 9000 shots in my career. I've lost almost 300 games. 26 times, I've been trusted to take the game-winning shot and missed. I've failed over and over and over again in my life. And that is why I succeed"

– Michael Jordan

Acknowledgments

To my...wife? (I am not married.)

And my...children? (Read the previous sentence.)

...without whom this book has been completed within 3-4 months. (Else it might have taken a year or two—pun intended!)

On a serious note, I would like to dedicate this book to the kid who taught me to live life freely. Shreyu (Shreyansh, my sister Jigisha's baby boy) showed me the power of innocence and smiles. I've had a completely different perspective of life since he has arrived.

Special thanks to Priyanka Agashe for supporting and encouraging me all the time. Please don't overrate me as a person (all sisters do that). Sorry for being *khadoos*. I would also like to dedicate this book to my father, who is an *avid* reader. He loves books so much that he reads these technical books and notes down all the quotes at the beginning of each chapter. I want to say thanks and share my gratitude for everything I've been blessed with.

I would like to thank my parents, Jigisha and Nitesh, *dada* and *dadi*, Vinay Kher, my teachers, friends, family members, Aakanksha "Akkus" Deshpande (thanks Mother India for always telling me "*koshish karne valo ki haar nahi hoti*"), Hemant and Priyanka, Mihir P and Anupama S, Yohan Wadia, Jyoti-Kanika Bhatia (you always remember special occasions *Jyotiben*), Rohini Gaonkar, Rohan C, Mayur Mothliya, Chintan Solaki, Navrang O, Dharmesh R, and Ashish B.

I am also thankful to Palak S, Subhrajyoti M, Siddharth B, Nirali Kotak, Sumukh, Bijal, Ragni, Beena, Arpan V, Parth S, Bibhas S, Paresh P, Nirav V, Vimal K, Paras Shah, Vishal R, Sharvil P, Sourabh M, Viral I, Vijay Y, Amit R, Manisha Y, Gowri, Saurabh S, Nishchal S, and Kushal V, who have always helped me and made my life easier at specific points in the past year or so. I'm not sure we will ever meet again in life, so I'm trying to thank all those who helped me, knowingly or unknowingly. Apologies if I have missed any names.

About the Reviewer

Allan Espinosa is a DevOps practitioner living in Tokyo. He is an active open source contributor to various distributed systems tools, such as Docker and Chef. He maintains several Docker images for popular open source software that were popular even before the official release from the upstream open source groups themselves. In his career, Allan has worked on large distributed systems containing hundreds to thousands of servers in production. He has built scalable applications on various platforms, ranging from large supercomputing centers in the US to production enterprise systems in Japan. Allan can be contacted through his Twitter handle `@AllanEspinosa`. His personal website at `http://ae spinosa.github.io` contains several blog posts on Docker and distributed systems in general.

I would like to thank my wife, Kana, for her continuous support, which allowed me to spend significant time with this review project.

www.PacktPub.com

For support files and downloads related to your book, please visit www.PacktPub.com.

Did you know that Packt offers eBook versions of every book published, with PDF and ePub files available? You can upgrade to the eBook version at www.PacktPub.com and as a print book customer, you are entitled to a discount on the eBook copy. Get in touch with us at service@packtpub.com for more details.

At www.PacktPub.com, you can also read a collection of free technical articles, sign up for a range of free newsletters and receive exclusive discounts and offers on Packt books and eBooks.

https://www.packtpub.com/mapt

Get the most in-demand software skills with Mapt. Mapt gives you full access to all Packt books and video courses, as well as industry-leading tools to help you plan your personal development and advance your career.

Why subscribe?

- Fully searchable across every book published by Packt
- Copy and paste, print, and bookmark content
- On demand and accessible via a web browser

Table of Contents

Preface

DevOps is part of almost every discussion in the project team, sales team, customer engagements, and so on. Yes, it is a Culture but customers are asking for Proof of Concepts of automation that can be utilized in the Application Life Cycle Management. Even though DevOps is in early stage and it is about changing the existing culture that invites resistance, still it is wise to follow what Socrates said:

"The secret of change is to focus all your energy not on fighting the old, but on building the new."

The reason behind the culture shift is to keep pace with evolution with ongoing revolution, innovations, and business demands in the highly dynamic and competitive market.

Main objective is to manage frequent releases effectively. The faster you fail, the faster you recover. To fail early is far better than to fail at the end of the phase where roll back is very difficult. By automating repetitive processes, you standardized the management of application lifecycle and avoid error prone manual processes.

In this book, we will cover all the key components of DevOps such as Continuous Integration, Cloud Computing, Configuration Management, Continuous Delivery, and Continuous Deployment; how to automate build integration, provision resources in cloud environment such as AWS and Microsoft Azure, use containers for application deployment, use Chef configuration management tool to set up runtime environment for application deployment; deploying web application into virtual machines configured with Chef, AWS Elastic Beanstalk, Microsoft Azure Web Apps, and Docker containers; application monitoring with Nagios, New Relic, and Native Cloud Monitoring features as well.

For Continuous Integration, we have used Jenkins 2. Orchestration of end to end automation is managed by Pipeline.

Jenkins 2 is aimed to claim Continuous Delivery space also. It brings a new setup experience and interesting UI improvements, and Pipeline as code while maintaining backward compatibility with existing Jenkins installations.

What this book covers

Chapter 1, *Getting Started–DevOps Concepts, Tools, and Technologies*, gives insights into DevOps movement, challenges for developers team, challenges for operations team, challenges faced by organizations, waterfall and agile model, importance of collaboration, cloud computing, reason to go for DevOps, benefits of DevOps, DevOps lifecycle, build automation, continuous integration and its best practices, configuration management, continuous delivery and continuous deployment and its best practices, continuous monitoring, and continuous feedback. It also covers an overview of code repositories, Maven, Jenkins 2.0, Chef, AWS, Microsoft Azure, Docker, Nagios, Hygieia DevOps Dashboard, overview of Sample JEE application.

Chapter 2, *Continuous Integration with Jenkins 2*, describes in details on overview of continuous integration, Jenkins 2.0 installation, Java and Maven configuration in Jenkins, creating and configuring build job for Java application with Maven, Dashboard View plugin, managing nodes, email notifications based on build status, and Jenkins and Sonar integration

Chapter 3, *Building the Code and Configuring the Build Pipeline*, covers built-in delivery pipelines using a domain-specific language (DSL), Build Pipeline plugin, deploying a WAR file in the web server.

Chapter 4, *Installing and Configuring Chef*, gives insight on Chef configuration management tool, hosted Chef, installing and configuring Chef workstation, and converging Chef node using Chef workstation.

Chapter 5, *Installing and Configuring Docker*, covers overview of Docker container, understanding difference between virtual machines and containers, installation and configuration of Docker on CentOS, creating the first Docker container, and managing containers.

Chapter 6, *Cloud Provisioning and Configuration Management with Chef*, gives insight into Chef and cloud provisioning, installing knife plugins for Amazon Web Services and Microsoft Azure, and creating and configuring virtual machine in Amazon Web Services and Microsoft Azure.

Chapter 7, *Deploying Application in AWS, Azure, and Docker*, covers prerequisites—to deploy application on Remote Server, use tomcat manager app, deploying application in Tomcat Docker container, deploying application in AWS Elastic Beanstalk, and deploying application in Microsoft Azure web apps.

Chapter 8, *Monitoring Infrastructure and Applications*, provides overview of monitoring, Nagios monitoring tool and quick start on it, installation of Nagios, configuring monitoring of AWS EC2 instance, AWS Elastic Beanstalk monitoring, Microsoft Azure web app service monitoring, Microsoft Azure application insights, and monitoring web application and Tomcat server with New Relic.

Chapter 9, *Orchestrating Application Deployment*, describes in detail how to orchestrate different build jobs for continuous integration, configuration management, continuous delivery and so on. It will cover creating parameterized build jobs for end to end automation, configuring Build Pipeline for Orchestration of Build Job, executing Build Pipeline for Application Deployment Automation, Steps for Deployment in Amazon Elastic Beanstalk (Platform as a Service), Steps for Deployment in Microsoft Azure Web Apps (Platform as a Service), steps to implement end to end automation in Visual Studio Team Server and TFS online for Continuous Integration, Continuous Delivery and Continuous Deployment, and Steps for Deployment in Docker containers. It also gives a brief introduction on Hygieia—DevOps Dashboard and how to run it.

What you need for this book

This book assumes that you are familiar with at least java programming language. Knowledge of core java and JEE is essential considering this book to gain better insight. Having a strong understanding of deployment of a web application in application server such as tomcat will help you to understand the flow quickly.

As application development lifecycle will cover lot of tools in general; it is essential to have some knowledge of repositories such as svn, git and so on. IDE tools such as Eclipse; build tools such as ant and maven. Knowledge of code analysis tools will make job easier in configuration and integration, however it is not extremely vital to perform exercises given in the book. Most of the configuration steps are mentioned clearly.

You will be walked through the steps required to install Jenkins 2, Chef Configuration Management tool. In order to be immediately successful, you will need administrative access to a host that runs a modern version of Linux; CentOS 6.x is what will be used for demonstration purposes. If you are a more experienced reader, then a recent release of almost any distribution will work just as well (but you may be required to do a little bit of extra work that is not outlined in the book). If you do not have access to a dedicated Linux host, a virtual host (or hosts) running inside of virtualization software such as VirtualBox or VMware workstation will work.

For AWS and Microsoft Azure, you can use the free trial and one-month free access respectively. Additionally, you will need access to the Internet to download plugins that you do not already have, as well as an installation of the Jenkins 2.

Who this book is for

This book is especially aimed at technical readers. No prior experience with Continuous Integration, Cloud Computing, Configuration Management, Continuous Delivery, and Continuous Deployment is assumed. You may be novice or experienced with Continuous Integration tools such as Jenkins, Atlassian Bamboo, and so on. In any case, if you may want to bring the visualization of end to end automation to the reality and actually see:

- How to can you extend Continuous Integration to integrate with Configuration Management tools
- How to provision resources in AWS and Microsoft Azure Environment
- How to deploy Web Application in the different Cloud Environments

This book covers Continuous Integration, Cloud Computing, Configuration Management, Continuous Delivery, and Continuous Deployment for Sample Spring based application. The main objective is to see end to end automation and implement it one technology stack that can be extended further based on the understanding.

Additionally, different Cloud service models such as PaaS and IaaS of different Cloud Service Providers such as AWS and Microsoft Azure has been used. Docker containers are also used for application deployment. Infrastructure Monitoring with Nagios, Application Monitoring with New Relic, and native Monitoring features provided by AWS and Microsoft Azure are also covered.

Conventions

In this book, you will find a number of text styles that distinguish between different kinds of information. Here are some examples of these styles and an explanation of their meaning.

Code words in text, database table names, folder names, filenames, file extensions, pathnames, dummy URLs, user input, and Twitter handles are shown as follows: "Now let's edit the `pom.xml` file."

A block of code is set as follows:

```
echo 'Hello from Pipeline Demo'
 stage 'Compile'
 node {
   git url: 'https://github.com/mitesh51/spring-petclinic.git'
   def mvnHome = tool 'Maven3.3.1'
   sh "${mvnHome}/bin/mvn -B compile"
 }
```

When we wish to draw your attention to a particular part of a code block, the relevant lines or items are set in bold:

```
<role rolename="manager-gui"/>
<role rolename="manager-script"/>
<user username="admin" password="cloud@123" roles="manager-script" />
```

New terms and **important words** are shown in bold. Words that you see on the screen, for example, in menus or dialog boxes, appear in the text like this: "Go to **Advanced Project Options**."

Warnings or important notes appear in a box like this.

Tips and tricks appear like this.

Reader feedback

Feedback from our readers is always welcome. Let us know what you think about this book—what you liked or disliked. Reader feedback is important for us as it helps us develop titles that you will really get the most out of. To send us general feedback, simply e-mail feedback@packtpub.com, and mention the book's title in the subject of your message. If there is a topic that you have expertise in and you are interested in either writing or contributing to a book, see our author guide at www.packtpub.com/authors.

Customer support

Now that you are the proud owner of a Packt book, we have a number of things to help you to get the most from your purchase.

Downloading the example code

You can download the example code files for this book from your account at `http://www.packtpub.com`. If you purchased this book elsewhere, you can visit `http://www.packtpub.com/support` and register to have the files e-mailed directly to you.

You can download the code files by following these steps:

1. Log in or register to our website using your e-mail address and password.
2. Hover the mouse pointer on the **SUPPORT** tab at the top.
3. Click on **Code Downloads & Errata**.
4. Enter the name of the book in the **Search** box.
5. Select the book for which you're looking to download the code files.
6. Choose from the drop-down menu where you purchased this book from.
7. Click on **Code Download**.

Once the file is downloaded, please make sure that you unzip or extract the folder using the latest version of:

- WinRAR / 7-Zip for Windows
- Zipeg / iZip / UnRarX for Mac
- 7-Zip / PeaZip for Linux

The code bundle for the book is also hosted on GitHub at `https://github.com/PacktPublishing/DevOps-for-Web-Development`. We also have other code bundles from our rich catalog of books and videos available at `https://github.com/PacktPublishing/`. Check them out!

Downloading the color images of this book

We also provide you with a PDF file that has color images of the screenshots/diagrams used in this book. The color images will help you better understand the changes in the output. You can download this file from `https://www.packtpub.com/sites/default/files/downloads/DevOpsforWebDevelopment_ColorImages.pdf`.

Errata

Although we have taken every care to ensure the accuracy of our content, mistakes do happen. If you find a mistake in one of our books—maybe a mistake in the text or the code—we would be grateful if you could report this to us. By doing so, you can save other readers from frustration and help us improve subsequent versions of this book. If you find any errata, please report them by visiting http://www.packtpub.com/submit-errata, selecting your book, clicking on the **Errata Submission Form** link, and entering the details of your errata. Once your errata are verified, your submission will be accepted and the errata will be uploaded to our website or added to any list of existing errata under the Errata section of that title.

To view the previously submitted errata, go to https://www.packtpub.com/books/content/support and enter the name of the book in the search field. The required information will appear under the **Errata** section.

Piracy

Piracy of copyrighted material on the Internet is an ongoing problem across all media. At Packt, we take the protection of our copyright and licenses very seriously. If you come across any illegal copies of our works in any form on the Internet, please provide us with the location address or website name immediately so that we can pursue a remedy.

Please contact us at copyright@packtpub.com with a link to the suspected pirated material.

We appreciate your help in protecting our authors and our ability to bring you valuable content.

Questions

If you have a problem with any aspect of this book, you can contact us at questions@packtpub.com, and we will do our best to address the problem.

1
Getting Started – DevOps Concepts, Tools, and Technologies

"The first rule of any technology used in a business is that automation applied to an efficient operation will magnify the efficiency. The second is that automation applied to an inefficient operation will magnify the inefficiency."

-Bill Gates

DevOps is not a tool or technology; it is an approach or culture that makes things better. This chapter describes in detail how DevOps solves different problems of the traditional application—delivery cycle. It also describes how it can be used to make development and operations teams efficient and effective in order to make time to market faster by improving culture. It also explains key concepts essential for evolving DevOps culture.

You will learn about the DevOps culture, its lifecycle and key concepts, and tools, technologies, and platforms used for automating different aspects of application lifecycle management.

In this chapter, we will cover the following topics:

- Understanding the DevOps movement
- The DevOps lifecycle—it's all about "continuous"
- Continuous integration
- Configuration management

- Continuous delivery/continuous deployment
- Continuous monitoring
- Continuous feedback
- Tools and technologies
- Overview of a sample Java EE application

Understanding the DevOps movement

Let's try to understand what DevOps is. Is it a real, technical word? No, because DevOps is not just about technical stuff. It is also neither simply a technology nor an innovation. In simple terms, DevOps is a blend of complex terminologies. It can be considered as a concept, culture, development and operational philosophy, or a movement.

To understand DevOps, let's revisit the old days of any IT organization. Consider there are multiple environments where an application is deployed. The following sequence of events takes place when any new feature is implemented or bug fixed:

1. The development team writes code to implement a new feature or fix a bug. This new code is deployed to the development environment and generally tested by the development team.
2. The new code is deployed to the QA environment, where it is verified by the testing team.
3. The code is then provided to the operations team for deploying it to the production environment.
4. The operations team is responsible for managing and maintaining the code.

Let's list the possible issues in this approach:

- The transition of the current application build from the development environment to the production environment takes weeks or months.
- The priorities of the development team, QA team, and IT operations team are different in an organization and effective, and efficient co-ordination becomes a necessity for smooth operations.
- The development team is focused on the latest development release, while the operations team cares about the stability of the production environment.
- The development and operations teams are not aware of each other's work and work culture.

- Both teams work in different types of environments; there is a possibility that the development team has resource constraints and they therefore, use a different kind of configuration. It may work on the `localhost` or in the dev environment

- The operations team works on production resources and there will, therefore, be a huge gap in the configuration and deployment environments. It may not work where it needs to run – in the production environment.

- Assumptions are key in such a scenario, and it is improbable that both teams will work under the same set of assumptions.

- There is manual work involved in setting up the runtime environment and configuration and deployment activities. The biggest issue with the manual application–deployment process is its nonrepeatability and error-prone nature.

- The development team has the executable files, configuration files, database scripts, and deployment documentation. They provide it to the operations team. All these artifacts are verified on the development environment and not in production or staging.

- Each team may take a different approach for setting up the runtime environment and the configuration and deployment activities, considering resource constraints and resource availability.

- In addition, the deployment process needs to be documented for future usage. Now, maintaining the documentation is a time-consuming task that requires collaboration between different stakeholders.

- Both teams work separately and hence there can be a situation where both use different automation techniques.

- Both teams are unaware of the challenges faced by each other and hence may not be able to visualize or understand an ideal scenario in which the application works.

- While the operations team is busy in deployment activities, the development team may get another request for a feature implementation or bug fix; in such a case, if the operations team faces any issues in deployment, they may try to consult the development team, who are already occupied with the new implementation request. This results in communication gaps, and the required collaboration may not happen.

- There is hardly any collaboration between the development team and the operations team. Poor collaboration causes many issues in the application's deployment to different environments, resulting in back-and-forth communication through e-mail, chat, calls, meetings, and so on, and it often ends in quick fixes.

- Challenges for the development team:
    - The competitive market creates on-time delivery pressure.
    - They have to take care of production-ready code management and new feature implementation.
    - The release cycle is often long and hence the development team has to make assumptions before the application deployment finally takes place. In such a scenario, it takes more time to fix the issues that occurred during deployment in the staging or production environment.

- Challenges for the operations team:
    - **Resource contention**: It's difficult to handle increasing resource demands
    - **Redesigning or tweaking**: This is needed to run the application in the production environment
    - **Diagnosing and rectifying**: They are supposed to diagnose and rectify issues after application deployment in isolation

DevOps with the changing times

Time changes everything. In the modern era, customers expect and demand extremely quick response, and we need to deliver new features continuously to stay in business. Users and customers today have rapidly changing needs; they expect 24/7 connectivity and reliability and access services over smartphones, tablets, and PCs. As software product vendors—irrespective of whether in the development and/or operations—organizations need to push updates frequently to satisfy customers' needs and stay relevant. In short, organizations are facing the following challenges:

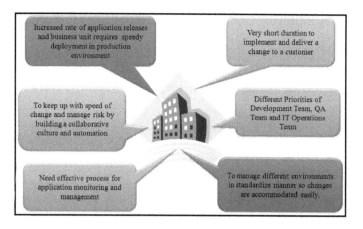

A change in the behavior of customers or market demand affects the development process.

The waterfall model

The waterfall model follows sequential application design process for software development. It comes with good control but lacks revisions. It is a goal based development but without any scope of revision. The waterfall model has long been used for software development:

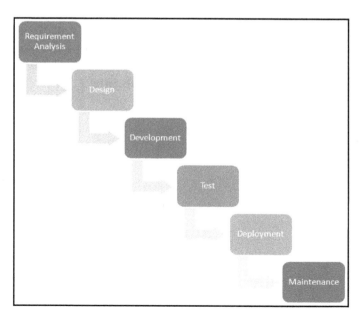

It has its advantages, as follows:

- Easy to understand
- Easy to manage—the input and output of each phase is defined
- Sequential process—order is maintained
- Better control

However, it is only useful in scenarios where requirements are predefined and fixed. As it is a rigid model with a sequential process, we can't go back to any phase and change things. It has its share of disadvantages, as follows:

- No revision
- No outcome or application package until all phases are completed
- Not possible to integrate feedback until all phases are completed
- Not suitable for changing requirements
- Not suitable for long-term and complex projects

The agile model

Inefficient estimation, long time to market, and other issues led to a change in the waterfall model, resulting in the agile model. Agile development or the agile methodology is a method of building an application by empowering individuals and encouraging interactions, giving importance to working software, customer collaboration—using feedback for improvement in subsequent steps—and responding to change in an efficient manner. It emphasizes customer satisfaction through continuous delivery in small interactions for specific features in short timelines or **sprints**.

The following diagram illustrates the working mechanism of agile:

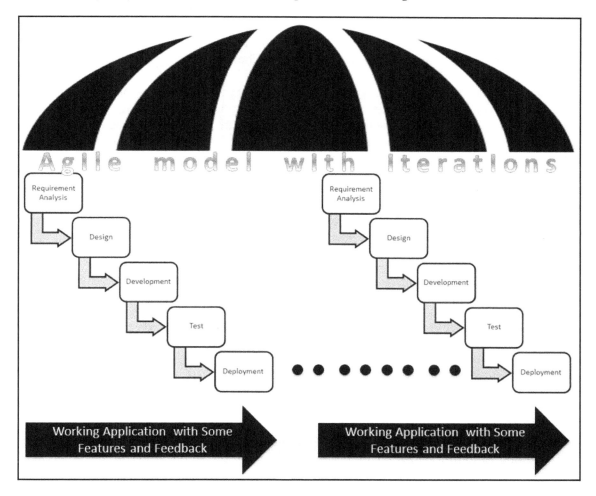

One of the most attractive benefits of agile development is continuous delivery in short time frames or, in agile terms, **sprints**. Now, it is not a one-time deployment, but multiple deployments. Why? After each sprint, a version of the application with some features is ready for showcasing. It needs to be deployed in specific environments for demonstration, and thus, deployment is no longer a one-time activity.

It is very essential from an organization's perspective to meet changing demands of customers. To make it more efficient, communication and collaboration between all cross-functional teams is essential. Many organizations have adopted the agile methodologies.

In such a case, traditional manual deployment processes work as speed barriers for incremental deployments. Hence, it is necessary to change other processes as well along with a change in the application development methodology. One key can't be used for all locks; similarly, the waterfall model is not suitable for all projects. We need to understand that agile is customer focused and feedback is vital. Changes happen based on customer feedback, and release cycles may increase. Just imagine a scenario where inputs are high but input processing is slow. Consider an example of a shoe company where one department prepares shoes and another department works on final touches and packaging. What would happen if the packaging process were slow and inefficient? Shoes would pile up in the packaging department. Now let's add a twist to this situation. What if the shoe-making department brings new machines and improves the process of making shoes? Let's say it makes the shoe-making process two to three times faster. Imagine the state of the packaging department. Similarly, cloud computing and DevOps have gained momentum, which increases the speed of delivery and improves the quality of the end product. Thus, the agile approach of application development, improvement in technology, and disruptive innovations and approaches have created a gap between development and operations teams.

Collaboration

DevOps attempts to fill these gaps by developing a partnership between the development and operations teams. The DevOps movement emphasizes communication, collaboration, and integration between software developers and IT operations. DevOps promotes collaboration, and collaboration is facilitated by automation and orchestration in order to improve processes. In other words, DevOps essentially extends the continuous development goals of the agile movement to continuous integration and release. DevOps is a combination of agile practices and processes leveraging the benefits of cloud solutions. Agile development and testing methodologies help us meet the goals of continuously integrating, developing, building, deploying, testing, and releasing applications. It provides a mechanism for constant feedback from different teams and stakeholders. It also provides transparency in the form of a platform for collaboration across teams, such as business analysts, developers, and testers. In short, agile and DevOps are compatible and increase each other's value.

One of the most popular sayings is that practice makes a man perfect. What if that saying were applied to a production-like environment? It is much easier to repeat the entire process as there are no last minute—surprises, and most of the issues in deployment have already been experienced and dealt with. The development team supports operational requirements such as deploy scripts, diagnostics, and load and performance testing from the beginning of the application—delivery lifecycle, and the operations team provides knowledgeable support and feedback before, during, and after deployment. The remedy is to integrate the testing, deployment, and release activities into the development process. This is done by performing all activities multiple times and making then an ongoing part of development so that by the time you are ready to release your system into production there is little to no risk, because the deployment process has already been rehearsed on many different environments in progressively more production-like environments.

Cloud computing – the disruptive innovation

A major challenge is managing the infrastructure for all environments. Virtualization and cloud environments can help you get started with this. The cloud helps us overcome this hurdle by providing flexible on-demand resources and environments. It provides distributed access across the globe and helps in the effective utilization of resources. The cloud provides a repository of software—tools that can be used on an on-demand basis. We can clone environments and reproduce required versions as and when required. The entire development, test, and production environments can be monitored and managed using the facilities provided by cloud providers. With the advent of cloud computing, it is easy to recreate every piece of infrastructure used by an application using automation. This means that operating systems, OS configuration, runtime environments and configuration, infrastructure configuration, and so forth can all be managed. In this way, it is easy to recreate the production environment exactly in an automated fashion. Thus, DevOps on cloud brings in the best-of-breed solution from both agile development and cloud solutions. It helps in providing a distributed agile environment in the cloud, leading to continuous accelerated delivery.

Why DevOps?

DevOps is effective because of new methodologies, automation tools, agile resources of cloud service providers, and other disruptive innovations, practices, and technologies. However, it is not only about tools and technology-DevOps is more about culture than tools or technology alone.

"Technology is just a tool. In terms of getting the kids working together and motivating them, the teacher is the most important."

-Bill Gates

There is an urgent need of a huge change in the way development and operations teams collaborate and communicate. Organizations need to have a change in culture and have long term business goals that include DevOps in their vision. It is important to establish the pain points and obstacles experienced by different teams or business units and use that knowledge for refining business strategy and fixing goals.

"People always fear change. People feared electricity when it was invented, didn't they? People feared coal; they feared gas-powered engines… There will always be ignorance, and ignorance leads to fear. But with time, people will come to accept their silicon masters."

-Bill Gates

If we identify the common issues faced by different sections of an organization and change the strategy to bring more value, then it makes sense. It can be a stepping stone in the direction of DevOps. With old values and objectives, it is difficult to adopt any new path. It is very important to align people with the new process first. For example, a team has to understand the value of the agile methodology; else, they will resist using it. They might resist it because they are comfortable with the old process. Hence, it is important to make them realize the benefit as well as empowering them to bring about the change.

"Change is hard because people overestimate the value of what they have—and underestimate the value of what they may gain by giving that up."

-James Belasco and Ralph Stayer

Self-dependent teams bring out the best in them when they are empowered. We also need to understand that power comes with accountability and responsibility. Cross-functional teams work together and enhance quality by providing their expertise in the development process; however, it is not an isolated function. Communication and collaboration across teams makes quality way higher.

The end objective of the DevOps culture is continuous improvement. We learn from our mistakes, and it becomes experience. Experience helps us identify robust design patterns and minimize errors in processes. This leads to an enhancement of productivity, and hence, we achieve new heights with continuous innovations.

"Software innovation, like almost every other kind of innovation, requires the ability to collaborate and share ideas with other people, and to sit down and talk with customers and get their feedback and understand their needs."

-Bill Gates

The benefits of DevOps

This diagram covers all the benefits of DevOps:

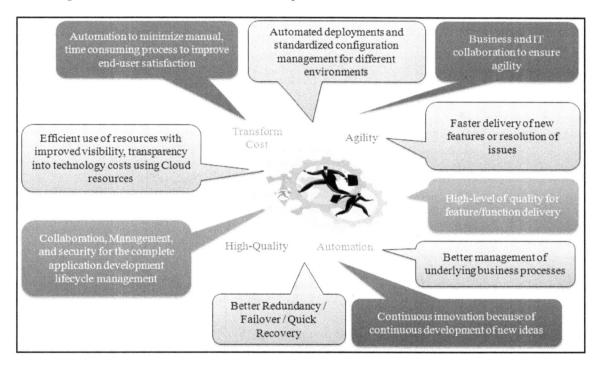

Collaboration among different stakeholders brings many business and technical benefits that help organizations achieve their business goals.

The DevOps lifecycle – it's all about "continuous"

Continuous Integration (CI), **Continuous Testing** (CT), and **Continuous Delivery** (CD) are significant part of DevOps culture. CI includes automating builds, unit tests, and packaging processes while CD is concerned with the application delivery pipeline across different environments. CI and CD accelerate the application development process through automation across different phases, such as build, test, and code analysis, and enable users achieve end-to-end automation in the application delivery lifecycle:

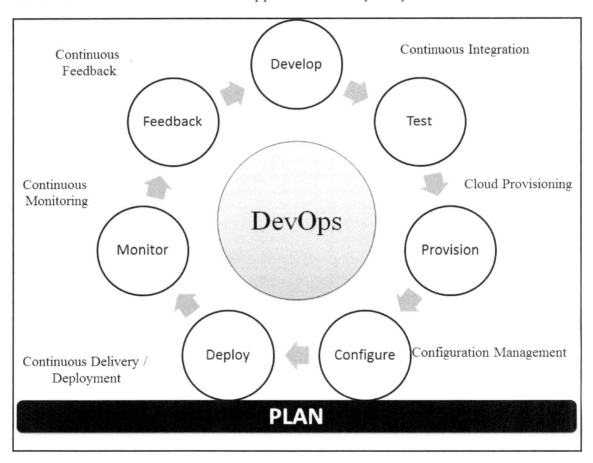

Continuous integration and continuous delivery or deployment are well supported by cloud provisioning and configuration management. Continuous monitoring helps identify issues or bottlenecks in the end-to-end pipeline and helps make the pipeline effective.

Continuous feedback is an integral part of this pipeline, which directs the stakeholders whether are close to the required outcome or going in the different direction.

"Continuous effort – not strength or intelligence – is the key to unlocking our potential"
-Winston Churchill

The following diagram shows a mapping of different parts of an application delivery pipeline with the toolset for Java web applications:

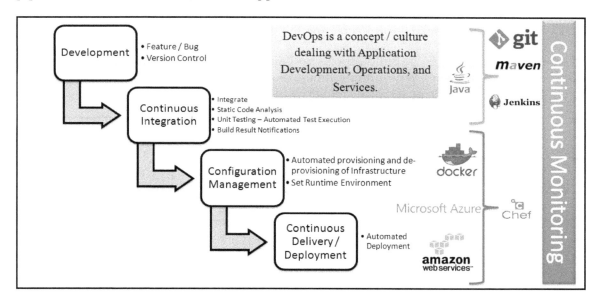

We will use a sample Spring application throughout this book for demonstration purposes, which is why the toolset is related to Java.

Build automation

An automated build helps us create an application build using build automation tools such as Apache Ant and Apache Maven. An automated build process includes the following activities:

- Compiling source code into class files or binary files
- Providing references to third-party library files
- Providing the path of configuration files
- Packaging class files or binary files into WAR files in the case of Java
- Executing automated test cases
- Deploying WAR files on local or remote machines
- Reducing manual effort in creating the WAR file

Maven and Ant automate the build process and make it simple, repeatable, and less error prone as it is a create-once-run-multiple-times concept. Build automation is the base of any kind of automation in the application delivery pipeline:

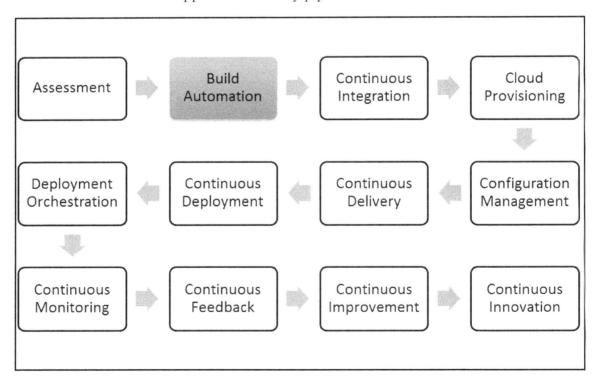

Build automation is essential for continuous integration and the rest of the automation is effective only if the build process is automated. All CI servers, such as Jenkins, Atlassian, and Bamboo use build files for continuous integration and creating their application-delivery pipeline.

Continuous integration

What is continuous integration? In simple words, CI is a software engineering practice where each check-in made by a developer is verified by either of the following:

- **Pull mechanism**: Executing an automated build at a scheduled time
- **Push mechanism**: Executing an automated build when changes are saved in the repository

This step is followed by executing a unit test against the latest changes available in the source code repository:

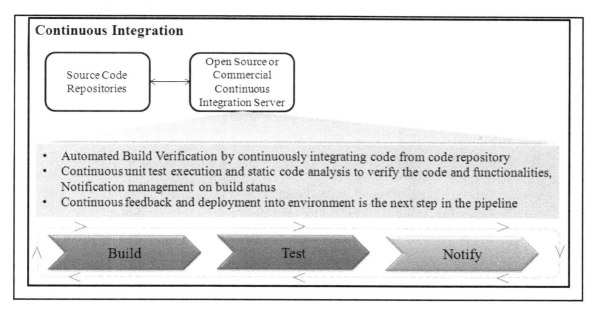

The main benefit of continuous integration is quick feedback based on the result of build execution. If it is successful, all is well; else, assign responsibility to the developer whose commit has broken the build, notify all stakeholders, and fix the issue.

 Read more about CI at `http://martinfowler.com/articles/continuous Integration.html`.

So why is CI needed? Because it makes things simple and helps us identify bugs or errors in the code at a very early stage of development, when it is relatively easy to fix them. Just imagine if the same scenario takes place after a long duration and there are too many dependencies and complexities we need to manage. In the early stages, it is far easier to cure and fix issues; consider health issues as an analogy, and things will be clearer in this context.

Continuous integration is a development practice that requires developers to integrate code into a shared repository several times a day. Each check-in is then verified by an automated build, allowing teams to detect problems early.

CI is a significant part and in fact a base for the release-management strategy of any organization that wants to develop a DevOps culture.

Following are immediate benefits of CI:

- Automated integration with pull or push mechanism
- Repeatable process without any manual intervention
- Automated test case execution
- Coding standard verification
- Execution of scripts based on requirement
- Quick feedback: build status notification to stakeholders via e-mail
- Teams focused on their work and not in the managing processes

Jenkins, Apache Continuum, Buildbot, GitLabCI, and so on are some examples of open source CI tools. AnthillPro, Atlassian Bamboo, TeamCity, Team Foundation Server, and so on are some examples of commercial CI tools.

Best practices

We will now be looking at best practices that can be useful when considering a continuous integration implementation:

- Maintain a code repository such as Git or SVN.
- Check-in third-party JAR files, build scripts, other artifacts, and so on into the code repository.
- Execute builds fully from the code repository: Use a clean build.
- Automate the build using Maven or Ant for Java.
- Make the build self-testing: Create unit tests.
- Commit all changes at least once a day per feature.
- Every commit should be built to verify the integrity of changes.
- Authenticate users and enforce access control (authentication and authorization).
- Use alphanumeric characters for build names and avoid symbols.
- Keep different build jobs to maintain granularity and manage operations in a better way. A single job for all tasks is difficult when trying to troubleshoot. It also helps to assign build execution to slave instances, if that concept is supported by CI server.
- Backup the home directory of the CI server regularly as it contains archived builds and other artifacts too, which may be useful in troubleshooting.
- Make sure the CI server has enough free disk space available as it stores a lot of build-related details.
- Do not schedule multiple jobs to start at the same time, or use a master-slave concept, where specific jobs are assigned to slave instances so that multiple build jobs can be executed at the same time.
- Set up an e-mail, SMS, or Twitter notification to specific stakeholders of a project or an application. It is advisable to use customized e-mails for specific stakeholders.
- It is advisable to use community plugins.

Cloud computing

Cloud computing is regarded as a groundbreaking innovation of recent years. It is reshaping the technology landscape. With breakthroughs made in appropriate service and business models, cloud computing has expanded to its role as a backbone for IT services. Based on experience, organizations improved from dedicated servers to consolidation and then to virtualization and cloud computing:

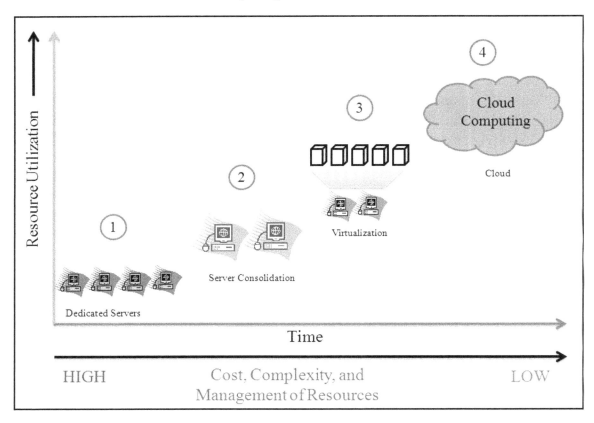

Cloud computing provides elastic and unlimited resources that can be efficiently utilized at the time of peak load and normal load with a pay-per-use pricing model. The pay-as-you-go feature is a boon for development teams that have faced resource scarcity for years. It is possible to automate resource provisioning and configuration based on your requirements, which has reduced a lot of manual effort. For more information, refer to *NIST SP 800-145, The NIST Definition of Cloud Computing* at `http://nvlpubs.nist.gov/nistpubs/Legacy/SP/nistspec ialpublication8-145.pdf`.

It has opened various opportunities in terms of the availability of application—deployment environments, considering three service models and four deployment models as shown in the following diagram:

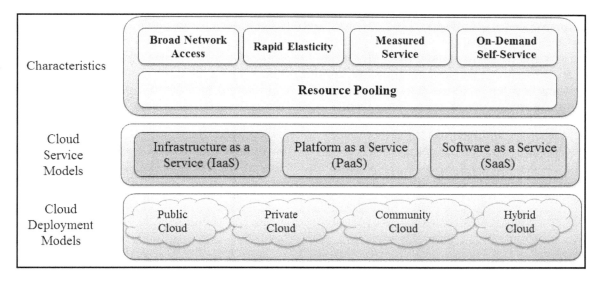

There are four cloud deployment models, each addressing specific requirements:

- **Public cloud**: This cloud Infrastructure is available to the general public
- **Private cloud**: This cloud Infrastructure is operated for and by a single organization
- **Community cloud**: This cloud infrastructure is shared by specific community that has shared concerns
- **Hybrid cloud**: This cloud infrastructure is a composition of two or more cloud models

Cloud computing is pivotal if we want to achieve our goals of automation to inculcate DevOps culture in any organization. Infrastructure can be treated similar to code while creating resources, configuring them, and managing resources using configuration-management tools. Cloud resources play an essential role in the successful adoption of DevOps culture. Elastic, scalable, and pay-as-you-go resource consumption enables organizations to use the same type of cloud resources in different environments. The major problems in all the environments are inconsistency and limited capacity. Cloud computing solves this problem as well as those of economic benefits.

Configuration management

Configuration management(CM) manages changes in the system or, to be more specific, the server runtime environment. Let's consider an example where we need to manage multiple servers with same kind of configuration. For example, we need to install Tomcat on each server. What if we need to change the port on all servers or update some packages or provide rights to some users? Any kind of modification in this scenario is a manual and, if so, error-prone process. As the same configuration is being used for all the servers, automation can be useful here. Automating installation and modification in the server runtime environment or permissions brings servers up to spec effectively.

CM is also about keeping track or versions of details related to the state of specific nodes or servers. It is a far better situation when we nee and update themselves. A centralized change can trigger this, or nodes can communicate with the CM server about whether they need to update themselves. CM tools make this process efficient when only changed behavior is updated, and the entire installation and modification isn't applied again to the server nodes.

There are many popular configuration management tools in the market, such as Chef, Puppet, Ansible, and Salt. Each tool is different in the way it works, but the characteristics and end goal are the same: to bring standardized behavior to the state changes of specific nodes without any errors.

Continuous delivery/continuous deployment

Continuous delivery and **continuous deployment** are used interchangeably more often than not. However, there is a small difference between them. Continuous delivery is a process of deploying an application in any environment in an automated fashion and providing continuous feedback to improve its quality. Continuous deployment, on the other hand, is all about deploying an application with the latest changes to the production environment. In other words, we can say that continuous deployment implies continuous delivery, but the converse isn't true:

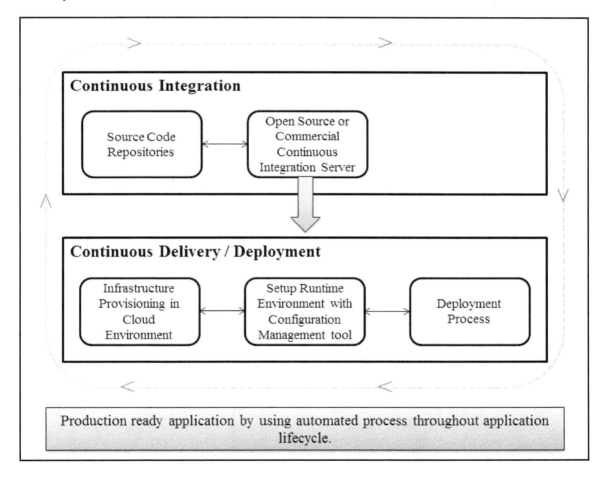

Continuous delivery is significant because of the incremental releases after short spans of implementation, or sprint in agile terms. To deploy a feature-ready application from development to testing may include multiple iterations in a sprint due to changes in the requirements or interpretation. However, at the end of a sprint, the final, feature-ready application is deployed to the production environment. Like we discussed about having multiple deployments in a testing environment even for a short span of time, it is advisable to automate such a thing. Scripts to create infrastructure and runtime environments for all environments are useful. It is easier to provision resources in such environments.

For example, to deploy an application in Microsoft Azure, we need the following resources:

- The Azure web app configured with specific types of resources
- A storage account to store **BACPAC** files to create the database

Then, we need to follow these steps:

1. Create a SQL Server instance to host the database.
2. Import BACPAC files from the storage account to create a new database.
3. Deploy the web application to Microsoft Azure.

In this scenario, we may consider to use a configuration file for each environment with respect to naming conventions and paths. However, we need similar types of resources in each environment. It is possible that the configuration of resources changes according to the environment, but that can be managed in a configuration file for each environment. Automation scripts can use configuration files based on the environment and create resources and deploy an application into it. Hence, repetitive steps can be easily managed by an automated approach, and this is helpful both in continuous delivery and continuous deployment.

Best practices for continuous delivery

The following are some common practices we should follow to implement continuous delivery:

- Plan to automate everything in an application delivery pipeline: Consider a situation where just a single commit only is required to deploy an application in the target environment. It should include compilation, unit test execution, code verification, notification, instance provisioning, setting up runtime environment, and deployment. You must remember to automate:
    - Repetitive tasks
    - Difficult tasks
    - Manual tasks
- Develop and test the newly implemented bug fixes in a production-like environment; it is possible now with pay-per-use resources provided by cloud computing.
- Deploy frequently in the development and test environments to gain experience and consistency.

> *Continuous Delivery: Reliable Software Releases through Build, Test, and Deployment Automation*: `http://martinfowler.com/books/continuousDe livery.html`.
>
> *Continuous Delivery vs Continuous Deployment*: `http://continuousdelivery.com/21/8/continuous-delivery-vs-continuous-deployment/`.
>
> *Continuous Delivery versus Continuous Deploy*: `http://devops.com/215/1/3/continuous-delivery-versus-continuous-deploy/`.

Continuous monitoring

Continuous monitoring is a backbone of end-to-end delivery pipeline, and open source monitoring tools are like toppings on an ice cream scoop. It is desirable to monitor at almost every stage in order to have transparency about all the processes, as shown in the following diagram. It also helps us troubleshoot quickly.

Monitoring should be a well thought-out implementation of a plan and it should a part of each of the component mentioned in the following diagram. Consider monitoring practices for continuous integration to continuous delivery/deployment:

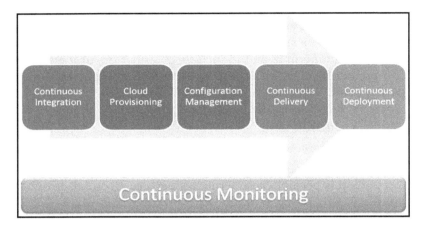

There is a likely scenario where end-to-end deployment is implemented in an automated fashion but issues arise due to coding problems, query-related problems, infrastructure related issues, and so on. We can consider different types of monitoring, as shown in the following diagram:

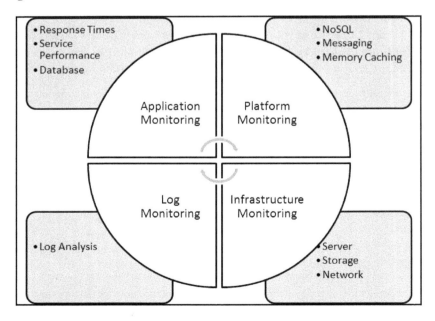

However, there is normally a tendency to monitor only infrastructure resources. The question one must ask is whether it is enough or whether we must focus on other types of monitoring as well. To answer this question, we must have a monitoring strategy in place in the planning stage itself. It is always better to identify stakeholders, monitoring aspects, and so on based on the culture and experience of an organization.

 Continuous monitoring demystified: `http://searchsecurity.techtarget.com/feature/Continuous-monitoring-demystified`

Continuous feedback

Continuous feedback is the last important component in the DevOps culture and provides a means of improvement and innovation. Feedback always provides improvement if it comes from stakeholders who know what they need and how the outcome should be. Feedback from the customer after deployment activities can serve as inputs to developers for improvement, as shown in the following diagram, and its correct integration will make the customer happy:

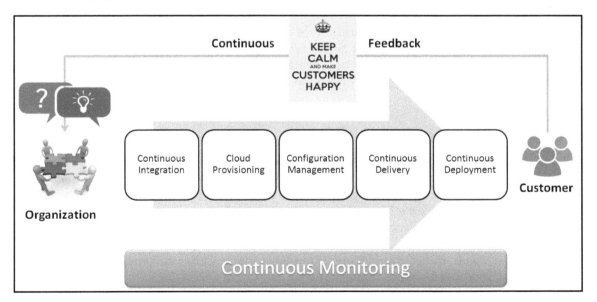

Here, we are considering a situation where a feature implementation is provided to the stakeholders and they provide their feedback. In the waterfall model, the feedback cycle is very long and hence developers may not be aware about whether the end product is what the customer asked for or whether the interpretation of what needs to be delivered was changed somewhere. In agile or DevOps culture, a shorter feedback cycle makes a major difference as stakeholders can actually see the result of a small implementation phase, and hence, the outcome is verified multiple times. If customers are not satisfied, then feedback is available at a stage where it is not very tedious to change things. In the waterfall model, this would've been a disaster as feedback used to be received very late. With time and dependencies, the complexity increases and changes in such situations takes a long time. In addition to this, no one remembers what they wrote 2 months back. Hence, a faster feedback cycle improves the overall process and connects endpoints as well as finding patterns in mistakes, learning lessons, and using improved patterns. However, continuous feedback not only improves the technical aspects of implementation but also provides a way to assess current features and whether they fit into the overall scenario or there is still room for improvement. It is important to realize that continuous feedback plays a significant role in making customers happy by providing an improved experience.

Tools and technologies

Tools and technologies play an important role in the DevOps culture; however, it is not the only part that needs attention. For all parts of the application delivery pipeline, different tools, disruptive innovations, open source initiatives, community plugins, and so on are required to keep the entire pipeline running to produce effective outcomes.

Code repositories – Git

Subversion is a version control system that is used to track all the changes made to files and folders. Using this, you can keep track of the applications being built. Features added months ago can also be tracked using the version code. It is all about tracking the code. Whenever any new features added or new code made, it is first tested and then committed by the developer. Then, the code is sent to the repository to track the changes, and a new version is given to it. A comment can also be made by the developer so that other developers can easily understand changes that were made. Other developers only have to update their checkout to see the changes made.

Advantages

The following are some advantages of using source code repositories:

- Many developers can work simultaneously on the same code
- If a computer crashes, the code can still be recovered as it had been committed in the server
- If a bug occurs, the new code can be easily reverted to the previous version

Git is an open source distributed version control system designed to handle small to enormous projects with speed and efficiency. It is easy to learn and has good performance. It comprises a full-fledged repository and version control tracking capabilities independent of a central server or network access. It was developed and designed by Linus Torvalds in 2005.

Characteristics

The following are some significant characteristics of Git:

- It provides support for nonlinear development
- It is compatible with existing systems and protocols
- It ensures the cryptographic authentication of history
- It has well-designed pluggable merge strategies
- It consists of toolkit-based designs
- It supports various merging techniques, such as **resolve**, **octopus**, and **recursive**

Differences between SVN and Git

SVN and Git are both very popular source code repositories; however, Git is getting more popular in recent times. Let's look at the major differences between them:

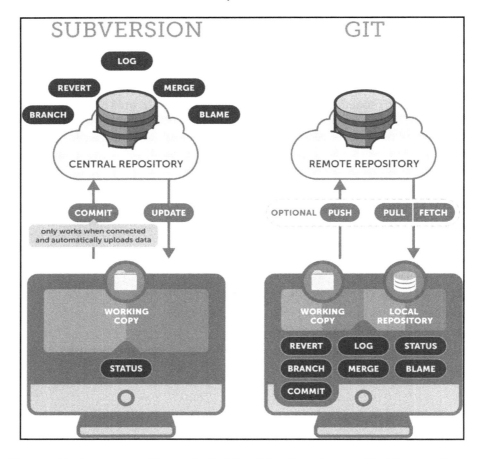

Detailed description of Subversion and Git is illustrated in the following table:

Subversion	Git
Centralized version control system	Distributed version control system
Snapshot of a specific version of the project is available on the developer's machine	Complete clone of a full-fledged repository is available on the developer's machine
Perform operations such as commit, merge, blame, and revert and verifies branch and log from a central repository	Perform operations such as commit, merge, and blame and verifies branch and log from a local repository, along with pull and push operation to a remote repository if the developer needs to share work with others
URLs are used for trunks, branches, or tags: `https://<URL/IP Address>/svn/trunk/AntExample1/`	`.git` is the root of projects, and commands are used to address branches and not URLs: `git@github.com:mitesh51/game-of-life.git`
An SVN workflow: Active feature implementation is developed within branches subdirectories ↓ Feature Implementation is finished ↓ Featured branch subdirectory is merged into trunk ↓ Featureed Branch subdirectory is removed ↓ Trunk-latest stable release of a project	A Git workflow: History of all branches and tags within the .git directory ↓ The latest stable release is available within the master branch ↓ Active feature implementation is developed in separate branch ↓ Featured branch subdirectory is merged into trunk ↓ Featureed Branch subdirectory is removed

File changes are included in the next commit	File changes have to be marked explicitly and only then are they included in the next commit
Committed work is directly transferred to the central repository, and hence, direct connection to the repository must be available	Committed work is not directly transferred to the remote repository and committed to local repository, and to share it with other developers, we need to push it to the remote repository, in which case we need a connection to the remote repository
Each commit gets ascending revision numbers	Each commit gets commit hashes rather than ascending revision numbers
Application directory: .svn db src test toplink-mw war build build.properties build readme warfile	Application directory: .git gameoflife-acceptance gameoflife-build gameoflife-core gameoflife-deploy gameoflife-web infinitest.filters pom README.markdown

.svn directory structure:	.git directory structure:

> .svn
 	
Name
 	
  pristine
  tmp
  entries
  format
  wc
	> .git
	
	Name
	
	  hooks
	  info
	  logs
	  objects
	  refs
	  COMMIT_EDIT
	  config
	  description
	  HEAD
	  index
	  packed-refs

Short learning curve	Long learning curve

Build tools – Maven

Apache Maven is a build tool with the Apache 2.0 license. It is used for Java projects and can be used in a cross-platform environment. It can be also be used for Ruby, Scala, C#, and other languages.

The following are the important features of Maven:

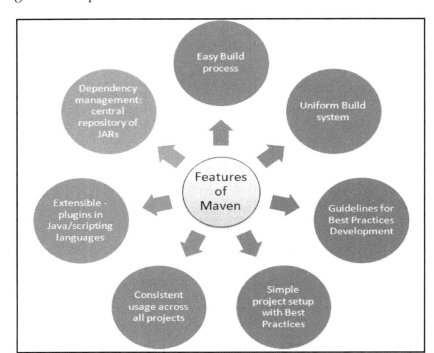

A **Project Object Model** (**POM**) XML file contains information about the name of the application, owner information, how the application distribution file can be created, and how dependencies can be managed.

Example pom.xml file

The `pom.xml` file has predefined targets, such as validate, generate-sources, process-sources, generate-resources, process-resources, compile, process-test-sources, process-test-resources, test-compile, test, package, install, and deploy.

The following is an example of a sample `pom.xml` file used in Maven:

```xml
<?xml version="1.0" encoding="UTF-8"?>
<project xmlns="http://maven.apache.org/POM/4.0.0" xmlns:xsi="http://www.w3.org/2001/XMLSchema-instance" xsi:schemaLocation="
http://maven.apache.org/POM/4.0.0 http://maven.apache.org/maven-v4_0_0.xsd">
    <modelVersion>4.0.0</modelVersion>
    <groupId>org.springframework.samples</groupId>
    <artifactId>spring-petclinic</artifactId>
    <version>1.0.0-SNAPSHOT</version>

    <name>petclinic</name>
    <packaging>war</packaging>

    <properties>

    <dependencies>

    <!-- Maven plugin versions are mentioned in order to guarantee the build reproducibility in the long term -->
    <build>
        <defaultGoal>install</defaultGoal>
        <testResources>
          <testResource>
            <!-- declared explicitly so Spring config files can be placed next to their corresponding JUnit test class  -->
            <directory>${project.basedir}/src/test/java</directory>
          </testResource>
          <testResource>
            <directory>${project.basedir}/src/test/resources</directory>
          </testResource>
        </testResources>
        <plugins>
    </build>
        <reporting>

    <url>demopetclinic</url>
</project>
```

Continuous integration tools – Jenkins

Jenkins was originally an open source continuous integration software written in Java under the MIT License. However, Jenkins 2 an open source automation server that focuses on any automation, including continuous integration and continuous delivery.

Jenkins can be used across different platforms, such as Windows, Ubuntu/Debian, Red Hat/Fedora, Mac OS X, openSUSE, and FreeBSD. Jenkins enables users to utilize continuous integration services for software development in an agile environment. It can be used to build freestyle software projects based on Apache Ant and Maven 2/Maven 3. It can also execute Windows batch commands and shell scripts.

It can be easily customized with the use of plugins. There are different kinds of plugins available for customizing Jenkins based on specific needs for setting up continuous integration. Categories of plugins include source code management (the Git, CVS, and Bazaar plugins), build triggers (the Accelerated Build Now and Build Flow plugins), build reports (the Code Scanner and Disk Usage plugins), authentication and user management (the Active Directory and GitHub OAuth plugins), and cluster management and distributed build (Amazon EC2 and Azure Slave plugins).

 To know more about Jenkins please refer *Jenkins Essentials* `https://www.p acktpub.com/application-development/jenkins-essentials`.

Jenkins accelerates the software development process through automation:

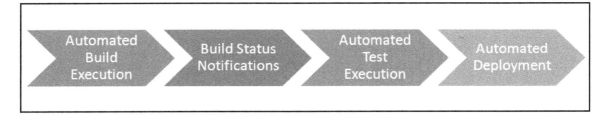

Key features and benefits

Here are some striking benefits of Jenkins:

- Easy install, upgrade, and configuration.
- **Supported platforms**: Windows, Ubuntu/Debian, Red Hat/Fedora/CentOS, Mac OS X, openSUSE, FreeBSD, OpenBSD, Solaris, and Gentoo.
- Manages and controls development lifecycle processes.
- **Non-Java projects supported by Jenkins**: Such as .NET, Ruby, PHP, Drupal, Perl, C++, Node.js, Python, Android, and Scala.
- A development methodology of daily integrations verified by automated builds.

- Every commit can trigger a build.
- Jenkins is a fully featured technology platform that enables users to implement CI and CD.
- The use of Jenkins is not limited to CI and CD. It is possible to include a model and orchestrate the entire pipeline with the use of Jenkins as it supports shell and Windows batch command execution. Jenkins 2.0 supports a delivery pipeline that uses a **Domain-Specific Language** (**DSL**) for modeling entire deployments or delivery pipelines.
- The pipeline as code provides a common language-DSL-to help the development and operations teams to collaborate in an effective manner.
- Jenkins 2 brings a new GUI with stage view to observe the progress across the delivery pipeline.
- Jenkins 2.0 is fully backward compatible with the Jenkins 1.x series.
- Jenkins 2 now requires Servlet 3.1 to run.
- You can use embedded **Winstone-Jetty** or a container that supports Servlet 3.1 (such as Tomcat 8).
- GitHub, Collabnet, SVN, TFS code repositories, and so on are supported by Jenkins for collaborative development.
- **Continuous integration**: Automate build and the test automated testing (continuous testing), package, and static code analysis.
- Supports common test frameworks such as HP ALM Tools, JUnit, Selenium, and MSTest.
- For continuous testing, Jenkins has plugins for both; Jenkins slaves can execute test suites on different platforms.
- Jenkins supports static code analysis tools such as code verification by CheckStyle and FindBug. It also integrates with Sonar.
- **Continuous delivery and continuous deployment**: It automates the application deployment pipeline, integrates with popular configuration management tools, and automates environment provisioning.
- To achieve continuous delivery and deployment, Jenkins supports automatic deployment; it provides a plugin for direct integration with IBM uDeploy.
- **Highly configurable**: Plugins-based architecture that provides support to many technologies, repositories, build tools and test tools; it has an open source CI server and provides over 400 plugins to achieve extensibility.
- **Supports distributed builds**: Jenkins supports "master/slave" mode, where the workload of building projects is delegated to multiple slave nodes.

- It has a machine-consumable remote access API to retrieve information from Jenkins for programmatic consumption, to trigger a new build, and so on.
- It delivers a better application faster by automating the application development lifecycle, allowing faster delivery.

The Jenkins build pipeline (quality gate system) provides a build pipeline view of upstream and downstream connected jobs, as a chain of jobs, each one subjecting the build to quality-assurance steps. It has the ability to define manual triggers for jobs that require intervention prior to execution, such as an approval process outside of Jenkins. In the following diagram **Quality Gates and Orchestration** of **Build Pipeline** are illustrated:

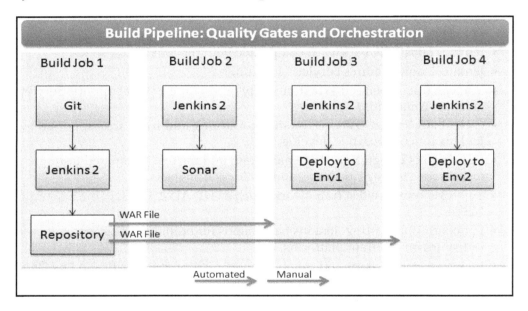

Jenkins can be used with the following tools in different categories as shown here:

Language	Java	.Net
Code repositories	Subversion, Git, CVS, StarTeam	Subversion, Git, CVS, StarTeam
Build tools	Ant, Maven	NAnt, MS Build
Code analysis tools	Sonar, CheckStyle, FindBugs, NCover, Visual Studio Code Metrics, PowerTool	Sonar, CheckStyle, FindBugs, NCover, Visual Studio Code Metrics, PowerTool
Continuous integration	Jenkins	Jenkins

Continuous testing	Jenkins plugins (HP Quality Center 10.00 with the QuickTest Professional add-in, HP Unified Functional Testing 11.5x and 12.0x, HP Service Test 11.20 and 11.50, HP LoadRunner 11.52 and 12.0x, HP Performance Center 12.xx, HP QuickTest Professional 11.00, HP Application Lifecycle Management 11.00, 11.52, and 12.xx, HP ALM Lab Management 11.50, 11.52, and 12.xx, JUnit, MSTest, and VsTest)	Jenkins plugins (HP Quality Center 10.00 with the QuickTest Professional add-in, HP Unified Functional Testing 11.5x and 12.0x, HP Service Test 11.20 and 11.50, HP LoadRunner 11.52 and 12.0x, HP Performance Center 12.xx, HP QuickTest Professional 11.00, HP Application Lifecycle Management 11.00, 11.52, and 12.xx, HP ALM Lab Management 11.50, 11.52, and 12.xx, JUnit, MSTest, and VsTest)
Infrastructure provisioning	Configuration management tool-Chef	Configuration management tool-Chef
Virtualization/cloud service provider	VMware, AWS, Microsoft Azure (IaaS), traditional environment	VMware, AWS, Microsoft Azure (IaaS), traditional environment
Continuous delivery/deployment	Chef/deployment plugin/shell scripting/Powershell scripts/Windows batch commands	Chef/deployment plugin/shell scripting/Powershell scripts/Windows batch commands

Configuration management tools – Chef

Software Configuration Management (SCM) is a software engineering discipline comprising tools and techniques that an organization uses to manage changes in software components. It includes technical aspects of the project, communication, and control of modifications to the projects during development. It also called software control management. It consists of practices for all software projects ranging from development to rapid prototyping and ongoing maintenance. It enriches the reliability and quality of software.

Chef is a configuration management tool used to transform infrastructure into code. It automates the building, deploying, and managing of the infrastructure. By using Chef, infrastructure can be considered as code. The concept behind Chef is that of reusability. It uses recipes to automate the infrastructure. Recipes are instructions required for configuring databases, web servers, and load balances. It describes every part of the infrastructure and how it should be configured, deployed, and managed. It uses building blocks known as resources. A resource describes parts of the infrastructure, such as the template, package, and files to be installed.

These recipes and configuration data are stored on Chef servers. The Chef client is installed on each node of the network. A node can be a physical or virtual server.

As shown in the following diagram, the Chef client periodically checks the Chef server for the latest recipes and to see whether the node is in compliance with the policy defined by the recipes. If it is out of date, the Chef client runs them on the node to bring it up to date:

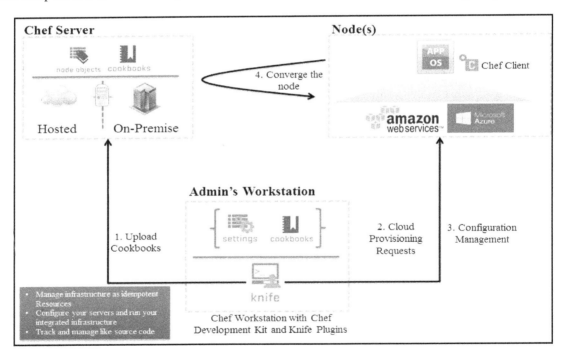

Features

The following are some important features of the Chef configuration management tool:

- The Chef server:
    - It manages a huge number of nodes
    - It maintains a blueprint of the infrastructure
- The Chef client:
    - It manages various operating systems, such as Linux, Windows, Mac OS, Solaris, and FreeBSD
    - It provides integration with cloud providers
    - It is easy to manage the containers in a versionable, testable, and repeatable way
    - Chef provides an automation platform to continuously define, build, and manage cloud infrastructure used for deployment
    - It enables resource provisioning and the configuration of resources programmatically, and it will help in the deployment pipeline in order to automate provisioning and configuration

The following three basic concepts of Chef will enable organizations to quickly manage any infrastructure:

- Achieving the desired state
- Centralized modeling of IT infrastructure
- Resource primitives that serve as building blocks

 To learn more about Chef refer *Learning Chef* `https://www.packtpub.com/networking-and-servers/learning-chef`.

Cloud service providers

AWS and Microsoft Azure are popular public cloud providers right now. They provide cloud services in different areas, and both have their strong areas. Based on the organization's culture and past partnerships, either can be considered after a detailed assessment based on requirements.

The following is a side-by-side comparison:

	AWS	**Microsoft Azure**
Virtual machines	Amazon EC2	Virtual machine
PaaS	Elastic Beanstalk	Azure Web Apps
Container services	Amazon EC2 Container Services	Azure Container Services
RDBMS	Amazon RDS	Azure SQL Database
NoSQL	DynamoDB	DocumentDB
BIG Data	Amazon EMR	HD Insight
Networking	Amazon VPC	Virtual network
Cache	Amazon Elasticache	Azure RadisCache
Import/export	Amazon import/export	Azure import/export
Search	Amazon CloudSearch	Azure Search
CDN	CloudFront	Azure CDN
Identity and access management	AWS IAM and Directory Services	Azure Active Directory
Automation	AWS OpsWorks	Azure Automation

Amazon Web Services: http://aws.amazon.com/.
Microsoft Azure: https://azure.microsoft.com

Container technology

Containers use OS-level virtualization, where the kernel is shared between isolated user-spaces. Docker and OpenVZ are popular open source example of OS—level virtualization technologies.

Docker

Docker is an open source initiative to wrap code, the runtime environment, system tools, and libraries. Docker containers share the kernel they are running on and hence start instantly and in a lightweight manner. Docker containers run on Windows as well as Linux distributions. It is important to understand how containers and virtual machines are different. Here is a comparison table of virtual machines and containers:

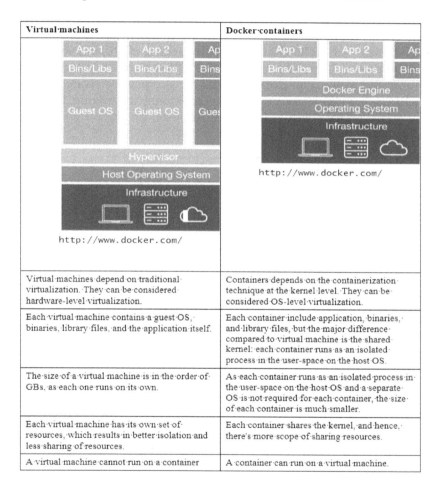

Virtual machines	Docker containers
Virtual machines depend on traditional virtualization. They can be considered hardware-level virtualization.	Containers depends on the containerization technique at the kernel level. They can be considered OS-level virtualization.
Each virtual machine contains a guest OS, binaries, library files, and the application itself.	Each container include application, binaries, and library files, but the major difference compared to virtual machine is the shared kernel: each container runs as an isolated process in the user-space on the host OS.
The size of a virtual machine is in the order of GBs, as each one runs on its own.	As each container runs as an isolated process in the user-space on the host OS and a separate OS is not required for each container, the size of each container is much smaller.
Each virtual machine has its own set of resources, which results in better isolation and less sharing of resources.	Each container shares the kernel, and hence, there's more scope of sharing resources.
A virtual machine cannot run on a container	A container can run on a virtual machine.

 You can download Docker by visiting `https://github.com/docker/dock`
`er`.

Monitoring tools

There are many open source tools available for monitoring resources. **Zenoss** and **Nagios** are two of the most popular open source tools and have been adopted by many organizations.

Zenoss

Zenoss is an agentless and open source management platform for applications, servers, and networks released under the GNU **General Public License** (**GPL**) version 2 and is based on the Zope application server. Zenoss Core consists of the extensible programming language Python, object-oriented web server Zope, monitoring protocol network, graph and log time series data by RRD tool, MySQL, and event-driven networking engine Twisted. It provides an easy-to-use web portal to monitor alerts, performance, configuration, and inventory. In the following diagram, Zenoss features are illustrated:

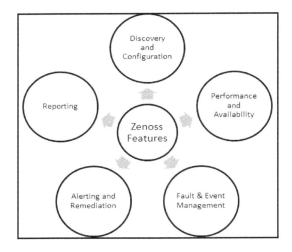

 You can visit Zenoss Core 5 website at http://www.zenoss.org/.

Nagios

Nagios is a cross-platform and open source monitoring tool for infrastructure and networks. It monitors network services such as FTP, HTTP, SSH, and SMTP. It monitors resources, detects problems, and alerts stakeholders. Nagios can empower organizations and service providers to identify and resolve issues in a way that outages have minimal impact on the IT infrastructure and processes, hence ensuring highest adherence to SLAs. Nagios can monitor cloud resources such as compute, storage, and network.

> You can get more information by navigating to Nagios official website at h
> ttps://www.nagios.org/.

Deployment orchestration/continuous delivery – Jenkins

The build pipeline, also called the **deployment** or **application delivery** pipeline, can be used to achieve end-to-end automation for all operations, including continuous integration, cloud provisioning, configuration management, continuous delivery, continuous deployment, and notifications. The following Jenkins plugins can be used for overall orchestration of all the activities involved in end-to-end automation:

- **Continuous integration**: Jenkins
- **Configuration management**: Chef
- **Cloud service providers**: AWS, Microsoft Azure
- **Container technology**: Docker
- **Continuous delivery/deployment**: ssh

End-to-end orchestration: Jenkins plugins

Here is a sample representation of end-to-end automation using different tools:

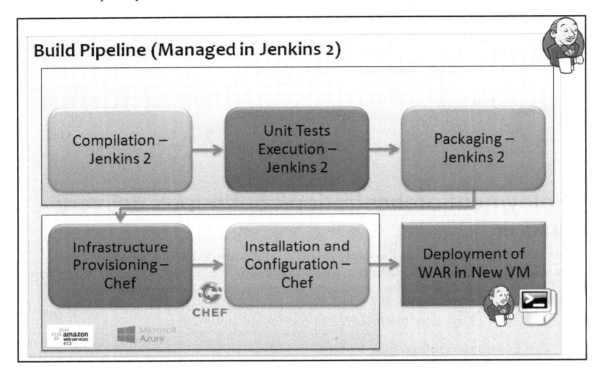

Jenkins can be used to manage unit testing and code verification; Chef can be used for setting up a runtime environment; Knife plugins can be used for creating a virtual machine in AWS or Microsoft Azure; the build pipeline or deployment pipeline plugins in Jenkins can be used for managing deployment orchestration.

From a single pipeline dashboard, we can view the status of all the builds that are configured in the pipeline. Each build in the pipeline is a kind of quality gate. If one build fails, then the execution won't go further. Additional dimensions can be added, such as notification based on compilation failures, unit test failures, or for unsuccessful deployment. The final deployment can be based on some sort of permission from a specific stakeholder. Consider a scenario for a parameterized build or promoted build concept-what should we do? All will be revealed in the chapters to follow!

The DevOps dashboard

One of the most liked components of DevOps culture is the dashboard or GUI that provides a combined status of all end-to-end activities. For automation tools, an easy-to-use web GUI is handy for managing resources. For end-to-end automation in application deployment activities, multiple open source or commercial tools are used. There is a high possibility that a single product may not be used for all activities, for example, Git or SVN as the repository, Jenkins as the CI server, and IBM UrbanCode Deploy as the deployment orchestration tool. In such a scenario, it is easier if there is a single-pane-of-glass view where we can track multiple tools for a specific application.

Hygieia is an open source DevOps dashboard that provides a way to track the status of a deployment pipeline. It basically tracks six different areas as of now, including features (Jira, VersionOne), code repository (GitHub, Subversion), builds (Jenkins, Hudson), quality (Sonar, Cucumber/Selenium), monitoring, and deployment (IBM UrbanCode Deploy). Following is a sample image of configured DevOps dashboard:

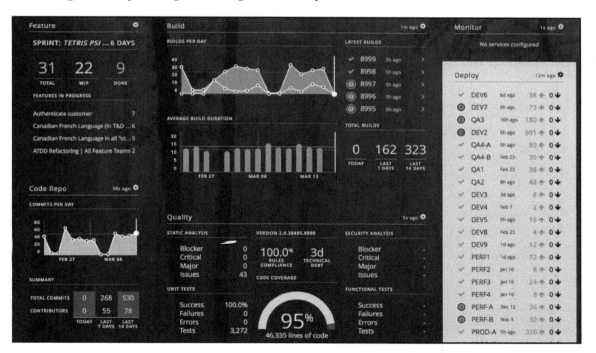

Download Hygieia from here `https://github.com/capitalone/Hygieia`.

An overview of a sample Java EE application

We are going to use PetClinic, available on GitHub. It is a sample spring application with JUnit test cases already written for it.

A sample Spring-based application `https://github.com/spring-projects/spring-petclinic`.

The PetClinic sample application can be used to build simple and robust database-oriented applications to demonstrate the use of Spring's core functionality. It is accessible via web browser:

A few use cases:

- Add a new pet owner, a new pet, and information pertaining to a visit to the pet's visitation history to the system
- Update the information pertaining to a pet and pet owner
- View a list of veterinarians and their specialties, a pet owner, a pet, and pet's visitation history

Once a WAR file is created, we can deploy it in Tomcat or another web server, and to verify it on the `localhost`, visit `http://localhost:8080/petclinic`. You will see something like this:

The list of tasks

These are the tasks we will try to complete in the rest of the chapters:

- Jenkins installation, configuration, UI personalization
- Java configuration (`JAVA_HOME`) in Jenkins
- Maven or Ant configuration in Jenkins
- Plugin installation and configuration in Jenkins
- Security (access control, authorization, and project-based security) in Jenkins
- Jenkins build configuration and execution
- Email notification configuration
- Deploying a WAR file to a web application server
- Creating and configuring a build/deployment pipeline
- Installing and configuring Chef
- Installing and configuring Docker
- Creating and configuring a virtual machine in AWS, Microsoft Azure, and containers
- Deploy a WAR file into a virtual machine and a container
- Configuring infrastructure monitoring
- Orchestrating the application delivery pipeline using Jenkins plugins

Self-test questions

1. Which of the following statements is not related to the development team in a traditional environment?
   - A competitive market creates pressure of on-time delivery of feature or bug fixing
   - Production-ready code management and new feature implementation
   - The release cycle is often long and hence the development team has to make assumptions before the application deployment finally takes place
   - Redesigning or tweaking is needed to run the application in a production environment

2. Which of the following are benefits of DevOps?
   - Collaboration, management, and security for the complete application development lifecycle management
   - Continuous innovation because of continuous development of new ideas
   - Faster delivery of new features or resolution of issues
   - Automated deployments and standardized configuration management for different environments
   - All of these

3. Which of the following are parts of the DevOps culture or application delivery pipeline?
   - Continuous integration
   - Cloud provisioning
   - Configuration management
   - Continuous delivery/deployment
   - Continuous monitoring
   - Continuous feedback

4. Which of the following are by-products of the DevOps culture or application delivery pipeline?
   - Continuous integration
   - Continuous delivery/deployment
   - Continuous monitoring
   - Continuous feedback
   - Continuous improvement
   - Continuous innovation

5. State whether the following statements are true or false:
   - Jenkins and Atlassian Bamboo are build automation tools
   - Apache Ant and Apache Maven are continuous integration tools
   - Chef is a configuration management tool
   - Build automation is essential for continuous integration and the rest of the automation is effective only if the build process is automated
   - Subversion is a distributed version control system
   - Git is a centralized version control system
   - AWS and Microsoft Azure are public cloud service providers

6. Which of the following are cloud deployment models according to NIST's definition of cloud computing?
   - Public cloud
   - Private cloud
   - Community cloud
   - Hybrid cloud
   - All of these

7. Which of the followings are cloud service models according to NIST's definition of cloud computing?
   - Software as a Service
   - Platform as a Service
   - Infrastructure as a Service
   - All of these

8. Which of the following are major components of a Chef installation?
   - Chef server/hosted chef
   - Chef workstation
   - Nodes
   - All of these

Summary

In this chapter, we learned about the difficulties faced by development and operations teams in a traditional environment and how agile development helps in such a scenario. What has changed after the arrival of agile development and what challenges has it brought with its arrival? We have covered the important aspects of the DevOps culture, including continuous integration and continuous delivery. We also covered details regarding cloud computing and configuration management that enhance the processes and help to adopt DevOps culture.

In terms of tools and technologies, we covered a brief overview of SVN, Git, Apache Maven, Jenkins, AWS, Microsoft Azure, Chef, Nagios, Zenoss, and the DevOps dashboard Hygieia.

In the next chapter, we will see how to install and configure Jenkins 2.0 and implement continuous integration using a sample Spring application available on GitHub.

It is the right time to quote *Charles Darwin* as it is relevant in the context of DevOps culture:

> *"It is not the most intellectual or the strongest species that survives, but the species that survives is the one that is able to adapt to or adjust best to the changing environment in which it finds itself."*

2
Continuous Integration with Jenkins 2

"The way to get started is to quit talking and begin doing."
-Walt Disney

Jenkins 2 has arrived. It comes with built-in support for delivery pipelines, improved usability, a new setup experience, and complete backward compatibility with existing Jenkins installations. We will be using Jenkins 2 in this book.

This chapter describes in detail how Jenkins plays an important role in continuous integration. It covers how to prepare a runtime environment for application lifecycle management and configure it with Jenkins. It manages all the aspects of running a build to create a distribution file or **Web application ARchive (WAR)** file for deployment by integrating with a source code repository such as SVN or Git for a sample Java EE application.

You will learn how to install and configure Jenkins, and you'll be able to get end-to-end experience in build job creation and configuration, static code analysis, notifications, Jenkins plugins, and so on as well as details on what exactly the sample application is all about.

In this chapter, we will cover the following topics:

- An introduction to Jenkins
- Installing Jenkins with plugins
- Configuring Java and Maven or Ant in Jenkins
- Creating and configuring a build job for a Java application with Maven
- The dashboard View plugin – overview and usage
- Sending e-mail notifications based on build status
- Integrating Jenkins and Sonar

Introduction

We all know what **Continuous Integration** (**CI**) is, right? It is the first step in our journey.

> *"The journey of a thousand miles begins with one step."*
> *-Lao Tzu, the father of Taoism*

In simple words, CI is a software engineering practice where each check-in made by a developer is verified by either of the following:

- **Pull mechanism**: Executing an automated build at a scheduled time
- **Push mechanism**: Executing an automated build when changes are saved in the repository

This step is followed by executing a unit test against the latest changes available in the source code repository.

Jenkins doesn't need the introduction; it is an open source and one the most popular CI tools available in the market. It helps in automating the repetitive task of CI. Jenkins makes the process effective and transparent.

> *"We are what we repeatedly do. Excellence, then, is not an act, but a habit."*
> *-Aristotle*

The next question you may ask is what makes Jenkins so popular. I already gave you one reason – can you recollect?

Yes, because it is open source. Open source tools come with predefined notions, but the Jenkins community is different, and Jenkins as a tool is quite different.

So, what are the other reasons for the popularity of Jenkins? Let's have a look:

- It is written in Java
- It provides extensibility with over 400 plugins for different integrations, such as the following:
    - Source code management
    - Build triggers
    - Build reports
    - Artifact uploaders
    - External site/tool integrations
    - UI plugins
    - Authentication and user management
    - Cluster management and distributed build
- It supports Java, .NET, Ruby, Groovy, Grails, PHP, Android, and iOS applications
- It is easy to use:
    - It has a simple learning curve
    - The user interface was already simple, and it has now improved after Jenkins 2 has been made available to the general public
- Easy installation
- Easy configuration

Installing Jenkins

Jenkins provides us with multiple ways to install it for all types of users. We can install it on at least the following operating systems:

- Ubuntu/Debian
- Windows
- Mac OS X
- OpenBSD
- FreeBSD
- openSUSE
- Gentoo
- CentOS/Fedora/Red Hat

One of the easiest options I recommend is to use a WAR file. A WAR file can be used with or without a container or web application server. Having Java is a must before we try to use a WAR file for Jenkins, which can be done as follows:

1. Download the `jenkins.war` file from `https://jenkins.io/`.

2. Open command prompt in Windows or a terminal in Linux, go to the directory where the `jenkins.war` file is stored, and execute the following command:

```
java - jar jenkins.war
```

3. Once Jenkins is fully up and running, as shown in the following screenshot, explore it in the web browser by visiting `http://localhost:8080.`:

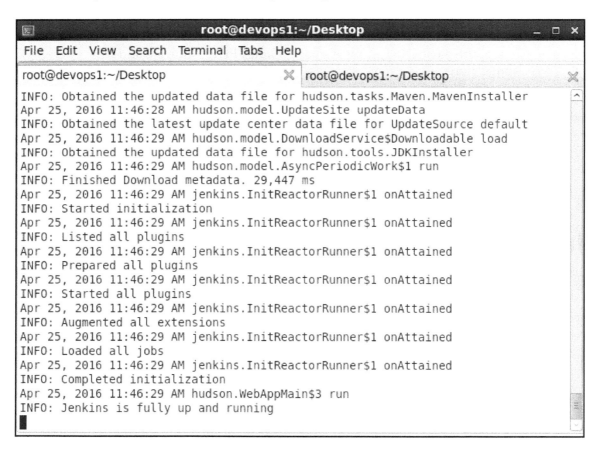

4. By default, Jenkins works on port `8080`. Execute the following command from the command-line:

```
java -jar jenkins.war --httpPort=9999
```

5. For HTTPS, use the following command:

```
java -jar jenkins.war --httpsPort=8888
```

6. Once Jenkins is running, visit the Jenkins home directory. In our case, we have installed Jenkins 2 on a CentOS 6.7 virtual machine.

7. Go to `/home/<username>/.jenkins`, as shown in the following screenshot. If you can't see the `.jenkins` directory, make sure hidden files are visible. In CentOS, press *Ctrl + H* to make hidden files visible:

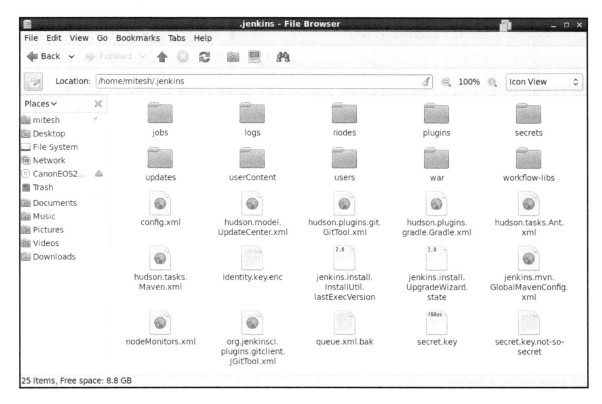

Setting up Jenkins

Now that we have installed Jenkins, let's verify whether Jenkins is running. Open a browser and navigate to `http://localhost:8080` or `http://<IP_ADDRESS>:8080`. If you've used Jenkins earlier and recently downloaded the Jenkins 2 WAR file, it will ask for a security setup.

To unlock Jenkins, follow these steps:

1. Go to the `.Jenkins` directory and open the `initialAdminPassword` file from the `secrets` subdirectory:

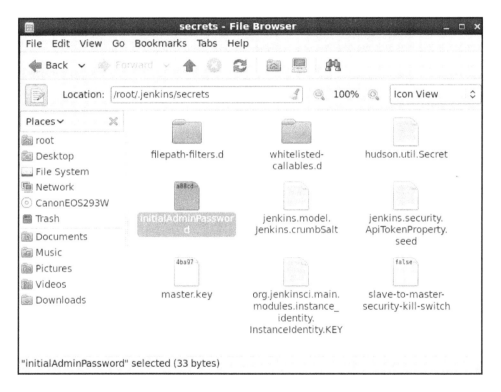

2. Copy the password from that file, paste it in the **Administrator password** box, and click on **Continue**, as shown here:

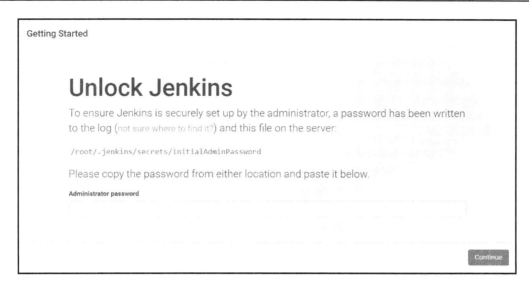

3. Clicking on **Continue** will redirect you to the **Customize Jenkins** page. Click on **Install suggested plugins**:

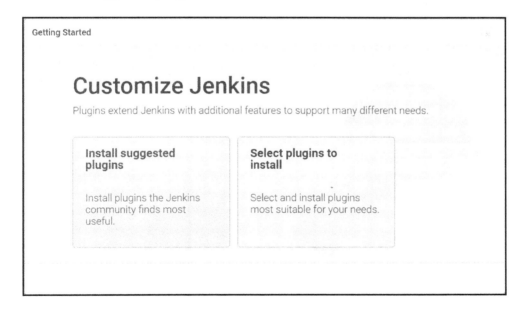

4. The installation of the plugins will start. Make sure that you have a working Internet connection:

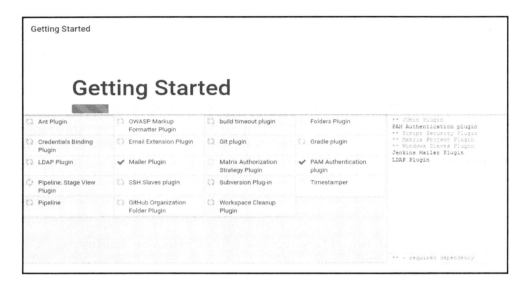

5. Once all the required plugins have been installed, you will see the **Create First Admin User** page. Provide the required details, and click on **Save and Finish**:

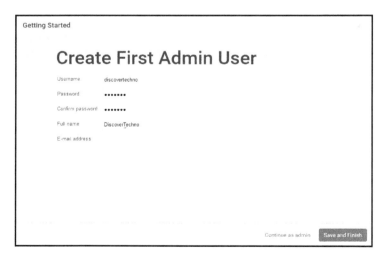

6. **Jenkins is ready!** Our Jenkins setup is complete. Click on **Start using Jenkins**:

 Get Jenkins plugins from `https://wiki.jenkins-ci.org/display/JENK INS/Plugins`.

The Jenkins dashboard

The Jenkins dashboard is a simple and powerful place where we can manage all builds and therefore manage the application delivery pipeline as well. Open `http://<localhost or IP address>:8080` from browser. Log in with the user credentials which we created earlier. It will direct us to the dashboard.

Let's understand the dashboard parameters:

- **New Item**: It is used to create a new build job, pipeline, or build flow in Jenkins 2:

- **Manage Jenkins**: It allows a Jenkins 2 administrator to manage plugins, users, security, nodes, credentials, global tool configuration, and so on:

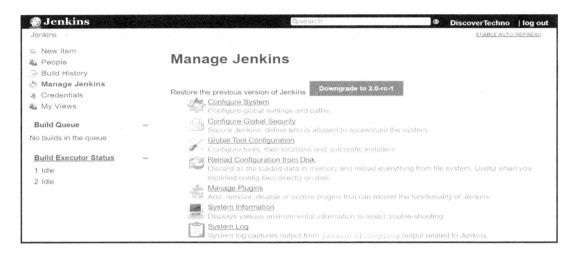

- To know about the existing nodes used for build execution, click on **Manage Nodes**. The **master** node entry will be available. It is the node where Jenkins is installed. We can add multiple slave nodes to distribute the load, which we will learn later in this chapter:

Now that we have installed Jenkins and become familiar with the Jenkins dashboard, the next step is to configure different tools that are used for build execution and create a base for continuous integration.

In the following sections, we will install and configure Java, Maven, and Ant.

Configuring Java and Maven in Jenkins

In Jenkins 2, the **Global Tool Configuration** section has been introduced, which is a good move. All major configurations related to external tools, their locations, and automatic installer tools can be made in this section. Earlier, these configurations were part of **Configure System**, which used to make that page bit cluttered.

Configuring Java

To configure Java, provide a **Name** and the **JAVA_HOME** path, or check **Install automatically** checkbox:

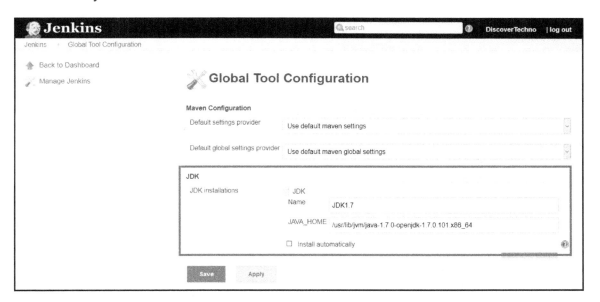

Configuring Maven

To configure Maven, download the Maven installer from `https://maven.apache.org/dow nload.cgi`, and extract it to the directory on your Jenkins virtual machine. In the **Global Tool Configuration** section, provide the **Name** and **MAVEN_HOME** path, or check **Install automatically** checkbox:

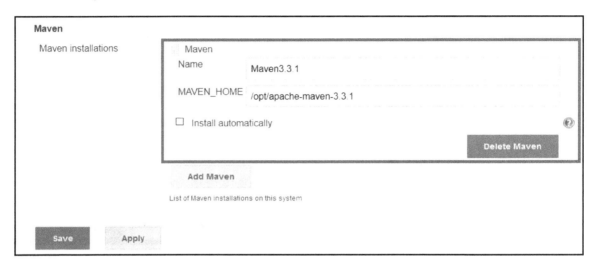

That's it! Our major configuration for running a simple build is done. Now, let's go to the home page of the Jenkins dashboard to create and configure a build job.

Creating and configuring a build job for a Java application with Maven

Jenkins builds configured with Maven understands how Maven works and what is required in terms of execution. It uses `pom.xml` to set up and create package files from the source files.

Now, let's perform steps to create and configure a new build job. Go to the Jenkins dashboard and click on **New Item**.

Go through all the available options of the types of jobs we can create. In our case, let's create a freestyle project for a demo:

1. **Enter an item name**, such as `PetClinic`, then select **Freestyle project**. Now click on **OK** to continue:

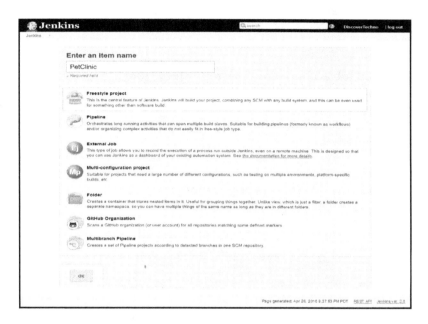

2. Let's verify what this operation does. Go to the Jenkins home directory, and navigate to the `jobs` directory. We can see that the directory has been created for the newly created job with the same name, as shown in the following screenshot:

Configuring and authenticating source code on GitHub

The next step is to configure a source code repository with the build job. We will use the open source Spring application hosted on GitHub, as explained in the previous chapter:

1. After that, we will get a URL similar to `https://github.com/mitesh51/spring-petclinic`.

2. Create a GitHub account and fork repository from `https://github.com/spring-projects/spring-petclinic`.

> Install Git on a virtual machine using the instructions available in the documentation:
> *Getting Started – Installing Git* (`https://git-scm.com/book/en/v2/Getting-Started-Installing-Git`).
> To download a Windows application navigate to `https://git-scm.com/` and click on **Downloads for Windows**.

3. Let's generate a new SSH key to use for authentication. Open a terminal on a CentOS virtual machine with Git installed.

4. Run `ssh-keygen -t rsa -b 4096 -C "your_email@example.com"`, substituting your GitHub e-mail address.

5. Press *Enter* when you are prompted with **Enter file in which to save the key**:

```
[mitesh@devops1 git]$ ssh-keygen -t rsa -b 4096 -C "          @gmail.com"
Generating public/private rsa key pair.
Enter file in which to save the key (/home/mitesh/.ssh/id_rsa):
Enter passphrase (empty for no passphrase):
Enter same passphrase again:
Your identification has been saved in /home/mitesh/.ssh/id_rsa.
Your public key has been saved in /home/mitesh/.ssh/id_rsa.pub.
The key fingerprint is:
d5:48:73:9f:94:d8:02:32:75:5d:c8:08:da:33:2b:5d mitesh.soni83@gmail.com
The key's randomart image is:
+--[ RSA 4096]----+
|        o.*oo*.+.|
|        * *+o*. |
|        . * E.o |
|         o =    |
|         S o    |
|          .     |
|                |
|                |
|                |
+----------------+
[mitesh@devops1 git]$ █
```

6. Add your SSH key to `ssh-agent`:

```
[mitesh@devops1 git]$ ssh-add ~/.ssh/id_rsa
Identity added: /home/mitesh/.ssh/id_rsa (/home/mitesh/.ssh/id_rsa)
[mitesh@devops1 git]$ █
```

7. Verify the newly generated keys in the `.ssh` folder:

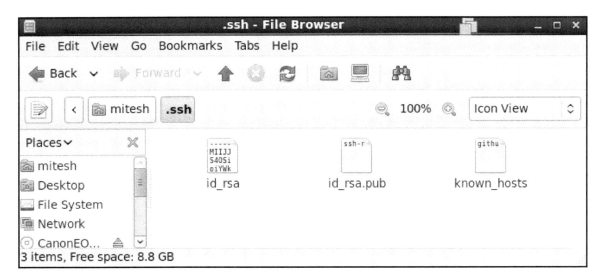

8. To configure your GitHub account to use the new SSH key, add it to your GitHub account. Visit your account page and click on **Settings**:

9. In the **Personal settings** sidebar, click on **SSH and GPG keys**. Click on **New SSH key**:

10. Open `/.ssh/id_rsa.pub` in a text editor your virtual machine, and copy the content:

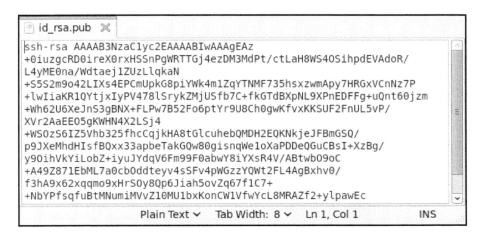

11. In the **Title** field, add a descriptive label for the new key, and paste the copied key content in the **Key** field. Click on **Add SSH key**:

12. Verify the added SSH key:

13. Now, let's verify authentication. Open terminal and type `ssh -T git@github.com` and press *Enter*. If we get successfully authenticated then we can access Git repository without credentials:

Configuring build job

Now that Git authentication is done with, let's configure a PetClinic build job:

1. Click on the **PetClinic** build job on the Jenkins dashboard. Then, click on the **Configure** link. You'll see the following page as shown here:

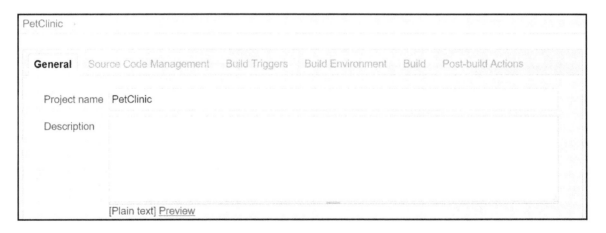

2. Under **Source Code Management**, provide the GitHub URL for the sample Spring project we forked earlier, as shown in the following screenshot:

3. We will configure**Build Triggers** and the **Build Environment** as shown here:

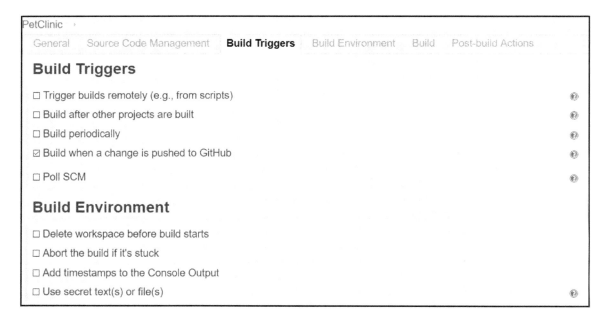

4. Under **Build**, click on **Add build step** and select**Invoke top-level Maven** targets. Select the **Maven Version** we configured in **Global Tools Configuration**. Enter the **Maven target** and click on **Save**:

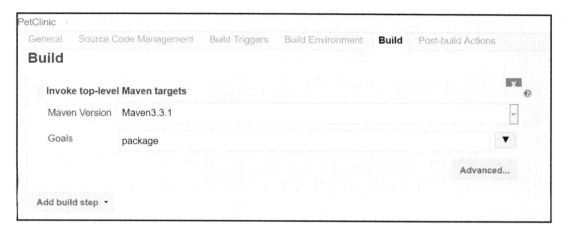

5. Let's manually trigger the build by clicking on **Build Now**. After the build is complete, you'll see this:

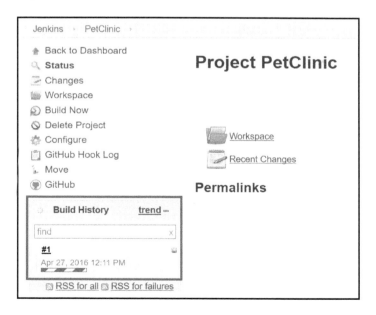

6. Click on the build number, the one with the # symbol. Open **Console Output**. Verify the Git operations executing before **Maven target** execution:

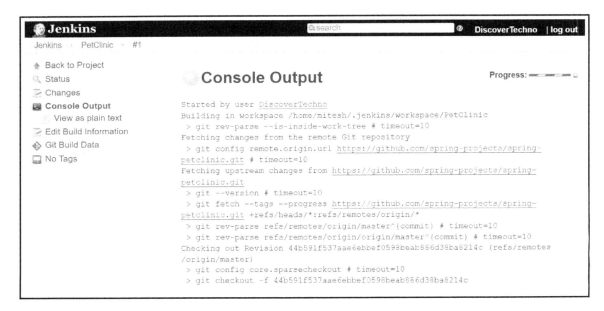

7. Once source code is available in the build job's workspace, the **Maven target** will be executed and the WAR file created. Verify the build status:

```
Jenkins    PetClinic    #1

                              [INFO]
                              [INFO] --- maven-war-plugin:2.3:war (default-war) @ spring-petclinic ---
                              [INFO] Packaging webapp
                              [INFO] Assembling webapp [spring-petclinic] in [/home/mitesh/.jenkins/workspace
                              /PetClinic/target/spring-petclinic-4.2.5-SNAPSHOT]
                              [INFO] Processing war project
                              [INFO] Copying webapp resources [/home/mitesh/.jenkins/workspace/PetClinic
                              /src/main/webapp]
                              [INFO] Webapp assembled in [12697 msecs]
                              [INFO] Building war: /home/mitesh/.jenkins/workspace/PetClinic/target
                              /petclinic.war
                              [INFO] ------------------------------------------------------------
                              [INFO] BUILD SUCCESS
                              [INFO] ------------------------------------------------------------
                              [INFO] Total time: 03:14 min
                              [INFO] Finished at: 2016-04-27T12:15:29-07:00
                              [INFO] Final Memory: 27M/214M
                              [INFO] ------------------------------------------------------------
                              Finished: SUCCESS

                              Page generated: Apr 27, 2016 12:12:13 PM PDT  REST API  Jenkins ver. 2.0
```

8. To verify the workspace of a build job, click on the **Workspace** link. Verify all the files available in the workspace. We can find these files in the .jenkins folder under the specific build job:

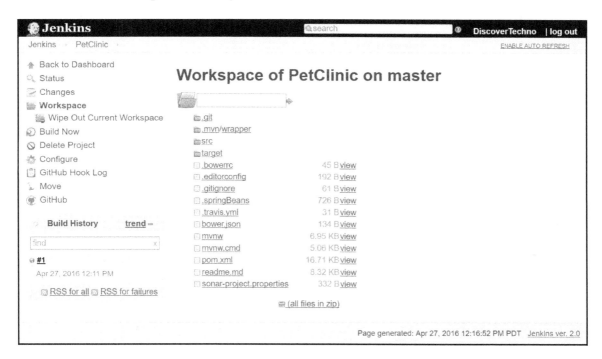

Configuring JUnit

Our sample application has JUnit test cases, and to execute them, we need to configure JUnit-related settings in the build job configuration:

1. Under **Post-build Actions**, select **Publish JUnit test result report**.
2. Provide a path for **Test report XMLs** based on the workspace.

3. Click on **Apply** and then click on **Save**:

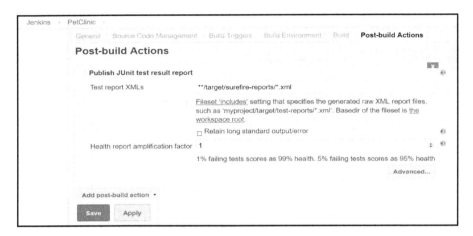

4. After you've configured the JUnit settings for the build, wait for a scheduled build execution, or click on **Build Now**.

5. Verify the build status on the Jenkins dashboard and you will see the **Test Result** link with a small summary. Click on **Test Result**:

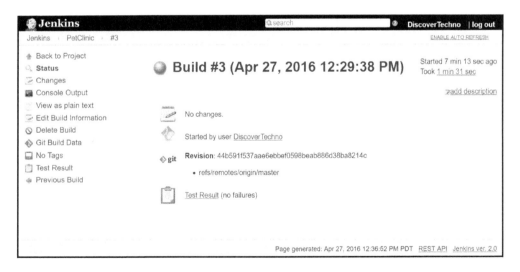

6. Verify all test execution statuses package wise. The page also provides information related to duration and failed test cases:

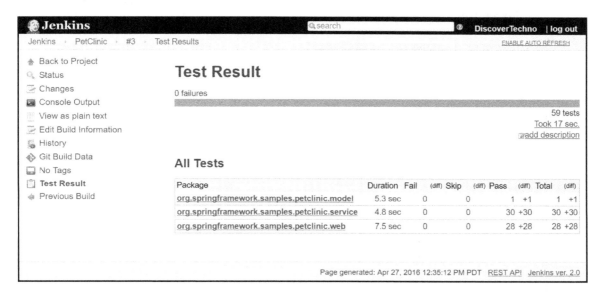

In the next section, we will cover the **Dashboard View** plugin, which helps us customize the view for build jobs.

The Dashboard View plugin – overview and usage

Dashboard View plugin provides a different view implementation, based on a portal kind of layout. We can select different build jobs to be included in a new view and configure different portlets for the view.

To configure it, follow these steps:

1. Go to **Plugin Manager** from **Manage Jenkins,** and click on the **Available** tab. Search for the `Dashboard View` plugin and click on **Install without restart**:

2. Once the plugin has been installed successfully, we can create a new view by clicking on the + sign on the Jenkins dashboard.

3. Enter a **View name**, select the view type, and click on **OK**:

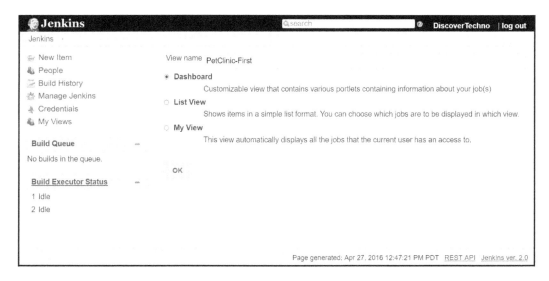

4. Click on **Edit** and configure **Dashboard Portlets** for the top, left column, right column, and bottom. We can use different portlets, such as **Test Statistics Chart**, and **Trends**:

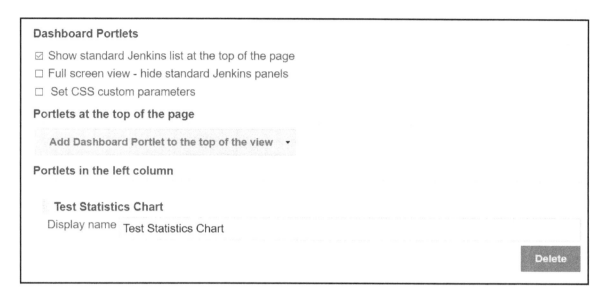

5. Add different portlets based on your requirements into the view, and save it. Here's a sample view:

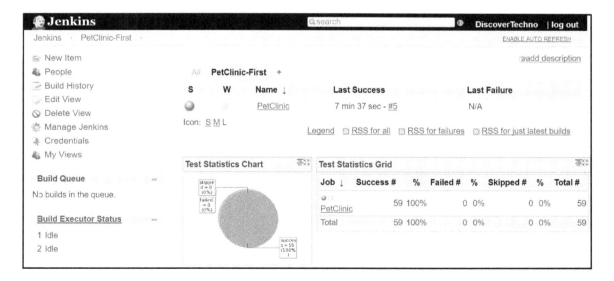

6. After we run the build job, we can find a test result chart on the build job's dashboard as well:

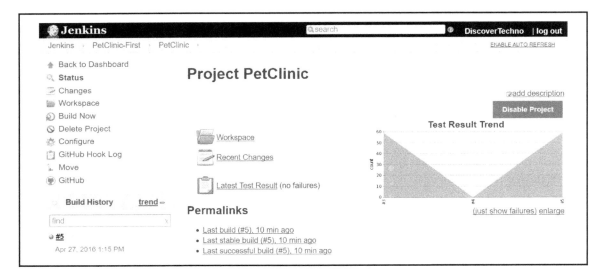

Now, we'll look at one of the most popular features of Jenkins: **distributed builds**.

Consider a scenario where you want different Java applications that need different JDK versions to compile source files. How do you manage such a situation effectively? We'll find out in the next section.

Managing nodes

Jenkins provides a master-slave concept for managing the aforementioned scenarios. We can assign different build jobs to different slaves in the build configuration and use the master-slave system to manage its overall lifecycle. The master node itself can execute the build if a slave node is not configured explicitly in the build job configuration.

There are quite a few reasons for using this feature:

- Build jobs require resources, and they compete for resource availability
- A different runtime environment is required for different build jobs
- It distributes the load across slave nodes

To make things clearer, we need not install Jenkins on the *slave nodes*. We only need to configure the slave nodes properly, which we will now cover.

The only requirements are the following:

- The configurations and runtime environment have to be available on the slave node
- The path needs to be configured correctly on the master node for the runtime environments or tools used by the slave node for execution.

Creating and configuring slave node in Jenkins 2

The following steps will guide you to create and configure a slave node in Jenkins 2:

1. Click on the **Manage Jenkins** link on the Jenkins dashboard:

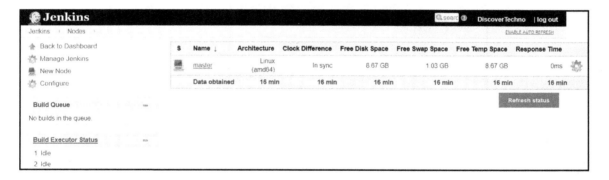

2. Verify that only the **master** node's entry is available. To add a new node, click on **New Node** in the left sidebar. Enter a node name in the **Node name** field, and click on **OK**:

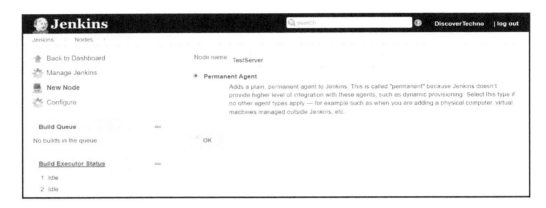

3. The next step is to configure the newly created node. Enter a **Remote root directory**, which will store details related to the build jobs on slave nodes. Give **Labels** to this node. Labels can be used to assign different build jobs to specific slave machines:

4. In Jenkins 2, on creating a slave node and configuring it, if you get the **slaveAgentPort.disabled** error, as shown in the following screenshot, you need to solve it before advancing to the next step:

5. To solve it, go to the **Manage Jenkins** page, and click on the **Configure Global Security** link. Select **Enable security**, and select **Fixed** or **Random** for **TCP port for JNLP agents**, and save the configuration:

6. The next step is to connect the Jenkins slave with the Jenkins master. We will connect the agent to Jenkins using the command-line:

7. Download the `slave.jar` file and put it on the slave node:

8. Execute the following code from the command-line on the slave node:

```
java -jar slave.jar -jnlpUrl
http://192.168.1.34:8080/computer/TestServer/slave-agent.jnlp -secret
65464e02c58c85b192883f7848ad2758408220bed2f3af715c01c9b01cb72f9b
```

```
Command Prompt - java -jar slave.jar -jnlpUrl http://192.168.1.34.8080/computer/TestServer/slave-agent.jnlp -secret 65464e02c58c85b192883f7848...    —    □    ✕

C:\Users\MItesh\Downloads>java -jar slave.jar -jnlpUrl http://192.168.1.34:8080/compu
ter/TestServer/slave-agent.jnlp -secret 65464e02c58c85b192883f7848ad2758408220bed2f3a
f715c01c9b01cb72f9b
May 04, 2016 5:30:44 PM hudson.remoting.jnlp.Main createEngine
INFO: Setting up slave: TestServer
May 04, 2016 5:30:44 PM hudson.remoting.jnlp.Main$CuiListener <init>
INFO: Jenkins agent is running in headless mode.
May 04, 2016 5:30:44 PM hudson.remoting.jnlp.Main$CuiListener status
INFO: Locating server among [http://192.168.1.34:8080/]
May 04, 2016 5:30:44 PM hudson.remoting.jnlp.Main$CuiListener status
INFO: Handshaking
May 04, 2016 5:30:44 PM hudson.remoting.jnlp.Main$CuiListener status
INFO: Connecting to 192.168.1.34:44559
May 04, 2016 5:30:44 PM hudson.remoting.jnlp.Main$CuiListener status
INFO: Trying protocol: JNLP3-connect
May 04, 2016 5:30:45 PM hudson.remoting.jnlp.Main$CuiListener status
INFO: Server didn't accept the handshake: Unknown protocol:Protocol:JNLP3-connect
May 04, 2016 5:30:45 PM hudson.remoting.jnlp.Main$CuiListener status
INFO: Connecting to 192.168.1.34:44559
May 04, 2016 5:30:45 PM hudson.remoting.jnlp.Main$CuiListener status
INFO: Trying protocol: JNLP2-connect
May 04, 2016 5:30:45 PM hudson.remoting.jnlp.Main$CuiListener status
INFO: Connected
```

9. Verify the status of the slave node from the Jenkins dashboard:

Agent TestServer (TestServer)

Connected via JNLP agent.

Created by DiscoverTechno

Labels

WindowsNode

Projects tied to TestServer

None

10. Now, we can see two nodes in the Jenkins dashboard:

Configuring the build job for master and slave node

The following steps will guide you to configure build jobs for master and slave nodes:

1. To configure the build job to run on the master, open its build configuration, and in **General** section, select **Restrict where this project can be run**.

2. In **Label Expression**, enter the label of the `Master` node:

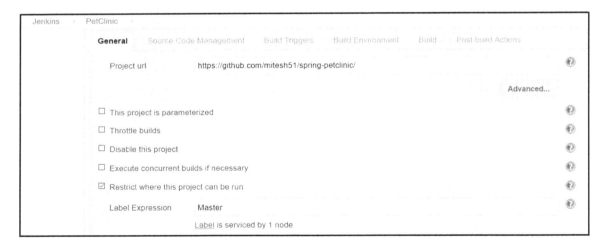

3. To configure the build job to run on the slave node, enter the label of the slave node in **Label Expression**. We can also configure the **JDK** or some other required path for build execution:

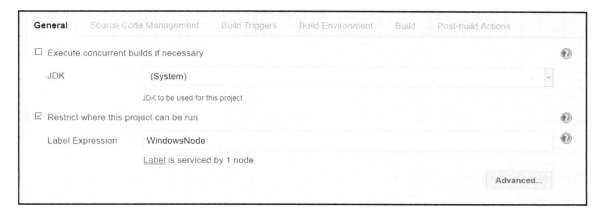

4. To configure tools specific to the slave node, click on **Configure** in the **Manage Nodes** section. In **Node Properties**, configure **Tool Locations** for the slave node, as shown in the following screenshot:

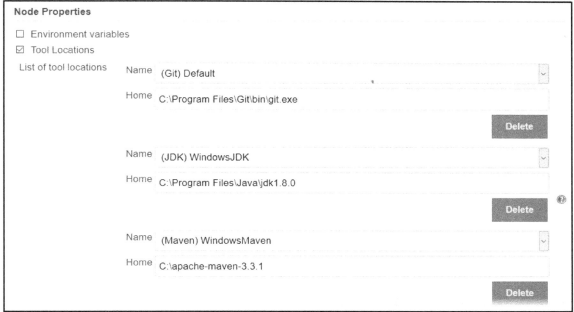

In the next section, we will see how to configure e-mail notifications.

Sending e-mail notifications based on build status

"Failure is simply the opportunity to begin again, this time more intelligently."
-Henry Ford

However, it is extremely vital to be aware of failure or at least to know when things fail so we can fix them and get rid of issues.

Notifications are always helpful in case of failures. Consider a scenario where a build failure or test case failure has to be notified to a specific set of stakeholders. In such a situation, it is desirable to have e-mail notifications.

We will use G-mail configuration for setting up e-mail notifications. Follow these steps:

1. Go to `https://www.google.com/settings/u/1/security/lesssecureapps` and click on **Turn on Access for less secure apps**, as shown here, to send e-mail notifications from Jenkins 2:

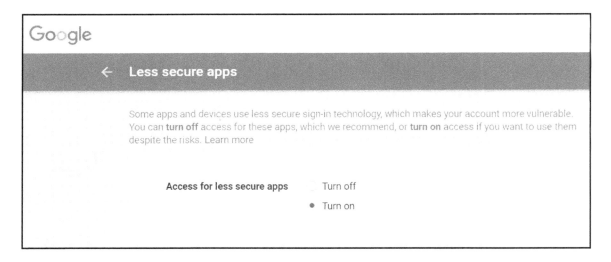

2. Do the following from the Jenkins dashboard:

1. Click on **Manage Jenkins,** and go to the **Configure System** section.

2. Go to the **E-mail Notification** subsection and enter the appropriate values for **SMTP Server** and **Default user e-mail suffix.**

3. Check the **Use SMTP Authentication** box, and enter a **User Name** and **Password.**

4. Check the **Use SSL** checkbox, and enter details for **SMTP Port** and **Reply-To Address.**

5. Finally, select **Test configuration by sending test e-mail.** If you set everything up correctly, you will see a message saying **Email was successfully sent**:

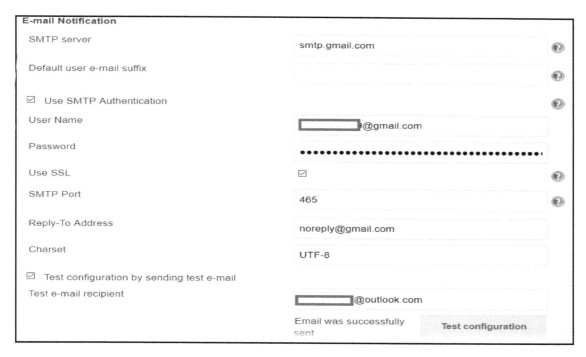

3. To verify e-mail notifications, simulate a failure in a build job. Open any build job and click on **Configure**.

4. In **Post-build Actions**, click on **Add Post-build Action** and configure it like this:

1. Select **E-mail Notification**.

2. Enter a list of **Recipients**.

3. Select **Send e-mail for every unstable build** and **Send separate e-mails to individuals who broke the build**:

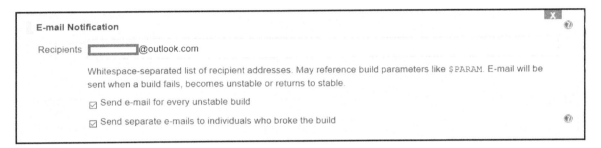

In our case, we execute a compile goal against the Maven build and we wanted to publish a JUnit test result to simulate a failure. We can see that the compilation of files is successful but the post-build action fails, and it triggers an e-mail notification based on the configuration:

```
[INFO] --------------------------------------------------------------
[INFO] BUILD SUCCESS
[INFO] --------------------------------------------------------------
[INFO] Total time: 21.332 s
[INFO] Finished at: 2016-04-28T19:44:26-07:00
[INFO] Final Memory: 25M/134M
[INFO] --------------------------------------------------------------
Recording test results
ERROR: Step 'Publish JUnit test result report' failed: No test report files were
found. Configuration error?
Sending e-mails to: [        ]@outlook.com
Finished: FAILURE
```

The following is the e-mail received. It contains a stack trace of the execution:

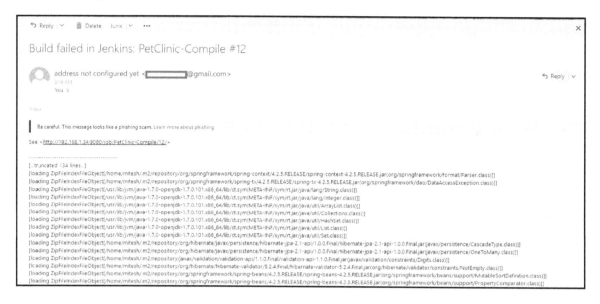

Consider a scenario where you want to send customized content in the e-mail. How would you achieve that?

Configure **Extended E-mail Notification**. Try it as an exercise.

Integrating Jenkins and Sonar

SonarQube is an open source tool for managing the code quality of an application. It manages seven axes of code quality, such as architecture and design, duplications, unit tests, potential bugs, complexities, coding rules, and comments. It covers programming languages and formats such as ABAP, C/C++, C#, COBOL, CSS, Erlang, Flex/ActionScript, Groovy, Java, JavaScript, JSON, Objective-C, PHP, PL/I, PL/SQL, Puppet, Python, RPG, Swift, VB.NET, Visual Basic 6, and XML. One of the most striking features is its extensibility. It is easy to cover new languages and add rule engines using an extension mechanism in the form of plugins.

To install the SonarQube plugin, follow these steps:

1. Go to **Manage Jenkins**, and click on **Manage Plugins**. Click on **Available**. Search for the **SonarQube** plugin, and install it by clicking on **Install without restart**:

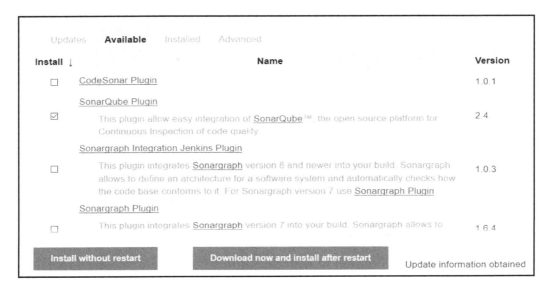

2. Download Sonar from `http://www.sonarqube.org/downloads/`.
3. Extract the installable directory from the ZIP file and go into the `bin` subdirectory.
4. Select the installable directory based on your OS, and run the `StartSona.*` file, as shown here:

```
D:\##DevOps Book\Installables\sonarqube-5.4\bin\windows-x86-64>StartSonar.bat
wrapper  | --> Wrapper Started as Console
wrapper  | Launching a JVM...
jvm 1    | Wrapper (Version 3.2.3) http://wrapper.tanukisoftware.org
jvm 1    |   Copyright 1999-2006 Tanuki Software, Inc.  All Rights Reserved.
jvm 1    |
jvm 1    | 2016.04.29 23:57:37 INFO  app[o.s.a.AppFileSystem] Cleaning or creating temp directory D:\##DevOps Book\Install
ables\sonarqube-5.4\temp
jvm 1    | 2016.04.29 23:57:38 INFO  app[o.s.p.m.JavaProcessLauncher] Launch process[search]: C:\Program Files\Java\jre1.8
.0_45\bin\java -Djava.awt.headless=true -Xmx1G -Xms256m -Xss256k -Djava.net.preferIPv4Stack=true -XX:+UseParNewGC -XX:+Use
ConcMarkSweepGC -XX:CMSInitiatingOccupancyFraction=75 -XX:+UseCMSInitiatingOccupancyOnly -XX:+HeapDumpOnOutOfMemoryError -
Djava.io.tmpdir=D:\##DevOps Book\Installables\sonarqube-5.4\temp -cp ./lib/common/*;./lib/search/* org.sonar.search.Search
Server C:\Users\MItesh\AppData\Local\Temp\sq-process7000722619322287622properties
jvm 1    | 2016.04.29 23:57:49 INFO  app[o.s.p.m.Monitor] Process[search] is up
jvm 1    | 2016.04.29 23:57:49 INFO  app[o.s.p.m.JavaProcessLauncher] Launch process[web]: C:\Program Files\Java\jre1.8.0_
45\bin\java -Djava.awt.headless=true -Dfile.encoding=UTF-8 -Djruby.management.enabled=false -Djruby.compile.invokedynamic=
false -Xmx768m -Xms256m -XX:MaxPermSize=160m -XX:+HeapDumpOnOutOfMemoryError -Djava.net.preferIPv4Stack=true -Djava.io.tmp
dir=D:\##DevOps Book\Installables\sonarqube-5.4\temp -cp ./lib/common/*;./lib/server/*;D:\##DevOps Book\Installables\sonar
qube-5.4\lib\jdbc\h2\h2-1.3.176.jar org.sonar.server.app.WebServer C:\Users\MItesh\AppData\Local\Temp\sq-process3019138822
364693273properties
jvm 1    | 2016.04.29 23:59:07 INFO  app[o.s.p.m.Monitor] Process[web] is up
```

5. Once Sonar is up and running, open a browser and visit `http://localhost:9000/` or `http://<IP_Address>:9000/`. You will get the Sonar dashboard:

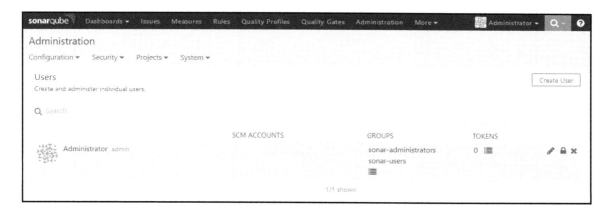

An important step for Jenkins 2 and Sonar integration is the **security token**:

1. Go to the **My Account** link in the top-right corner.
2. Click on the Security tab and then on **Generate Tokens**:

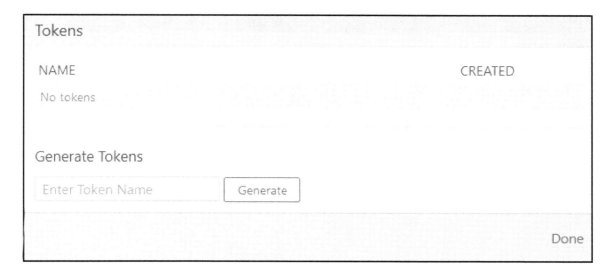

3. Enter a token name, and click on **Generate**. Copy the token value and click on **Done**:

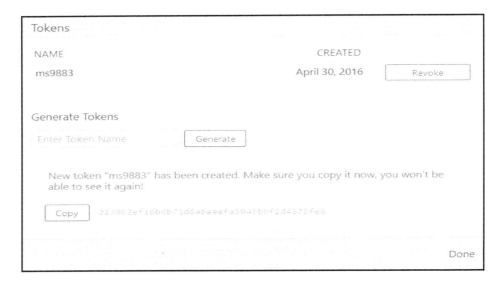

4. Verify the **TOKENS** column in the on dashboard:

5. Once we have a security token ready, we need to integrate Jenkins and Sonar:

6. In the **Manage Jenkins** section, click on **Configure System**, and add SonarQube servers. Here, provide a **Server URL** and **Server authentication token**, and save the settings:

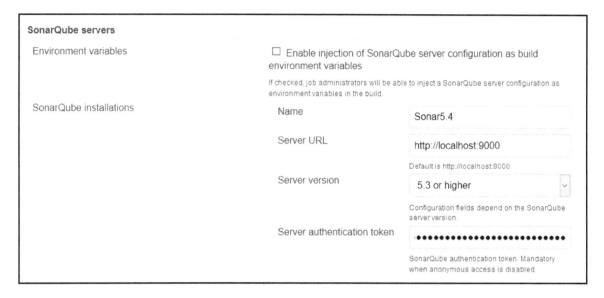

7. In **Global Tool Configuration**, configure **SonarQube Scanner installations** as well:

Once all Sonar-related installations and configurations are completed, we need to add a build step to execute **SonarQube Scanner**. Run the build job with these steps:

1. We need `sonar-project.properties` to configure Sonar with a specific application. In our sample application, the `sonar-project.properties` file is already available, as shown here:

```
# Required metadata
sonar.projectKey=java-sonar-runner-simple
sonar.projectName=Simple Java project analyzed with the SonarQube Runner
sonar.projectVersion=1.0

# Comma-separated paths to directories with sources (required)
sonar.sources=src

# Language
sonar.language=java

# Encoding of the source files
sonar.sourceEncoding=UTF-8
```

2. Verify the console output of a build job for Sonar execution:

```
D:\##DevOps Book\Installables\sonar-scanner-2.6
INFO: Scanner configuration file: D:\##DevOps Book\Installables\sonar-scanner-2.6\conf\sonar-scanner.properties
INFO: Project root configuration file: d:\jenkins\workspace\PetClinic-Test\sonar-project.properties
INFO: SonarQube Scanner 2.6
INFO: Java 1.8.0-ea Oracle Corporation (64-bit)
INFO: Windows 8.1 6.3 amd64
INFO: Error stacktraces are turned on.
INFO: User cache: C:\Users\MItesh\.sonar\cache
INFO: Load global repositories
INFO: Load global repositories (done) | time=1131ms
INFO: User cache: C:\Users\MItesh\.sonar\cache
INFO: Load plugins index
INFO: Load plugins index (done) | time=16ms
INFO: Download sonar-csharp-plugin-4.4.jar
INFO: Download sonar-java-plugin-3.10.jar
INFO: Download sonar-scm-git-plugin-1.0.jar
INFO: Download sonar-scm-svn-plugin-1.2.jar
INFO: Download sonar-javascript-plugin-2.10.jar
INFO: SonarQube server 5.4
INFO: Default locale: "en_US", source code encoding: "UTF-8"
INFO: Process project properties
INFO: Load project repositories
```

```
INFO: Load project repositories (done) | time=133ms
INFO: Apply project exclusions
INFO: Load quality profiles
INFO: Load quality profiles (done) | time=927ms
INFO: Load active rules
INFO: Load active rules (done) | time=4068ms
INFO: Publish mode
INFO: ------------ Scan Simple Java project analyzed with the
SonarQube Runner
INFO: Language is forced to java
INFO: Load server rules
INFO: Load server rules (done) | time=656ms
INFO: Base dir: d:\jenkins\workspace\PetClinic-Test
INFO: Working dir: d:\jenkins\workspace\PetClinic-Test\.sonar
INFO: Source paths: src
INFO: Source encoding: UTF-8, default locale: en_US
INFO: Index files
INFO: 56 files indexed
INFO: Quality profile for java: Sonar way
INFO: JaCoCoSensor: JaCoCo report not found :
d:\jenkins\workspace\PetClinic-Test\target\jacoco.exec
INFO: JaCoCoItSensor: JaCoCo IT report not found:
d:\jenkins\workspace\PetClinic-Test\target\jacoco-it.exec
INFO: Sensor JavaSquidSensor
INFO: Configured Java source version (sonar.java.source): none
INFO: JavaClasspath initialization...
INFO: Bytecode of dependencies was not provided for analysis of source
files, you might end up with less precise results. Bytecode can be provided
using sonar.java.libraries property
INFO: JavaClasspath initialization done: 1 ms
INFO: JavaTestClasspath initialization...
INFO: Bytecode of dependencies was not provided for analysis of test
files, you might end up with less precise results. Bytecode can be provided
using sonar.java.test.libraries property
INFO: JavaTestClasspath initialization done: 1 ms
INFO: Java Main Files AST scan...
INFO: 56 source files to be analyzed
INFO: 46/56 files analyzed, current file:
d:\jenkins\workspace\PetClinic-
Test\src\test\java\org\springframework\samples\petclinic\service\AbstractCl
inicServiceTests.java
INFO: Java Main Files AST scan done: 12107 ms
INFO: Java bytecode has not been made available to the analyzer. The
org.sonar.java.bytecode.visitor.DependenciesVisitor@4f1150f5,
org.sonar.java.checks.unused.UnusedPrivateMethodCheck@3fba233d are
disabled.
INFO: Java Test Files AST scan...
INFO: 0 source files to be analyzed
```

```
    INFO: Java Test Files AST scan done: 1 ms
    INFO: Sensor JavaSquidSensor (done) | time=15295ms
    INFO: Sensor Lines Sensor
    INFO: 56/56 source files have been analyzed
    INFO: 0/0 source files have been analyzed
    INFO: Sensor Lines Sensor (done) | time=28ms
    INFO: Sensor QProfileSensor
    INFO: Sensor QProfileSensor (done) | time=29ms
    INFO: Sensor SurefireSensor
    INFO: parsing d:\jenkins\workspace\PetClinic-Test\target\surefire-
reports
    INFO: Sensor SurefireSensor (done) | time=531ms
    INFO: Sensor SCM Sensor
    INFO: SCM provider for this project is: git
    INFO: 56 files to be analyzed
    INFO: 56/56 files analyzed
    INFO: Sensor SCM Sensor (done) | time=3754ms
    INFO: Sensor Code Colorizer Sensor
    INFO: Sensor Code Colorizer Sensor (done) | time=9ms
    INFO: Sensor CPD Sensor
    INFO: JavaCpdIndexer is used for java
    INFO: Sensor CPD Sensor (done) | time=303ms
    INFO: Analysis report generated in 1055ms, dir size=294 KB
    INFO: Analysis reports compressed in 629ms, zip size=191 KB
    INFO: Analysis report uploaded in 524ms
    INFO: ANALYSIS SUCCESSFUL, you can browse
http://localhost:9000/dashboard/index/java-sonar-runner-simple
    INFO: Note that you will be able to access the updated dashboard once
the server has processed the submitted analysis report
    INFO: More about the report processing at
http://localhost:9000/api/ce/task?id=AVRjchhfszI1jSgY1AZe
    INFO: ---------------------------------------------------------------
-------
    INFO: EXECUTION SUCCESS
    INFO: ---------------------------------------------------------------
-------
    INFO: Total time: 57.737s
    INFO: Final Memory: 52M/514M
    INFO: ---------------------------------------------------------------
-------
    Recording test results
    Finished: SUCCESS
```

3. Let's verify the Sonar UI at
   `http://localhost:9000/dashboard/index/java-sonar-runner-simple`.

4. In the **PROJECTS** section, we can find project details available now. Click on the project name:

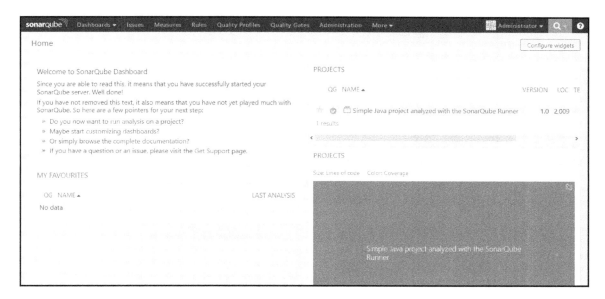

5. We can see the result of the analysis here. **Quality Gate** shows passed. It provides details about **Technical Debt**, **Duplications**, and **Structure** too:

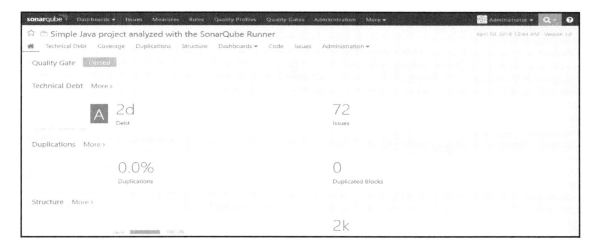

6. Quality gates can be defined in the Sonar dashboard. We have used the default quality gate here:

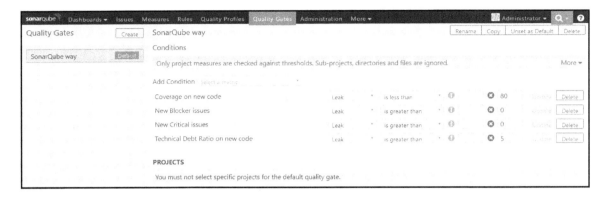

7. To verify **Lines of code**, **Complexity**, and **Comment lines** data, click on the **Structure** tab in the Sonar dashboard:

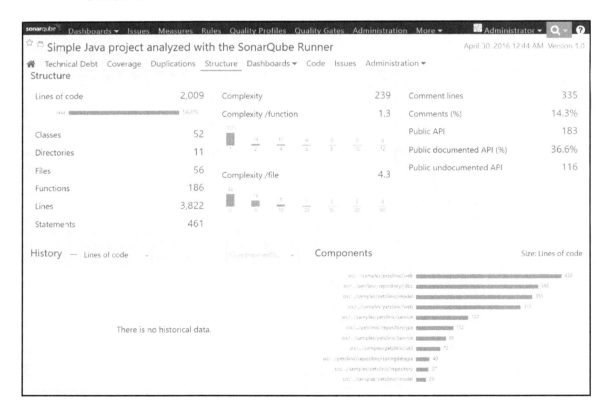

8. To get more insight into issues in specific files, click on the **Technical Debt** tab, and click on the bubbles on the chart:

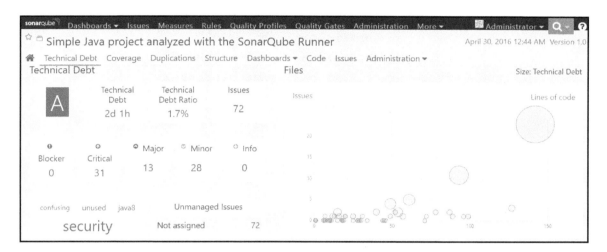

Sonar stores historical data in 24-hour slices.

Self-test questions

1. Jenkins is written in Java.

   - True
   - False

2. On which of the following operating systems can Jenkins be installed?

   - Ubuntu/Debian
   - Windows
   - Mac OS X
   - CentOS/Fedora/Red Hat
   - All of these

3. Which of the following commands can be used to change the default port on which Jenkins runs?

- ```
  java -jar jenkins.war --httpPort=9999
  ```
- ```
  java -jar jenkins.war --http=9999
  ```
- ```
  java -jar jenkins.war --https=9999
  ```
- ```
  java -jar jenkins.war --httpsPort=9999
  ```

4. Sonar stores historical data in 22-hour slices.

- True
- False

Summary

In this chapter, we learned about some new features in Jenkins 2, why Jenkins is so popular, and how to install it. We discussed the improvements with respect to security and plugin installations during setup and how to configure Java and Maven. We took a look at what happens in the background when we create a new job in Jenkins, how to authenticate with Git, and how to configure Git in Jenkins. We then performed a unit test execution in a sample Spring application and configured the Dashboard View plugin with different portlets for customized views. We then learned how to manage the master and slave nodes for load distribution and managing different environments as required, how to configure e-mail notifications for build status, and how to integrate Sonar and Jenkins.

In the next chapter, we will look at one of the most important aspects in terms of the orchestration of the end-to-end pipeline of application delivery. We will discuss the pipeline concept of Jenkins 2 and the build pipeline plugin.

It is the proper time to quote *Ralph Waldo Emerson*, as it is relevant in the context of failures during build execution in the process of continuous integration:

"Our greatest glory is not in never failing, but in rising up every time we fail."

3
Building the Code and Configuring the Build Pipeline

"Start wide, expand further, and never look back."

-Arnold Schwarzenegger

It is always better to start early and visualize the things we want to achieve. That is the objective of this chapter. It will be easy to realize the importance of this chapter when we are at the last line of the final chapter of this book.

One of the highlights of Jenkins 2 is built-in support for delivery pipelines. We know that Jenkins is a continuous integration server, but what if we wanted to use it for continuous delivery or continuous deployment too? Automation and orchestration both are equally important while dealing with the application delivery pipeline.

This chapter describes in detail how to create the pipelines of different jobs for a sample **Java Enterprise Edition** (**Java EE**) application. It will also cover the deployment of an application to a local web or application server and the configuration of a build pipeline for the lifecycle of continuous integration. This way, Jenkins users can model application delivery pipelines as the code. Once we make it into code, we can store in a code repository and it can be managed in a better way. An important benefit is a collaboration. As it can be stored in version control, different teams can reuse it for different operations, based on the environment.

Readers will learn how to manage the lifecycle of continuous integration, including pulling code from a code repository, building the code, executing unit tests, and static code analysis using different jobs.

We will cover the following topics:

- The built-in delivery pipelines of Jenkins 2
- Build pipeline configuration for end-to-end automation for managing the lifecycle of continuous integration
- Deploying a WAR file from Jenkins to a local Tomcat server

Creating built-in delivery pipelines

Jenkins 2 provides a way to create delivery pipelines using a **domain-specific language** (**DSL**).

The steps for creating a built-in delivery pipeline are as follows:

1. Go to the Jenkins dashboard and click on **New Item**.
2. Enter an item name, say `PetClinic-Pipeline`, and select **Pipeline**, as shown in the following screenshot, and click on **OK**:

3. In case you have an existing pipeline available, you can create a new pipeline by copying from it.

4. Go to **Advanced Project Options**. For the purpose of learning, input `echo 'Hello from Pipeline Demo'` in the **Script** box.

5. Click on **Save** to save the configuration:

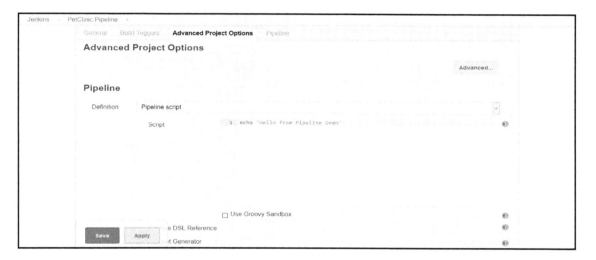

6. As we haven't created any stage, we will get a warning, as shown in the following screenshot. However, we can execute the pipeline for demo purposes:

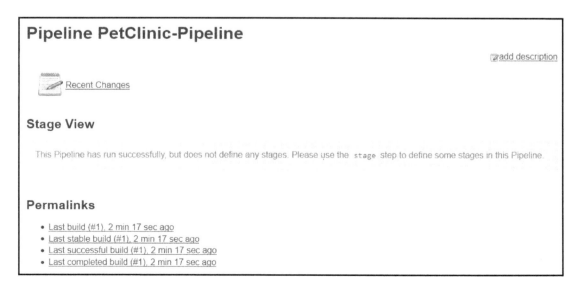

7. Click on the **Build Now**. Verify the **Console Output**. We can see the script execution completing successfully:

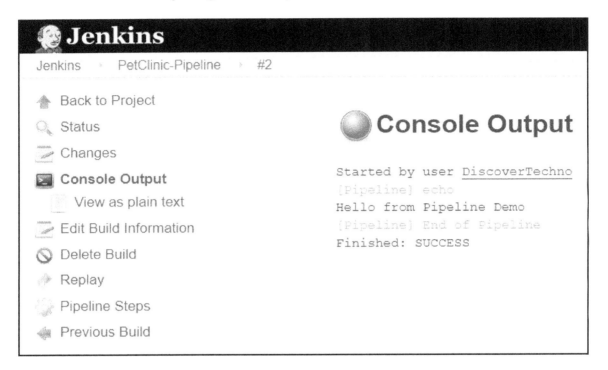

Creating scripts

Let's go step by step and learn how we can create a script. To make things easier, refer to the Pipeline DSL reference or use Snippet Generator. Select the checkbox, and then select a **Sample Step**. Provide specific parameters required by the step, and click on **Generate Groovy**.

Pipeline DSL Reference: `https://jenkins.io/doc/pipeline/steps/`
Snippet Generator: `https://jenkins.io/doc/pipeline/#using-snippet-generator`

Example 1 – creating a Groovy script to build a job

Here's how to create a Groovy script to build a job. It triggers a new downstream job to build:

Sample step	Parameters
build: Build a job	**Project to Build**: `PetClinic-Compile` **Parameters**: None Other configurations: Default

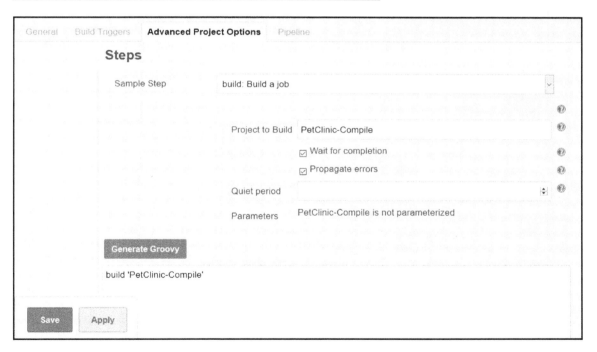

Example 2 – creating a build step to publish test reports

Creating a build step is used to configure post-build actions or in general build steps that are pipeline compatible, based on the drop-down list:

Sample step	Parameters
step: General Build Setup	**Build Step**: `Publish JUnit test result report` **Test Report XMLs**: `**/target/surefire-reports/TEST-*.xml` Other configurations: Default

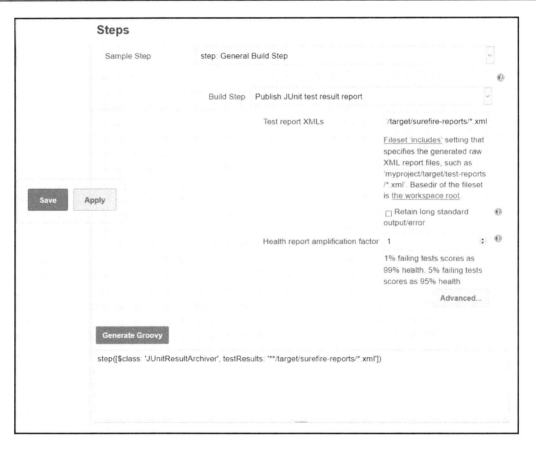

Example 3 – archiving build job artifacts

To archive build job artifacts, use the following parameters:

Sample step	Parameters
archive: Archive artifacts	**Includes**: This includes artifacts, using a comma separated list-matching Ant-style pattern for archiving artifacts **Excludes**: This excludes artifacts, using a comma separated list-matching Ant-style pattern for not archiving artifacts

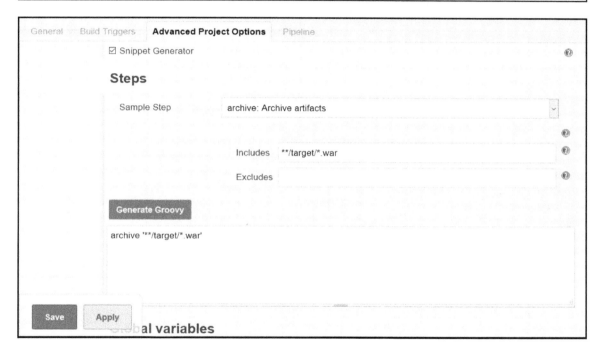

Example 4 – running a build step on a node

To run a build step on a specific node, we need to write a script. Use **Snippet Generator** and select a sample step node, and select the slave node label. Then, click on **Generate Groovy:**

Sample step	Parameters
node: Allocate node	**Label:** The label associated with slave node. Refer to `Chapter 2`, *Continuous Integration with Jenkins 2*. For more details on master-slave nodes in Jenkins 2

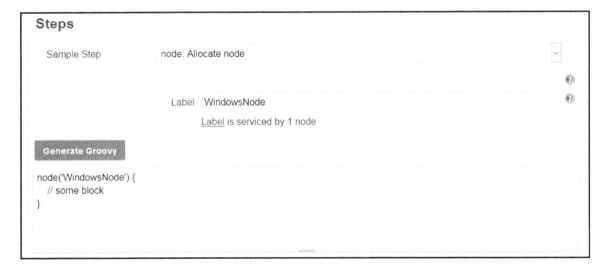

Example 5 – marking the definite steps of a build job

We will now create a Groovy script to mark definite sections of a build job as being controlled by limited concurrency:

Sample step	Parameters
stage: Stage	**Stage Name:** `Compile/Test/Deploy` Other configurations: Default

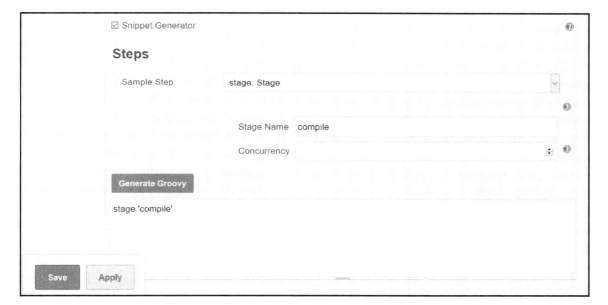

Creating a pipeline for compiling and executing test units

For demonstration purposes, let's try a simple scenario to create a pipeline for compiling source files and executing unit test cases:

1. Let's use the following script in the **Script** box:

```
echo 'Hello from Pipeline Demo'
stage 'Compile'
build 'PetClinic-Compile'
stage 'Test'
build 'PetClinic-Test'
```

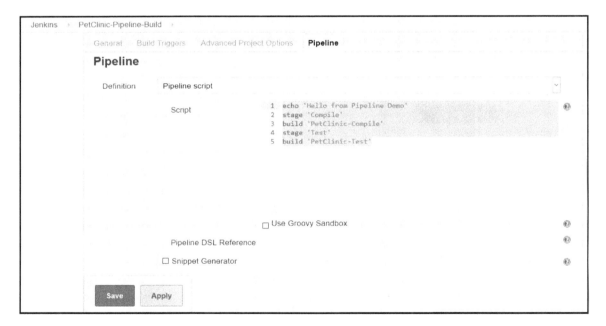

2. Click on **Build Now** and go to **Console Output** to verify the execution process:

3. Go to the build job's main page. We can see **Stage View** here. Remember, we have created two stages: one is **Compile** and the other is **Test**. **Stage View** provides instant visualization. It provides details such as build completion time, the node on which the build has been executed, and whether the build has executed successfully or failed:

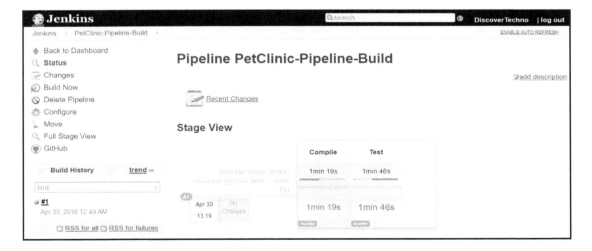

4. For a particular build execution, we can verify **Pipeline Steps** as well:

5. Click on **Full Stage View** to get a full-screen view, as shown in the following screenshot:

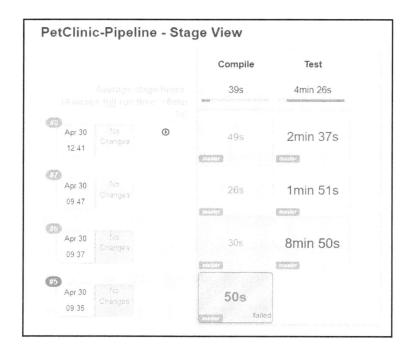

6. To obtain details specific to a stage, mouse over a specific stage, and it will show you the status of that stage's execution as well as the **Logs** link:

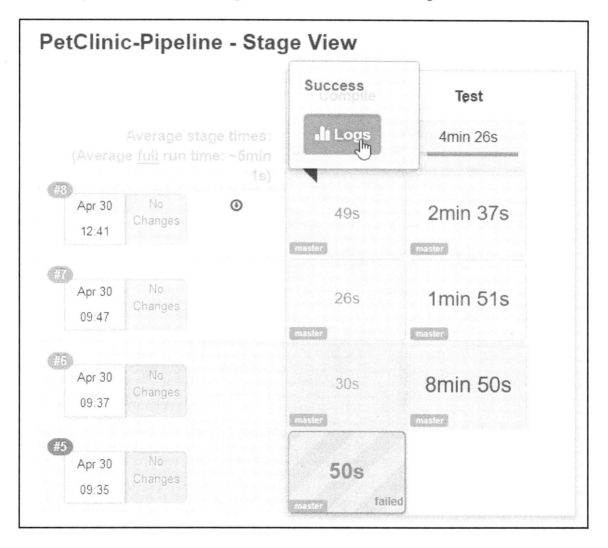

7. Click on the **Stage Logs** link, and it will provide log details respective to the stage. Click on the dropdown to obtain more details about the logs:

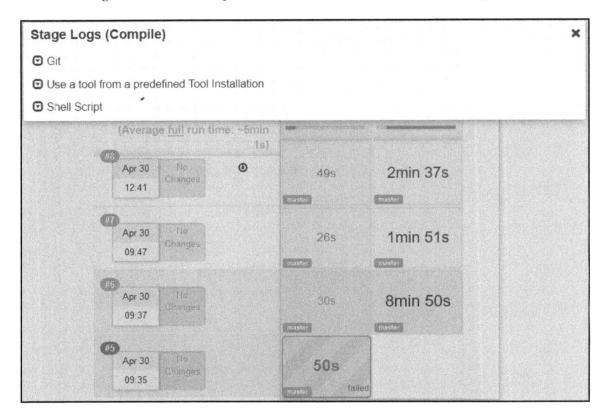

Now, let's consider a scenario where we want to execute different stages on different nodes.

1. Copy the following code and paste it in **Script** section:

```
echo 'Hello from Pipeline Demo'
stage 'Compile'
node {
  git url: 'https://github.com/mitesh51/spring-petclinic.git'
  def mvnHome = tool 'Maven3.3.1'
  sh "${mvnHome}/bin/mvn -B compile"
}
stage 'Test'
node('WindowsNode') {
  git url: 'https://github.com/mitesh51/spring-petclinic.git'
  def mvnHome = tool 'WindowsMaven'
```

```
        bat "${mvnHome}\\bin\\mvn -B verify"
        step([$class: 'ArtifactArchiver', artifacts: '**/target/*.war',
fingerprint: true])
        step([$class: 'JUnitResultArchiver', testResults:
'**/target/surefire-reports/TEST-*.xml'])
    }
```

2. Click on **Build Now** and verify the **Stage View**:

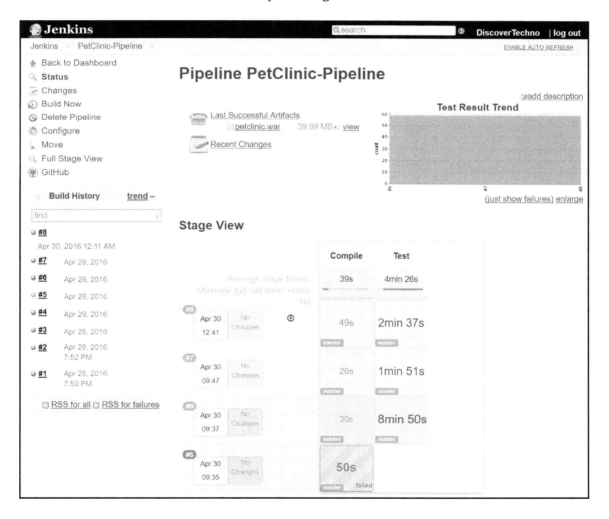

3. **Pipeline Steps** describes drill-down details of execution, as shown in the following screenshot:

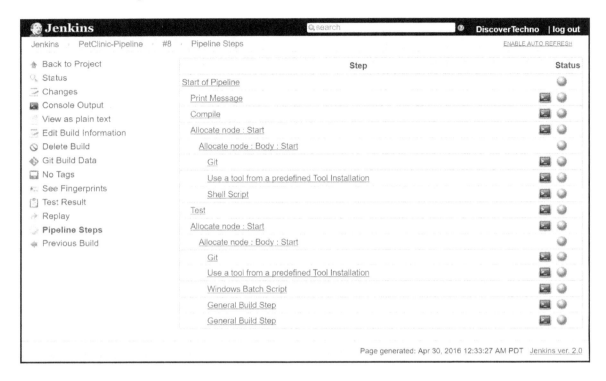

4. Let's verify stage logs for **Git** operation. Mouse over the **Compile** stage, and click on **logs**. Expand the **Git** dropdown, as shown in the following screenshot, to get more details:

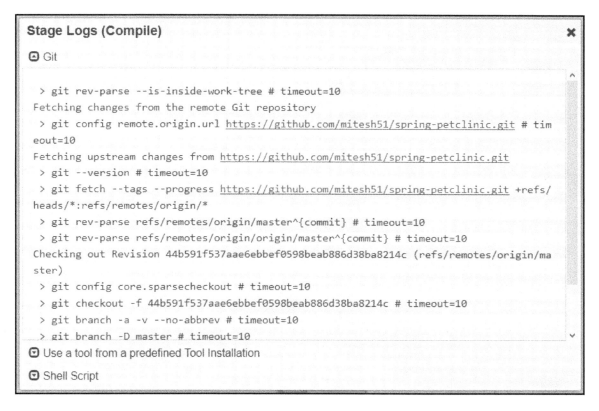

Can you guess what could be the potential issue with a Groovy script for creating pipeline?

Yes; again, it is code. It becomes difficult to manage it over time and hence it is always better to store it in a repository. In the **Pipeline Definition** section, there is an option to load the **Pipeline script from SCM**. We can select **Git** or **Subversion** for the **SCM**, and then we need to provide repository details and script file details:

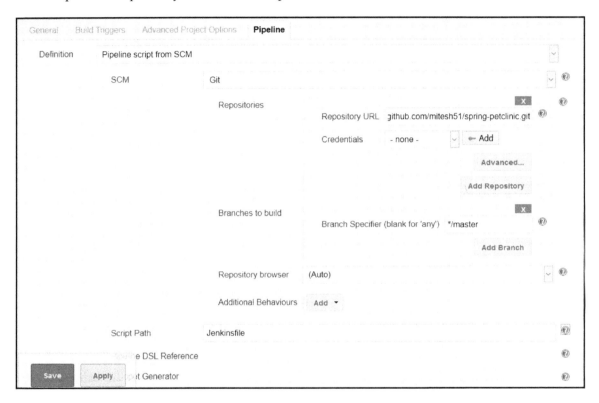

 For more details visit *Getting Started with Pipeline* from the Jenkins documentation: https://jenkins.io/doc/pipeline/

Using the Build Pipeline plugin

We have seen the built-in pipeline concept of Jenkins 2. It is a very flexible and powerful concept, but for that, we need to write a Groovy script. Another way that has an easy learning curve is to use the **Build Pipeline** plugin. It provides simple visualization of upstream and downstream build jobs. It also enables manual triggers for a situation where we need approval for executing a specific build. We can create a chain of jobs for end-to-end automation. Here, I'm assuming that you are aware of the concept of upstream and downstream build jobs.

To create a build pipeline, follow these steps:

1. Install the **Build Pipeline** plugin.
2. On the Jenkins dashboard, click on the plus sign, which will open a page to create a **Build Pipeline View**. Provide a **View name** for the build pipeline, and click on **OK**:

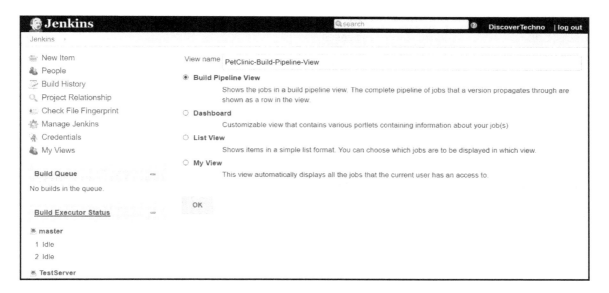

3. It is important to configure upstream and downstream build jobs:

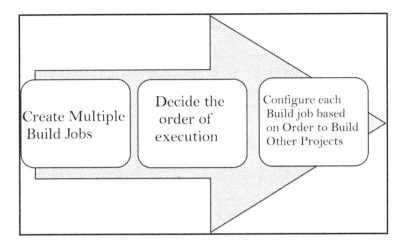

We have created multiple build jobs to compile the source code, verify the source code using Sonar, and to execute JUnit test cases.

We have defined the order as well: if compilation is successful, the other two build jobs will be executed. In our case, they are `PetClinic-Code` and `PetClinic-Test`.

Follow these steps to configure the build jobs:

1. Go to the configuration page of the `PetClinic-Compile` build job.
2. Go to the **Post-build Actions** section.
3. Enter the name of the build jobs in the **Project to build** textbox. You can provide a comma-separated list here.

4. Click on **Save** to save the configuration.

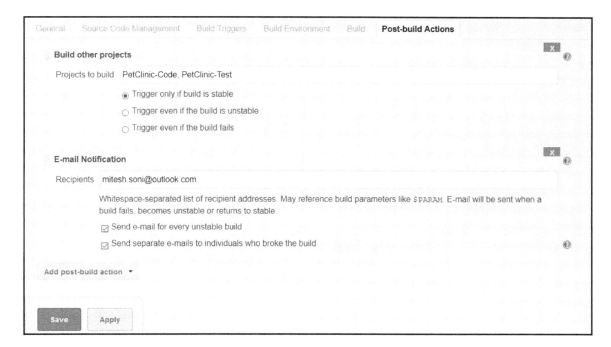

5. Verify the list of the **Downstream Projects** on the build job's main page:

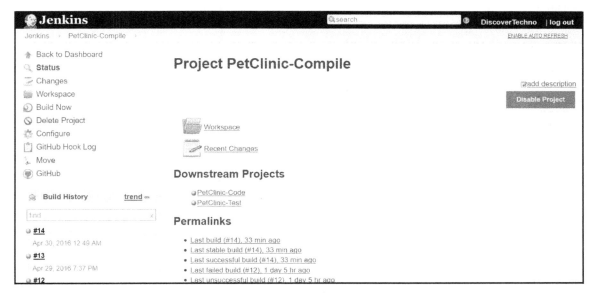

6. The next step is to configure the **Build Pipeline View** we created earlier. Use this table:

Property name	Property description
Name	The name of the build pipeline.
Description	The description is displayed on the **Build Pipeline View** page. It can be used to display details such as the pipeline, resources, the objective of the pipeline, and the flow.
Filter build queue	Only jobs in this specific view will be shown in the queue.
Filter build executors	This is used to show build executors that could execute the jobs in this view.
Build Pipeline View Title	The build pipeline view title to display on the Jenkins dashboard.
Layout	**Based on the upstream/downstream relationship**: This layout mode derives the pipeline structure based on the upstream/downstream trigger relationship between jobs.
Select Initial Job	This sets the initial or parent job in the build pipeline view. The rest of the build job will be considered based on the upstream/downstream relationship.
No Of Displayed Builds	The number of build pipelines to display in the view.
Restrict triggers to most recent successful builds	This is used to restrict the display of a **Trigger** button to only the most recent successful build pipelines.
Always allow manual trigger on pipeline steps	This is used to execute a successful pipeline step again, using the same parameter values if the build is parameterized.
Show pipeline project headers	This is used to show the pipeline definition header in the pipeline view.
Show pipeline parameters in project headers	This is used to list the parameters used to run the latest successful job in the pipeline's project headers.
Show pipeline parameters in revision box	This is used to list the parameters used to run the first job in each pipeline's revision box.
Refresh frequency (in seconds)	This provides the frequency in seconds with which the **Build Pipeline Plugin** updates the build lightbox.

URL for custom CSS files	Used for a custom CSS files if any.
Console Output Link Style	You can choose from **Lightbox**, **New Window**, or **This Window**.

7. We have selected the **PetClinic-Compile** build job in the **Select Initial Job** section as the initial job, as you can see here:

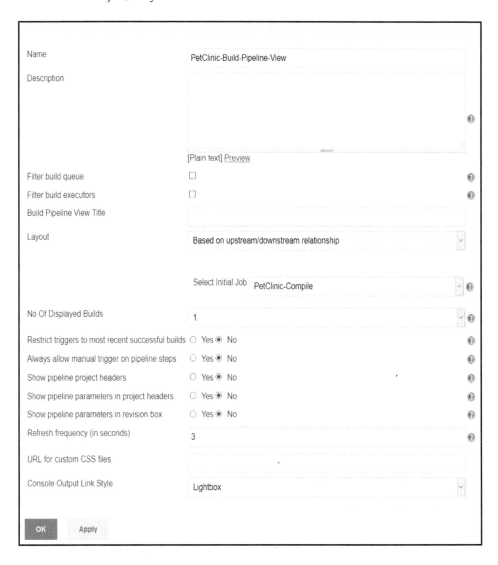

8. On the **PetClinic-Build-Pipeline-View** page, we can run the build pipeline by clicking on **Run**, view the history by clicking on **History**, configure the pipeline by clicking on **Configure**, and delete the pipeline using **Delete**. Click on **Run** to execute the build pipeline for the first time:

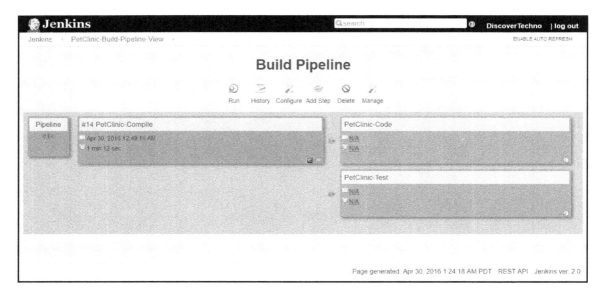

9. The following are the default color codes:

Color	Description
Red	Indicates failed execution of a build job
Green	Indicates successful execution of a build job
Blue	Indicates a build job that hasn't been executed
Yellow	Indicates a running build job

10. Now let's observe the execution of a build job in this pipeline, as shown in the following screenshot:

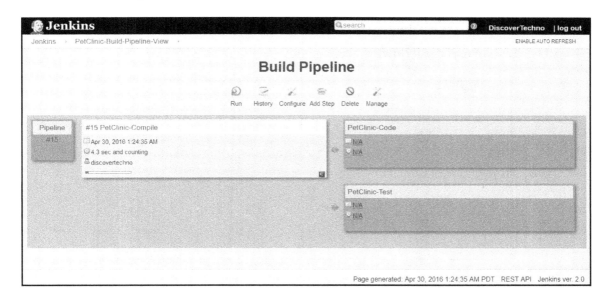

11. We can see all jobs in green as all the builds have been executed successfully:

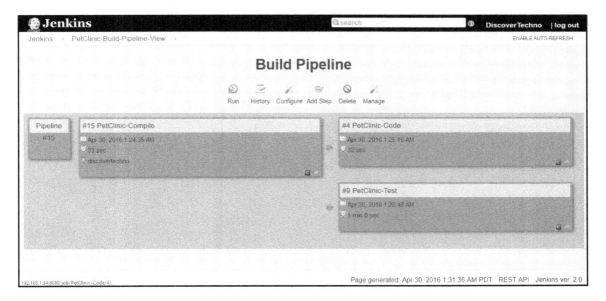

Manual trigger configuration makes sure that pipeline step doesn't execute automatically and requires manual intervention to execute next step. It can be very useful in the scenarios where you need to wait for the deployment in the specific environment or to wait for permission before deployment. Let's configure the build pipeline using a manual trigger:

1. As shown in the following screenshot, select Yes for all the options:

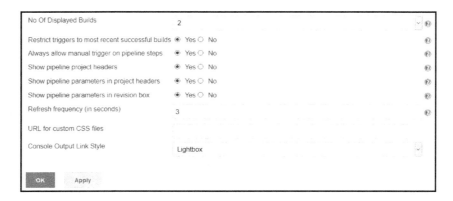

2. Let's save and verify the changes in the **Build Pipeline View** section. Verify the manual trigger and headers with the health details of each build job:

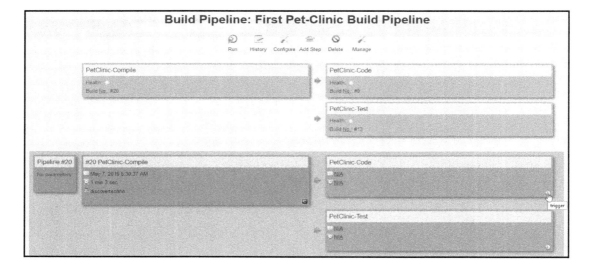

3. Verify the build history of **PetClinic-Build-Pipeline-View**, as shown in the following screenshot:

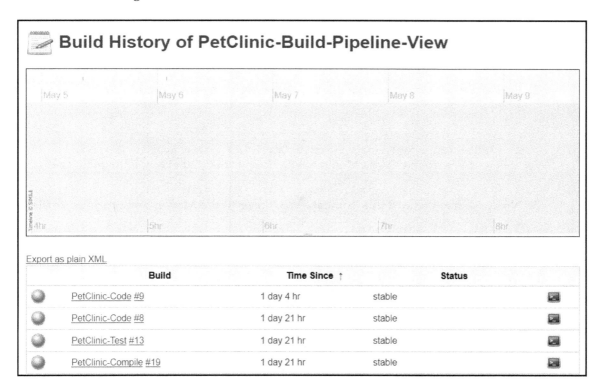

Build History of PetClinic-Build-Pipeline-View

| May 5 | May 6 | May 7 | May 8 | May 9 |

| 4hr | 5hr | 6hr | 7hr | 8hr |

Export as plain XML

	Build	Time Since ↑	Status	
⚪	PetClinic-Code #9	1 day 4 hr	stable	🖥
⚪	PetClinic-Code #8	1 day 21 hr	stable	🖥
⚪	PetClinic-Test #13	1 day 21 hr	stable	🖥
⚪	PetClinic-Compile #19	1 day 21 hr	stable	🖥

 the Build Pipeline plugin from `https://wiki.jenkins-ci.org/display/JENKINS/Build+Pipeline+Plugin`.

Deploying a WAR file. The most important thing in application life cycle management is the deployment of the packages. That is the business part of the whole exercise. The objective is to automate the process of deployment of the packages into web server or application server. Once the deployment process is automated, it can be easily integrated into end to end automation of application delivery.

For Maven and Tomcat integration, let's create an admin user. We will use admin user credentials to deploy an application to a Tomcat server:

1. Open `apache-tomcat-7.0.68\conf\tomcat-users.xml`, and add the following statements into it:

   Here we define roles such as manager-gui, manager-script. For this deployment, we will use manager-script role.

2. Create a user with the name `admin`, and assign a password and roles, as shown here:

   ```
   <role rolename="manager-gui"/>
   <role rolename="manager-script"/>
   <user username="admin" password="cloud@123" roles="manager-script"
   />
   ```

3. Now, we need to add this Tomcat `admin` user to the Maven `settings.xml` file:

   ```
   servers>
   server>
   id>tomcat-development-server</id>
   username>admin</username>
   password>password</password>
   /server>
   /servers>
   ```

4. Now let's edit the `pom.xml` file. Find the `Tomcat Plugin` block in `pom.xml`, and add following details. Make sure that the server name is the same one we provided in the `settings.xml` file of Maven as `id`:

   ```
   <plugin>
   <groupId>org.apache.tomcat.maven</groupId>
   <artifactId>tomcat7-maven-plugin</artifactId>
   <version>2.2</version>
   <configuration>
   <server>tomcat-development-server</server>
   <url>http://192.168.1.35:9999/manager/text</url>
   <warFile>target\petclinic.war</warFile>
   <path>/petclinic</path>
   </configuration>
   </plugin>
   ```

5. We can verify execution from the command-line using `mvn tomcat7:deploy` command. Maven will deploy the WAR file to Tomcat 7 using the Manager app at `http://localhost:8080/manager/text`, to the `/petclinic` path.

6. In the case of any failures because of a preexisting WAR file in the Tomcat `webapps` folder, use `tomcat7:redeploy`.

Let's create a build job in Jenkins and add a build step to invoke top-level Maven targets:

1. Use `tomcat7:redeploy` for **Goals** and Save it:

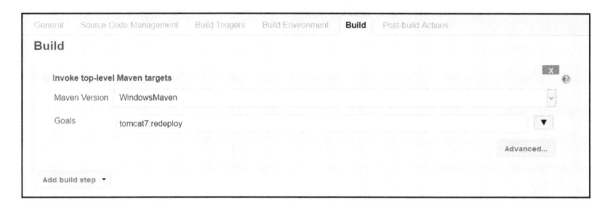

2. Execute the build by clicking on **Build Now**. Verify the deployment process in the console output:

```
[INFO] --- maven-war-plugin:2.3:war (default-war) @ spring-petclinic ---
[INFO] Packaging webapp
[INFO] Assembling webapp [spring-petclinic] in [d:\jenkins\workspace\PetClinic-Deploy\target\spring-
petclinic-4.2.5-SNAPSHOT]
[INFO] Processing war project
[INFO] Copying webapp resources [d:\jenkins\workspace\PetClinic-Deploy\src\main\webapp]
[INFO] Webapp assembled in [969 msecs]
[INFO] Building war: d:\jenkins\workspace\PetClinic-Deploy\target\spring-petclinic-4.2.5-SNAPSHOT.war
[INFO]
[INFO] <<< tomcat7-maven-plugin:2.2:redeploy (default-cli) < package @ spring-petclinic <<<
[INFO]
[INFO] --- tomcat7-maven-plugin:2.2:redeploy (default-cli) @ spring-petclinic ---
[INFO] Deploying war to http://192.168.1.35:9999/petclinic
Uploading: http://192.168.1.35:9999/manager/text/deploy?path=%2Fpetclinic&update=true
40002/40946 KB
40004/40946 KB
40006/40946 KB
40008/40946 KB
40010/40946 KB
40012/40946 KB
```

3. Once the WAR file has been uploaded, the build job will be completed successfully:

```
40940/40946 KB
40942/40946 KB
40944/40946 KB
40946/40946 KB
Uploaded: http://192.168.1.35:9999/manager/text/deploy?path=%2Fpetclinic&update=true (40946 KB at
9024.9 KB/sec)

[INFO] tomcatManager status code:200, ReasonPhrase:OK
[INFO] OK - Deployed application at context path /petclinic
[INFO] ------------------------------------------------------------------------
[INFO] BUILD SUCCESS
[INFO] ------------------------------------------------------------------------
[INFO] Total time: 58.469 s
[INFO] Finished at: 2016-05-07T23:41:13+05:30
[INFO] Final Memory: 38M/263M
[INFO] ------------------------------------------------------------------------
Finished: SUCCESS
```

When we use `tomcat7:deploy` or `tomcat7:redeploy`, it includes the package lifecycle in the execution. If we want to only deploy the WAR file, we can use `tomcat7:deploy-only`, as shown in the following console output:

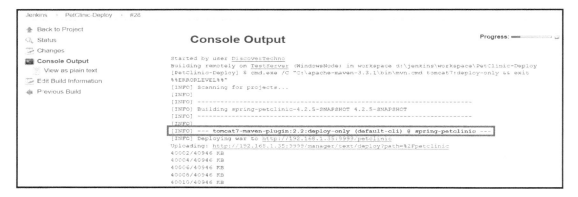

Integrating the deployment operation

Till now we have covered Pipeline or orchestration of different tasks and now let's integrate pipeline and deployment automation. By doing this, we will complete Continuous Integration and Continuous Delivery with orchestration. Let's try to integrate the deployment operation into the build pipeline.

We will need to perform the following tasks:

1. Compile source files.
2. Execute JUnit test cases.
3. Archive the artifact/WAR file: It is used to archive build artifacts, such as JAR files, WAR files, and ZIP files, so they can be downloaded later. Add **Post-build Actions** to `PetClinic-Test` to archive the artifact:

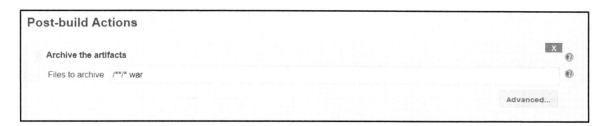

4. Execute the build job, as shown in the following screenshot, and verify whether it has been successfully archived or not. If you see **Finished: SUCCESS**, then the build job was successfully executed:

```
[INFO] --- maven-war-plugin:2.3:war (default-war) @ spring-petclinic ---
[INFO] Packaging webapp
[INFO] Assembling webapp [spring-petclinic] in [d:\jenkins\workspace\PetClinic-Test\target\spring-
petclinic-4.2.5-SNAPSHOT]
[INFO] Processing war project
[INFO] Copying webapp resources [d:\jenkins\workspace\PetClinic-Test\src\main\webapp]
[INFO] Webapp assembled in [2371 msecs]
[INFO] Building war: d:\jenkins\workspace\PetClinic-Test\target\spring-petclinic-4.2.5-SNAPSHOT.war
[INFO] ------------------------------------------------------------------------
[INFO] BUILD SUCCESS
[INFO] ------------------------------------------------------------------------
[INFO] Total time: 35.535 s
[INFO] Finished at: 2016-05-08T00:53:30+05:30
[INFO] Final Memory: 29M/271M
[INFO] ------------------------------------------------------------------------
Archiving artifacts
Recording test results
Warning: you have no plugins providing access control for builds, so falling back to legacy behavior
of permitting any downstream builds to be triggered
Triggering a new build of PetClinic-Deploy
Finished: SUCCESS
```

5. We need to add a build step to copy artifacts from **PetClinic-Test**. Check the **Copy Artifact Plugin** checkbox, and then click on **Install without restart**:

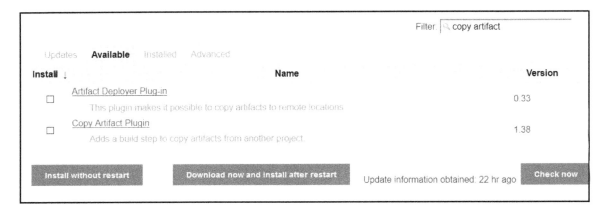

6. Configure the copy artifact plugin in the **PetClinic-Deploy** build job:

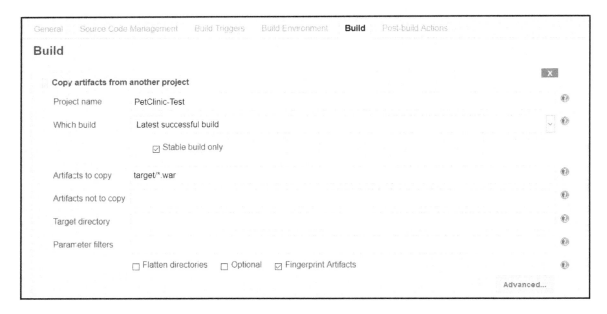

7. Verify the workspace directory. Go to the **PetClinic-Test**`target` directory. If a WAR file is there from a past build, remove it:

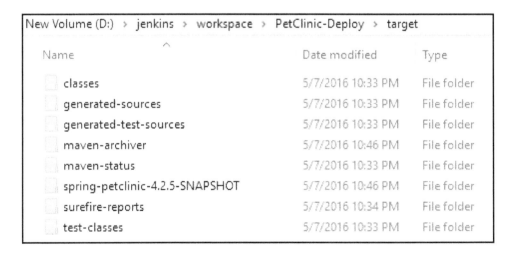

8. Verify the `target` directory of the `PetClinic-Deploy` folder. There is no WAR file:

9. Add **PetClinic-Deploy** as a downstream project to **PetClinic-Test**. Then, run the build pipeline:

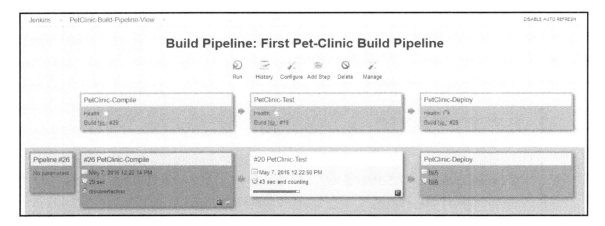

10. Verify the execution of the build pipeline. Click on the lightbox of any build job in the build pipeline. Verify the **PetClinic-Test** console output:

```
PetClinic-Build-Pipeline-View  >  PetClinic-Test  >  #20

                    Tests run: 59, Failures: 0, Errors: 0, Skipped: 0

        [INFO]
        [INFO] --- maven-war-plugin:2.3:war (default-war) @ spring-petclinic ---
        [INFO] Packaging webapp
        [INFO] Assembling webapp [spring-petclinic] in [d:\jenkins\workspace\PetClinic-Test\target\spring-
        petclinic-4.2.5-SNAPSHOT]
        [INFO] Processing war project
        [INFO] Copying webapp resources [d:\jenkins\workspace\PetClinic-Test\src\main\webapp]
        [INFO] Webapp assembled in [2371 msecs]
        [INFO] Building war: d:\jenkins\workspace\PetClinic-Test\target\spring-petclinic-4.2.5-SNAPSHOT.war
        [INFO] ------------------------------------------------------------------------
        [INFO] BUILD SUCCESS
        [INFO] ------------------------------------------------------------------------
        [INFO] Total time: 35.535 s
        [INFO] Finished at: 2016-05-08T00:53:30+05:30
        [INFO] Final Memory: 29M/271M
        [INFO] ------------------------------------------------------------------------
        Archiving artifacts
        Recording test results
        Warning: you have no plugins providing access control for builds, so falling back to legacy behavior
        of permitting any downstream builds to be triggered
        Triggering a new build of PetClinic-Deploy
        Finished: SUCCESS

                                           Page generated May 7, 2016 12 24 06 PM PDT   REST API   Jenkins ver. 2 0
```

Now, we will copy the archive file from one build and use it for deployment in another build. Once the **PetClinic-Test** build job execution has completed, follow these steps:

1. Verify the `target` folder in the workspace. You will see the WAR file in the `target` directory, as shown in the following screenshot:

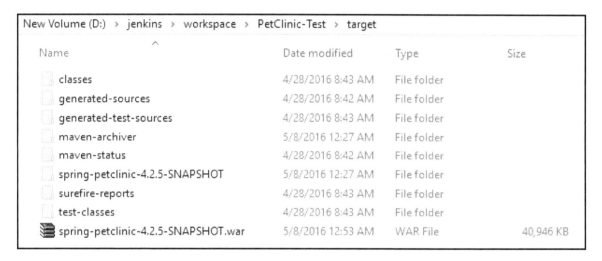

2. Verify the execution of the **PetClinic-Deploy** build job:

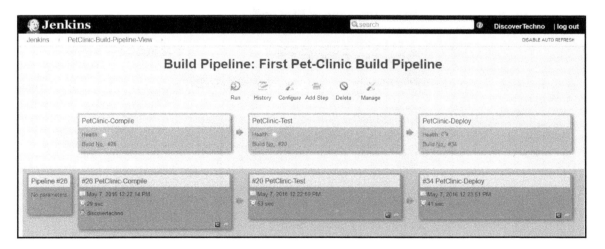

3. Verify the build job's status in the Jenkins dashboard:

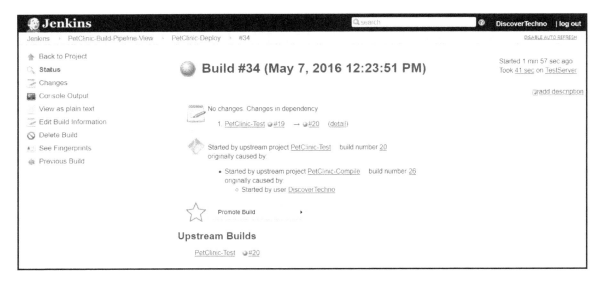

4. Click on the lightbox of **Build Pipeline View**; it will redirect you to the console output of a specific build job. Click on the **PetCLinic-Deploy** lightbox.
5. Verify the console output:

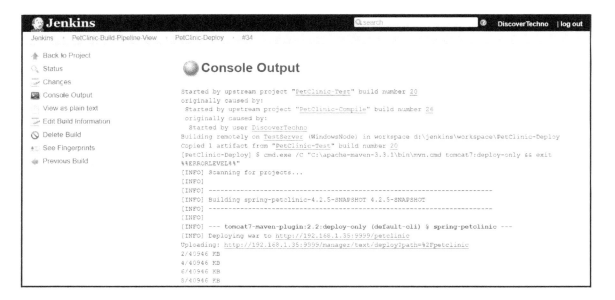

6. Verify that the successfully uploaded file adheres to the configuration:

```
PetClinic-Build-Pipeline-View    PetClinic-Deploy    #34
                    40922/40946 KB
                    40924/40946 KB
                    40926/40946 KB
                    40928/40946 KB
                    40930/40946 KB
                    40932/40946 KB
                    40934/40946 KB
                    40936/40946 KB
                    40938/40946 KB
                    40940/40946 KB
                    40942/40946 KB
                    40944/40946 KB
                    40946/40946 KB
                    Uploaded: http://192.168.1.35:9999/manager/text/deploy?path=%2Fpetclinic (40946 KB at 5678.2 KB/sec)

                    [INFO] tomcatManager status code:200, ReasonPhrase:OK
                    [INFO] OK - Deployed application at context path /petclinic
                    [INFO] ------------------------------------------------------------------------
                    [INFO] BUILD SUCCESS
                    [INFO] ------------------------------------------------------------------------
                    [INFO] Total time: 24.879 s
                    [INFO] Finished at: 2016-05-08T00:54:31+05:30
                    [INFO] Final Memory: 16M/154M
                    [INFO] ------------------------------------------------------------------------
                    Finished: SUCCESS

                                              Page generated: May 7, 2016 12:26:18 PM PDT   REST API   Jenkins ver. 2.0
```

As an exercise, try to use the build flow plugin.

Self-test questions

1. Which feature is one of the highlights of the Jenkins 2 release?

   - Built-in support for continuous integration
   - Built-in support for JUnit
   - Built-in support for delivery pipelines
   - Built-in support for Apache Maven

2. Which language is used to create delivery pipelines ?

   - Java
   - C++
   - C#
   - Domain-specific language

3. In the Build Pipeline plugin, what is the significance of blue color?

   - Indicatingfailed execution of a build job
   - Indicating successful execution of a build job
   - Indicating a build job that hasn't been executed
   - Indicating a running build job

Summary

In this chapter, we covered one of the latest features of Jenkins 2 and one of its highlights:built-in support for delivery pipelines. We learned how to use it in detail. We covered a simple Groovy script to build a job, generate a build step, archive build job artifacts, run a build step on a specific node, mark definite sections of a build as being controlled by limited concurrency, and so on. We walked through a scenario where we want to execute different stages on different nodes. Another similar plugin was installed and configured with an example:the Build Pipeline plugin.

In the next chapter, we will discuss one of the important pillars of DevOps culture-configuration management-using Chef. First, we will see how to install Chef on a workstation and configure it with hosted Chef. We will look at installing Tomcat using community Tomcat installation cookbooks.

4

Installing and Configuring Chef

"Give me six hours to chop down a tree and I will spend the first four sharpening the axe."
-Abraham Lincoln

We are going to see how Chef is useful in end-to-end automation of the application delivery lifecycle. Let's revisit the context. We want to create an end-to-end pipeline where the application source files are compiled, unit tests are executed, package file is created, a new virtual machine created, runtime environment is setup, and deployment is performed. Chef in our context plays a vital role, considering its many uses. We are going to use it for setting up our runtime environment and standardizing the process of configuration management rather than implementing a customized way to install tools using scripts. Centralized configuration management makes it easy to control and configure resources without complication.

This chapter describes in detail the configuration management tool Chef, the installation of its components and alternatives, and the configuration of components and convergence of a node for preparing a runtime environment for Java EE application using cookbooks. However, writing a cookbook and a detailed discussion of Chef components is out of the scope of this book as it will take up too much space.

You will learn how to install and configure Chef and converge a node based on cookbooks/roles.

We will cover the following topics:

- Getting started with Chef
- An overview of hosted Chef
- Installing and configuring a Chef workstation
- Converging a Chef node using a Chef workstation

Getting started with Chef

The Chef is one of the most popular configuration tools in the open source world. We discussed Chef briefly in `Chapter 1`, *Getting Started-DevOps Concepts, Tools, and Technology*.

Let's get hands-on with provisioning instances and configuration management. However, before that, we will need to understand the basics.

There are three major components of Chef:

- **The open source Chef server** or **hosted Chef**: The Chef server or hosted Chef is the pivotal component, which stores cookbooks and other important details of registered nodes. It is used to configure and manage nodes using Chef workstations.
- **Chef workstations**: A Chef workstation works as a local repository, and the **knife** plugin is installed on it. Knife is used to upload cookbooks to the Chef server and execute plugin commands.
- **Node**: A node is a physical or virtual machine in any environment where we need to configure runtime environments or perform operations using Chef configuration. The node communicates with the Chef server (open source or hosted),obtains configuration details related to itself, and then starts executing steps based on it. The Chef server can be installed on a physical machine or a virtual machine with an open source installable file, based on the operating system. Another, easier method to use is hosted Chef, where we need not install and configure a Chef server. We can use the SaaS offering from Chef. It allows up to five nodes. The biggest benefit is we need not manage a Chef server or upgrade it. Hence, we save ourselves from management and maintenance overhead.

Take a look at the Chef website `https://chef.io`. You will see the Chef homepage, as shown here:

There are a lot of details available here about Chef and cloud-related integration as well as knife plugins. We will create a hosted Chef account in the next section and configure it with a local workstation. To proceed, click on the **MANAGEMENT CONSOLE** link in the top right corner of the Chef website.

Overview of hosted Chef

We can use Chef server either by installing and managing Chef server on our own or we can use hosted Chef – SaaS offering to utilize in configuration management.

1. Click on **MANAGEMENT CONSOLE** or navigate to `https://manage.chef.io/login`. We are going to start from scratch, so click on **Click here to get started!**

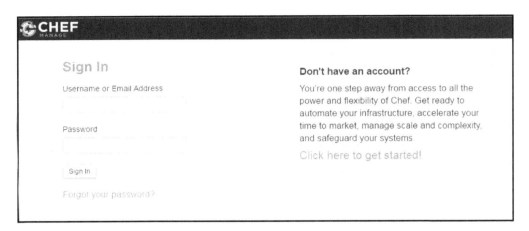

2. Enter your **Full Name**, **Company** name, **Email** address, and **Username** in the respective text boxes and check the box that says **I agree to the Terms of Service and the Master License and Services Agreement**. Then, click on the **Get Started** button:

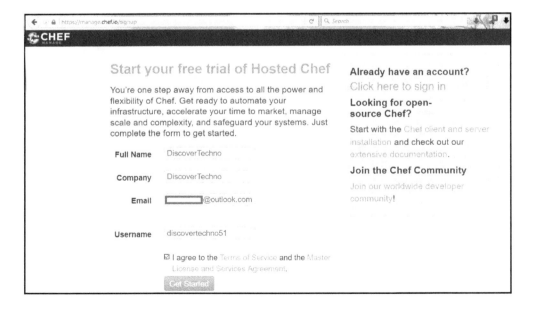

3. You will then see this message:

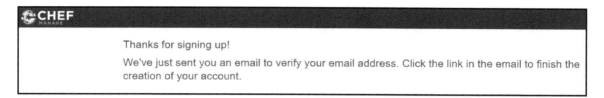

4. Open your e-mail inbox and click on the verification link to complete the creation of your hosted Chef account. You will get an **Email Verification Successful** message. After typing your password, click on **Create User** button:

5. The next task is to create an organization. Click on **Create New Organization**:

6. Provide the **Full Name** and **Short Name** of the organization, and click on the **Create Organization** button:

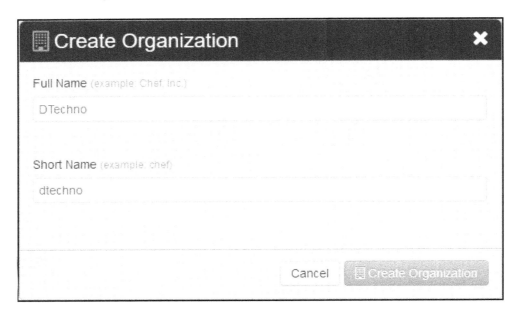

7. Bingo! You've just created your hosted Chef account, and you can now start using it. The next step is to download a starter kit:

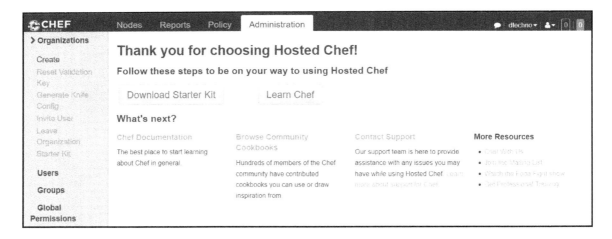

8. When you click on **Download Starter Kit**, your user and organization keys will be reset. Make sure to keep them in a safe place. On the confirmation dialog, click on **Proceed**:

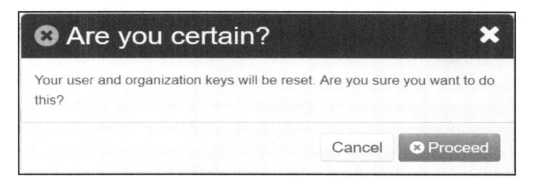

Let's have a quick walkthrough of the hosted Chef portal or dashboard

1. Click on **Nodes**; you will be shown an empty list as no node has been configured using the Chef server. Note this as we are going to see the same screen when we configure a node later.

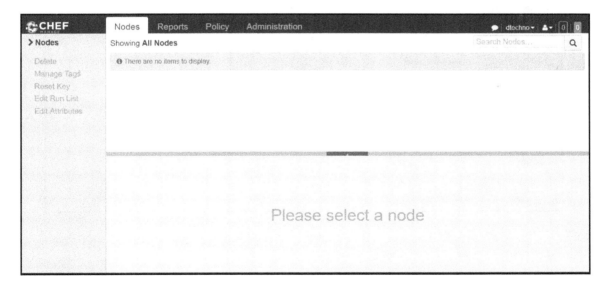

2. Now, navigate to **Administration** | **Users** and verify the user account created at the time of registration:

3. The **Reports** tab has no data as the convergence process hasn't taken place and no success or failure data is available:

Once we have a hosted Chef account available, the next step is to configure a Chef workstation:

1. First, download the Red Hat version of the Chef client from `https://downloads.chef.io/chef-client/redhat/` as we are going to use a CentOS virtual machine to act as our workstation.

2. Select your operating system type, select the Chef client version, and download the installation files:

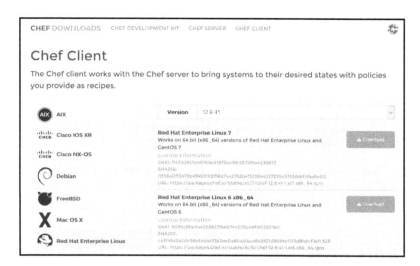

3. The Chef development kit is useful for installing development tools, and it can also be used to install knife plugins for AWS and Azure. Download it from `https ://downloads.chef.io/chef-dk/`:

In the next section, we will see how to configure a Chef workstation.

Installing and configuring a Chef workstation

Before installing a Chef client for preparing a workstation, let's try to verify whether the Chef client has been installed:

1. Execute the `chef-client –version` command to verify whether the Chef client has been installed:

```
[mitesh@devops1 Desktop]$ chef-client –version
bash: chef-client: command not found
```

2. As you can see in the output of the previous command, the Chef client is not installed. Now, navigate to the directory where the Chef client installable is stored using the `cd` command:

```
[mitesh@devops1 Desktop]$ cd chef/
[mitesh@devops1 chef]$ ls
chef-12.9.41-1.el6.x86_64.rpmchefdk-0.13.21-1.el6.x86_64.rpm
```

3. Run the downloaded Chef client RPM using `rpm –ivh chef-<version>.rpm`:

```
[mitesh@devops1 chef]$ rpm –ivh chef-12.9.41-1.el6.x86_64.rpm
warning: chef-12.9.41-1.el6.x86_64.rpm: Header V4DSA/SHA1
Signature,                key ID 83ef826a: NOKEY
error: can't create transaction lock on /var/lib/rpm/.rpm.lock
         (Permission denied)
```

4. Permission is denied, so use `sudo` to run the command, and verify the installation process:

```
[mitesh@devops1 chef]$ sudo rpm –ivh
chef-12.9.41-1.el6.x86_64.rpm
[sudo] password for mitesh:
warning: chef-12.9.41-1.el6.x86_64.rpm: Header V4DSA/SHA1
Signature,                key ID 83ef826a: NOKEY
Preparing...################################### [100%]
1:chef      ################################### [100%]
Thank you for installing Chef!
```

5. After successful installation, verify the Chef client version:

```
[mitesh@devops1 chef]$ chef-client --version
Chef: 12.9.41
```

The next step is to use the Chef starter kit that we downloaded while creating an account in hosted Chef:

1. Extract the chef-repo compressed file, and verify its contents. Copy the .chef directory into the root or user folder:

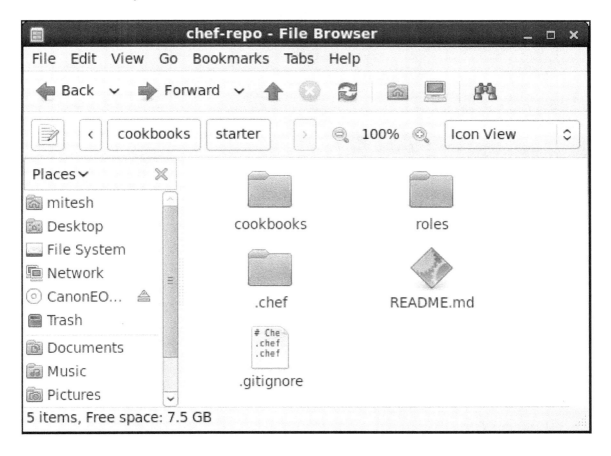

2. Verify the `cookbooks` folder, available in the `chef-repo` directory:

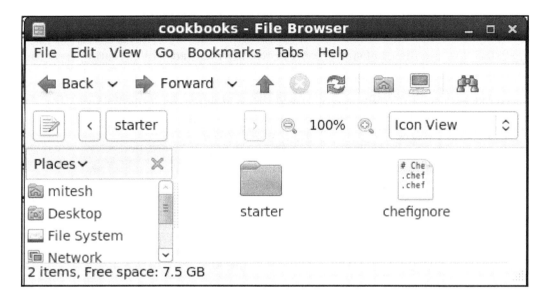

3. In the `.chef` directory, open the `knife.rb` file, which contains various configurations. All the configurations you need are already available. Adjust the path of the `cookbooks` directory if needed:

```
current_dir = File.dirname(__FILE__)
log_level                    :info
log_locationSTDOUT
node_name"discovertechno51"
client_key"#{current_dir}/discovertechno51.pem"
validation_client_name"dtechno-validator"
validation_key"#{current_dir}/dtechno-validator.pem"
chef_server_url"https://api.chef.io/organizations/dtechno"
cookbook_path                ["#{current_dir}/../cookbooks"]
```

 For more information on knife's configuration options, visit `http://docs.chef.io/config_rb_knife.html`.

4. With that, we've finished configuring our Chef workstation. The next step is using it to converge the node.

Converging a Chef node using a Chef workstation

In this section, we will try to setup runtime environment in node using Chef workstation.

First of all, let's login to the Chef workstation which setup:

1. Open the terminal and verify the IP address using `ifconfig`:

    ```
    [root@devops1 chef-repo]#ifconfig
    eth3      Link encap:EthernetHWaddr00:0C:29:D9:30:7F
    inetaddr:192.168.1.35Bcast:192.168.1.255Mask:255.255.255.0
    inet6addr: fe80::20c:29ff:fed9:307f/64 Scope:Link
              UP BROADCAST RUNNING MULTICAST  MTU:1500Metric:1
              RX packets:841351errors:0dropped:0overruns:0frame:0
              TX packets:610551errors:0dropped:0overruns:0carrier:0
    collisions:0txqueuelen:1000
              RX bytes:520196141 (496.0 MiB)  TX bytes:278125183
    (265.2                     MiB)
    lo        Link encap:Local Loopback
    inetaddr:127.0.0.1Mask:255.0.0.0
    inet6addr:  ::1/128 Scope:Host
              UP LOOPBACK RUNNING  MTU:65536Metric:1
              RX packets:1680errors:0dropped:0overruns:0frame:0
              TX packets:1680errors:0dropped:0overruns:0carrier:0
    collisions:0txqueuelen:0
              RX bytes:521152 (508.9 KiB)  TX bytes:521152 (508.9
    KiB)
    ```

2. Verify the knife version installed on the Chef workstation with `knife --version`:

    ```
    [root@devops1 chef]#knife --version
    Chef: 12.9.41
    ```

3. The `knife node list` command is used to obtain the list of nodes served by the Chef server in our case, hosted Chef. As we haven't converged any nodes, the list will be empty.

    ```
    [root@devops1 chef-repo]#knife node list
    ```

4. Create a virtual machine using VMware Workstation or VirtualBox. Install CentOS. Once the VM is ready, find its IP address and note it down.

5. On your Chef workstation, open a terminal and, using `ssh`, try to connect to the node or VM we just created:

```
[root@devops1 chef-repo]#sshroot@192.168.1.37
```

6. The authenticity of the host `192.168.1.37` can't be established:

```
RSA key fingerprint is 4b:56:28:62:53:59:e8:e0:5e:5f:54:08:c1:0c:1e:6c.
Are you sure you want to continue connecting (yes/no)? yes
Warning: Permanently added '192.168.1.37' (RSA) to the list of known
hosts.
root@192.168.1.37's password:
Last login: Thu May 28 10:26:06 2015 from 192.168.1.15
```

7. We now have an SSH session on the node from the Chef workstation. If you verify the IP address, you'll know that you are accessing a different machine by remote (SSH)access:

```
[root@localhost ~]#ifconfig
eth1      Link encap:EthernetHWaddr00:0C:29:44:9B:4B
inetaddr:192.168.1.37Bcast:192.168.1.255Mask:255.255.255.0
inet6addr: fe80::20c:29ff:fe44:9b4b/64 Scope:Link
          UP BROADCAST RUNNING MULTICAST  MTU:1500Metric:1
          RX packets:11252errors:0dropped:0overruns:0frame:0
          TX packets:6628errors:0dropped:0overruns:0carrier:0
collisions:0txqueuelen:1000
          RX bytes:14158681 (13.5 MiB)   TX bytes:466365 (455.4
KiB)
lo        Link encap:Local Loopback
inetaddr:127.0.0.1Mask:255.0.0.0
inet6addr: ::1/128 Scope:Host
          UP LOOPBACK RUNNING  MTU:65536Metric:1
          RX packets:59513errors:0dropped:0overruns:0frame:0
          TX packets:59513errors:0dropped:0overruns:0carrier:0
collisions:0txqueuelen:0
          RX bytes:224567119 (214.1 MiB)   TX bytes:224567119
(214.1                    MiB)

[root@localhost ~]#
```

8. Let's verify the node virtual machine. In my case, the VM already had the Chef client installed, so executing `rpm -qa *chef*`gave me the following result:

```
[root@localhost Desktop]#rpm -qa *chef*
chef-12.3.0-1.el6.x86_64
```

9. Let's remove the Chef client installation using `yum remove`:

```
[root@localhost Desktop]#yum remove chef-12.3.0-1.el6.x86_64
Loaded plugins: fastestmirror, refresh-packagekit, security
Setting up Remove Process
Resolving Dependencies
--> Running transaction check
---> Package chef.x86_64 0:12.3.0-1.el6 will be erased
--> Finished Dependency Resolution
Dependencies Resolved
================================================================
      Package        Arch           Version             Repository
Size
================================================================
    Removing:
      chef          x86_64         12.3.0-1.el6         installed
125 M
    Transaction Summary
================================================================
Remove          1 Package(s)
Installed size: 125 M
Is this ok [y/N]: y
Downloading Packages:
Running rpm_check_debug
Running Transaction Test
Transaction Test Succeeded
Running Transaction
  Erasing    : chef-12.3.0-1.el6.x86_641/1
  Verifying  : chef-12.3.0-1.el6.x86_641/1
Removed:
chef.x86_64 0:12.3.0-1.el6
Complete!
You have new mail in /var/spool/mail/root
```

10. We've removed the Chef client; to verify this, execute the following command:

```
[root@localhost Desktop]# chef-client -version
bash: chef-client: command not found
```

11. Let's remove the Tomcat installation as well if it has been installed on the node:

```
[root@localhost Desktop]# yum remove tomcat6
Loaded plugins: fastestmirror, refresh-packagekit, security
Setting up Remove Process
Resolving Dependencies
--> Running transaction check
---> Package tomcat6.x86_64 0:6.0.24-83.el6_6 will be erased
--> Processing Dependency: tomcat6 = 6.0.24-83.el6_6 for package:
```

```
tomcat6-
admin-webapps-6.0.24-83.el6_6.x86_64
    --> Running transaction check
    ---> Package tomcat6-admin-webapps.x86_64 0:6.0.24-83.el6_6 will be
erased
    --> Finished Dependency Resolution
    Dependencies Resolved


    ================================================================
     Package                    Arch       Version                 Repository
Size
    ================================================================
    Removing:
    tomcat6x86_64        6.0.24-83.el6_6            @updates      188 k
    Removing for dependencies:
    tomcat6-admin-webappsx86_64        6.0.24-83.el6_6        @updates      62
k

    Transaction Summary
    ================================================================
    Remove        2 Package(s)
    Installed size: 250 k
    Is this ok [y/N]: y
    Downloading Packages:
    Running rpm_check_debug
    Running Transaction Test
    Transaction Test Succeeded
    Running Transaction
      Erasing: tomcat6-admin-webapps-6.0.24-83.el6_6.x86_641/2
      Erasing: tomcat6-6.0.24-83.el6_6.x86_64   2/2
    warning: /etc/tomcat6/server.xml saved as
/etc/tomcat6/server.xml.rpmsave
    warning: /etc/tomcat6/logging.properties saved as
/etc/tomcat6/logging.properties.rpmsave
    warning: /etc/sysconfig/tomcat6 saved as /etc/sysconfig/tomcat6.rpmsave
      Verifying: tomcat6-admin-webapps-6.0.24-83.el6_6.x86_64   1/2
      Verifying: tomcat6-6.0.24-83.el6_6.x86_64   2/2
    Removed:
    tomcat6.x86_64 0:6.0.24-83.el6_6
    Dependency Removed:
    tomcat6-admin-webapps.x86_64 0:6.0.24-83.el6_6
    Complete!
    You have new mail in /var/spool/mail/root
```

12. Now, run the `yum remove tomcat6` command to verify whether Tomcat is still installed on the system:

```
[root@localhost Desktop]# yum remove tomcat6
Loaded plugins: fastestmirror, refresh-packagekit, security
```

```
Setting up Remove Process
No Match for argument: tomcat6
Loading mirror speeds from cached hostfile

 * base: centos.excellmedia.net
 * extras: centos.excellmedia.net
 * rpmforge: ftp.riken.jp
 * updates: centos.excellmedia.net
Package(s) tomcat6 available, but not installed.
No Packages marked for removal
```

13. Check whether the **Java Development Kit (JDK)** has been installed on the node:

```
[root@localhost Desktop]# java -version
java version "1.7.0_75"
OpenJDK Runtime Environment (rhel-2.5.4.0.el6_6-x86_64u75-b13)
OpenJDK 64-Bit Server VM (build 24.75-b04, mixed mode)
```

14. Exit the SSH session of the node's virtual machine. We now have control of the Chef workstation machine, and we will try to converge the node VM we just accessed remotely.

15. Use knife to converge the node. Provide the IP address/DNS name, user, password, and name of the node.

16. Verify the output:

```
[root@devops1 chef-repo]# knife bootstrap 192.168.1.37 -x root -P
cloud@123 -N tomcatserver
   Doing old-style registration with the validation key at
/home/mitesh/chef-repo/.chef/dtechno-validator.pem...
   Delete your validation key in order to use your user credentials
instead
   Connecting to 192.168.1.37
   192.168.1.37 -----> Installing Chef Omnibus (-v 12)
   192.168.1.37 downloading
https://omnitruck-direct.chef.io/chef/install.sh
   192.168.1.37   to file /tmp/install.sh.26574/install.sh
   192.168.1.37 trying wget...
   192.168.1.37 el 6 x86_64
   192.168.1.37 Getting information for chef stable 12 for el...
   192.168.1.37 downloading
https://omnitruck-direct.chef.io/stable/chef/metadata?v=12&p=el&pv=6&m=x86_
64
   192.168.1.37   to file /tmp/install.sh.26586/metadata.txt
   192.168.1.37 trying wget...
   192.168.1.37 sha1859bc9be9a40b8b13fb88744079ceef1832831b0
   192.168.1.37
sha256c43f48e5a2de56e4eda473a3ee0a80aa1aaa6c8621d9084e033d8b9cf3efc328
```

```
    192.168.1.37 url
https://packages.chef.io/stable/el/6/chef-12.9.41-1.el6.x86_64.rpm
    192.168.1.37 version12.9.41
    192.168.1.37 downloaded metadata file looks valid...
    192.168.1.37 downloading
https://packages.chef.io/stable/el/6/chef-12.9.41-1.el6.x86_64.rpm
    192.168.1.37    to file
/tmp/install.sh.26586/chef-12.9.41-1.el6.x86_64.rpm
    192.168.1.37 trying wget...

    192.168.1.37 Comparing checksum with sha256sum...
    192.168.1.37 Installing chef 12
    192.168.1.37 installing with rpm...
    192.168.1.37 warning:
/tmp/install.sh.26586/chef-12.9.41-1.el6.x86_64.rpm: Header V4DSA/SHA1
Signature, key ID 83ef826a: NOKEY
    192.168.1.37 Preparing...
######################################### [100%]
    192.168.1.37    1:chef
######################################### [100%]
    192.168.1.37 Thank you for installing Chef!
    192.168.1.37 Starting the first Chef Client run...
    192.168.1.37 Starting Chef Client, version 12.9.41
    192.168.1.37 Creating a new client identity for tomcatserver using the
validator key.
    192.168.1.37 resolving cookbooks for run list: []
    192.168.1.37 Synchronizing Cookbooks:
    192.168.1.37 Installing Cookbook Gems:
    192.168.1.37 Compiling Cookbooks...
    192.168.1.37 [2016-05-12T23:47:49-07:00] WARN: Node tomcatserver has an
empty run list.
    192.168.1.37 Converging 0 resources
    192.168.1.37
    192.168.1.37 Running handlers:
    192.168.1.37 Running handlers complete
    192.168.1.37 Chef Client finished, 0/0 resources updated in 37 seconds
```

17. There was no run list or role associated with the `knife` command, but the convergence was successful.

18. Let's verify our hosted Chef account. We can see the **Node Name** and **IP Address** in the **Nodes** section of dashboard, so open it and verify the details:

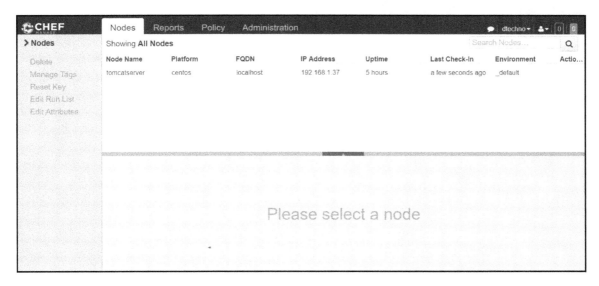

19. Select a node and click on the **Details** tab to get more information about the node, such as the **Attributes** associated with it and its **Permissions**, as shown in the following screenshot:

20. Verify the CPU attributes and other details of the node:

21. The convergence was successful, and we can see that in the **Reports** section of the hosted Chef account:

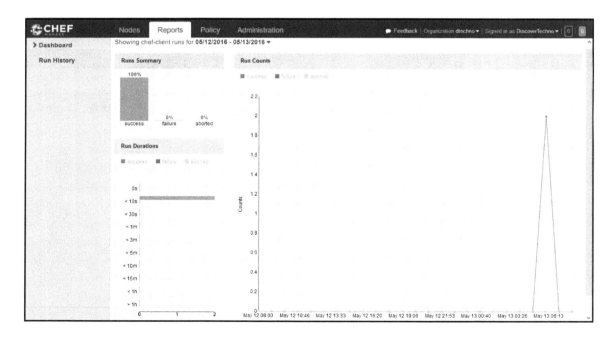

Installing software packages using cookbooks

Until now, we've seen how to created a hosted Chef account, how to configure a Chef workstation, and how to converge a node.

Now it is time to install software packages using cookbooks. To set up the runtime environment automatically, it's best to use the Chef community cookbooks:

1. Visit `https://github.com/chef-cookbooks` and find all the community cookbooks required to set up a runtime environment, as shown in the following screenshot:

2. We are using a sample Spring application, namely, PetClinic. We need to install Java and Tomcat to run a Java EE application such as this.
3. Download the Tomcat cookbook from `https://supermarket.chef.io/cookbooks/tomcat`, and navigate to the **Dependencies** section on that page. Without the dependencies uploaded to our Chef server, we can't upload the Tomcat cookbook to use it.

4. Download OpenSSL and Chef Sugar from `https://supermarket.chef.io/cook books/openssl` and `https://supermarket.chef.io/cookbooks/chef-sugar` respectively.

5. To install Java, download the cookbook from `https://supermarket.chef.io/co okbooks/java` and its dependency as well: `https://supermarket.chef.io/cook books/apt`. Extract all compressed files to the `cookbooks` directory:

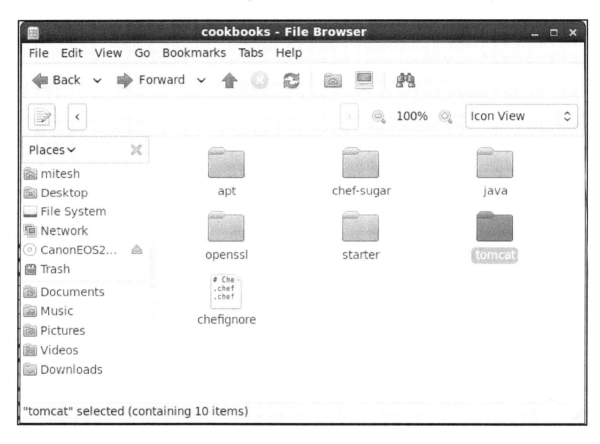

6. Go to `cookbooks` from the terminal and verify the subdirectories of the community cookbooks.

```
[root@devops1 cookbooks]# ls
apt   chefignore  chef-sugar  java  openssl  starter  tomcat
[root@devops1 cookbooks]# cd ..
```

7. Upload the `apt` cookbook with `knife cookbook upload apt`:

```
[root@devops1 chef-repo]# knife cookbook upload apt
Uploading apt            [3.0.0]
Uploaded 1 cookbook.
```

8. Verify from the **Cookbooks** section on the hosted Chef instance whether the **apt Cookbook** has been uploaded:

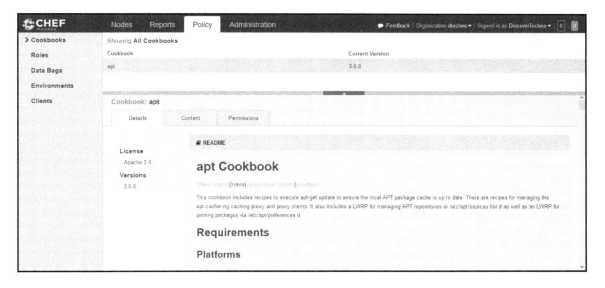

9. Make sure to upload all dependencies first, or it will give you an error. Upload all other cookbooks in order:

```
[root@devops1 chef-repo]# knife cookbook upload chef-sugar
Uploading chef-sugar     [3.3.0]
Uploaded 1 cookbook.
[root@devops1 chef-repo]# knife cookbook upload java
Uploading java           [1.39.0]
Uploaded 1 cookbook.
[root@devops1 chef-repo]# knife cookbook upload openssl
Uploading openssl        [4.4.0]
```

```
Uploaded 1 cookbook.
[root@devops1 chef-repo]# knife cookbook upload tomcat
Uploading tomcat          [0.17.0]
Uploaded 1 cookbook.
```

10. Check whether all the cookbooks have been uploaded from the hosted Chef account:

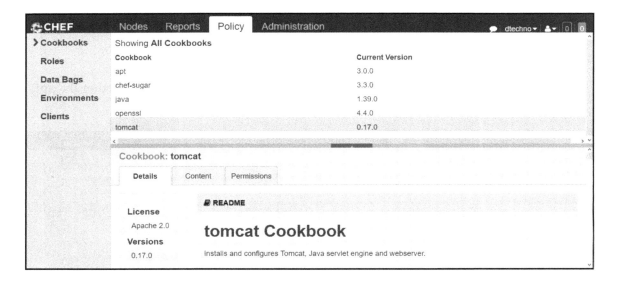

Creating a role

Once all cookbooks have been uploaded successfully, we need to create a role. A role is defined for a specific function and provides a path for different patterns and workflow processes.

For example, the web server role can consist of Tomcat server recipes and any custom attributes:

1. Go to **Policy| Roles | Create** to create a role. In the **Create Role** window, provide a **Name** and **Description** and then click on **Next**, as shown in the following screenshot:

2. A **Run List** keeps roles/recipes in a proper manner and order. We can say that it describes the specifications of a node. Select **tomcat** from the **Available Recipes** section, drag it to the **Current Run List** section, and click on **Create Role**:

3. Verify the newly added role details in the hosted Chef dashboard:

4. Now, we are ready to associate the role while converging the node. Add the role to the node with `knife node run_list add tomcatserver"role[v-tomcat]"`:

```
[root@devops1 chef-repo]# knife node run_list add tomcatserver"role[v-
tomcat]"
   tomcatserver:
   run_list: role[v-tomcat]
   [root@devops1 chef-repo]#
```

5. The role has now been associated with the node, and the next time the Chef client runs on the node, it will check whether it is in sync with its assignment. If not, it will execute the steps to bring the status in compliance with the role assigned.

```
[root@localhost Desktop]# chef-client
Starting Chef Client, version 12.9.41
resolving cookbooks for run list: ["tomcat"]
Synchronizing Cookbooks:
  - tomcat (0.17.0)
  - chef-sugar (3.3.0)
  - java (1.39.0)
  - apt (3.0.0)
  - openssl (4.4.0)
Installing Cookbook Gems:
Compiling Cookbooks...
```

```
.
.
.
Converging 3 resources
Recipe: tomcat::default
  * yum_package[tomcat6] action install
    - install version 6.0.24-94.el6_7 of package tomcat6
  * yum_package[tomcat6-admin-webapps] action install
    - install version 6.0.24-94.el6_7 of package tomcat6-admin-webapps
.
.<!-- A "Connector" using the shared thread pool-->
<!--
<Connector executor="tomcatThreadPool"
    -                port="8080" protocol="HTTP/1.1"
    -                connectionTimeout="20000"
    +                port="8080" protocol="HTTP/1.1"
    +                connectionTimeout="20000"
redirectPort="8443" />
    -    -->
    +    -->
.
.
  * service[tomcat6] action start
    - start service service[tomcat6]
  * execute[wait for tomcat6] action run
    - execute sleep 5
  * service[tomcat6] action enable
    - enable service service[tomcat6]
  * execute[wait for tomcat6] action run
    - execute sleep 5
  * execute[wait for tomcat6] action nothing (skipped due to action
:nothing)
  * service[tomcat6] action restart
    - restart service service[tomcat6]
  * execute[wait for tomcat6] action run
    - execute sleep 5
Running handlers:
Running handlers complete
Chef Client finished, 11/15 resources updated in 09 minutes 59 seconds
You have new mail in /var/spool/mail/root
[root@localhost Desktop]# service tomcat6 status
tomcat6 (pid 39782) is running...     [  OK  ]
You have new mail in /var/spool/mail/root
```

6. If you take a look at the output, we will come to know what exactly happens when convergence takes place.

7. Verify the **Reports** section in the hosted Chef account to obtain the latest details:

Now we know how to create a hosted Chef account, configure a workstation, and converge anode. This is the important piece, in the end-to-end automation as with the use of Chef configuration management tool, we have setup runtime environment that is required to run Java EE application.

Self-test questions

1. Which of these categories does Chef fall into?

   - Continuous integration
   - Configuration management
   - Both of these
   - Neither of these

2. What are the three main components of a Chef installation?

- Chef server
- Chef workstation
- Chef Node
- Cookbooks
- All of these
- None of these

3. Which command can be used to check the version of a Chef client?

- `chefclient -version`
- `chef-client -version`
- `chefclient --version`
- `chef-client --version`
- None of these

4. What is the name of the configuration file in Chef?

- `knife.java`
- `knife.py`
- `knife.rb`
- `knife.sh`
- None of these

5. Which command is used for listing a node as available on a Chef server?

- `knife node list`
- `knife client list`
- `knife node listing`
- `knife nodes list`
- None of these

Summary

In this chapter, we covered how we can create a hosted Chef account, configure a workstation, upload a community cookbook to a hosted Chef account, converge a node, use community cookbooks to install Tomcat, verify the convergence of a node on a hosted Chef account, and verify success and failure reports. Essentially, we are standardizing the process of setting up a runtime environment from a centralized location. Most of the configuration tools do almost similar things, and you can decide based on experience and other features which configuration management tool you want. Automating the repetitive process in any field is the key to increasing efficiency, and configuration management tools do exactly that in the end-to-end automation of application delivery. In this chapter, we automated installing tomcat and other runtime requirements for sample Java EE application so we can deploy the WAR file created by Continuous Integration process.

In the next chapter, we will discuss Docker, one of the most popular technologies in recent times. It is also one of the most disruptive innovations. We will see how Docker containers are different from virtual machines, how to install them, and some basics about the technology.

5
Installing and Configuring Docker

"If you cannot do great things, do small things in a great way."
-Napoleon Hill

Docker-yes, one of the hot topics of technical discussions in recent times. It is an open source, container-based technology and considered one of the disruptive innovations of recent times. Docker containers are isolated packages that contain the components required to run an application.

This chapter will describe container technology in detail and explain how it is different from virtual machines by comparing the benefits of both. It will give you an overview of Docker and its installation and configuration details; it will also cover how to create CentOS containers for application deployment.

We will also cover Docker Hub and the basic architecture of Docker. We will see how to use the Tomcat image available on Docker Hub and create a sample image with a Java and Tomcat installation and a Dockerfile.

We will cover the following topics:

- Overview of Docker containers
- Understanding the difference between virtual machines and containers
- Installation and configuration of Docker on CentOS
- Creating your first Docker container
- Managing containers

Overview of Docker containers

Docker is an open source initiative for OS virtualization that automates the deployment of applications inside software containers. It provides isolated user spaces and hence provides user-based processes, space, and filesystems. Behind the scenes, it shares the Linux host kernel. The following diagram illustrates the working mechanism of a Docker container:

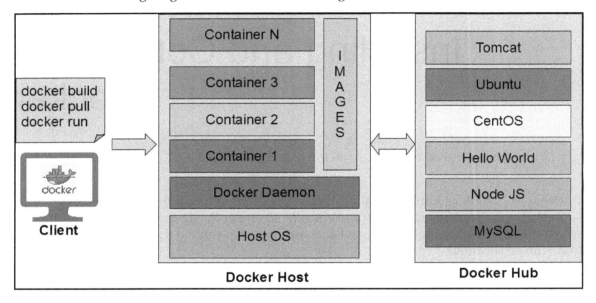

Docker has two main components, with a client-server architecture:

- **The Docker host**: The Docker host contains the Docker daemon, containers, and images. The **Docker engine** is an important component that provides the core Docker technology. This core Docker technology enables images and containers. When we install Docker successfully, we run a simple command. In our case, we will consider CentOS for the container. To run an interactive shell in the CentOS image, use `docker run -i -t <image> /bin/bash`:
  - The `-i` flag initiates an interactive container
  - The `-t` flag creates a pseudo-terminal that attaches `stdin` and `stdout`
  - The `<image>` is a CentOS image
  - `/bin/bash` starts a shell

- When we run this command, it verifies whether the CentOS image is available locally. If it is not available, it will download the image from Docker Hub.
- An image has a filesystem and parameter that can be used at runtime, while a container is an instance of an image with a state. It is simple to understand that containers change while images do not.
- **Docker Hub**: Docker Hub is a **Software as a Service (SaaS)** for sharing and managing Docker containers. It is a kind of centralized registry service provided by Docker. As a user, we can use it to build and ship applications. It allows us to create a pipeline to integrate with code repositories and for collaboration, image discovery, and automation.

1. Let's navigate to `https://hub.docker.com` and sign up by providing a username, e-mail, and password:

2. Activate your account by clicking on the activation link sent to your e-mail ID:

3. After successful activation, login to your Docker Hub account:

4. Following is the screenshot of the Docker **Dashboard**. Explore it as an exercise:

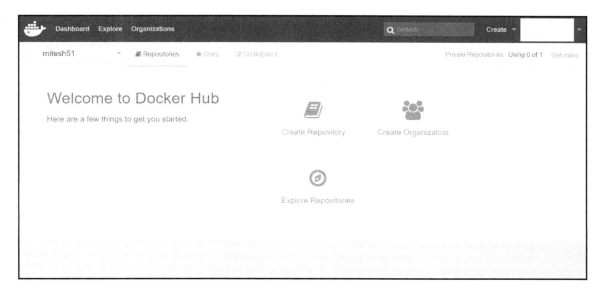

5. Click on **Repositories** to find images available in the public domain. Search for `centos`, and you will get a list of all CentOS images available on Docker Hub:

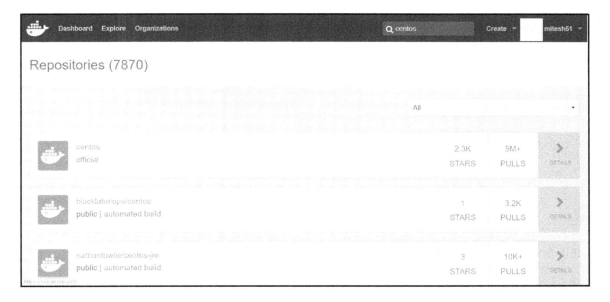

In the next section, we will see why containers are gaining so much attention by comparing them with virtual machines.

Understanding the difference between virtual machines and containers

In recent times, cloud computing has become part of almost all technical discussions. Virtual machines have served a lot of people in utilizing resources efficiently. However, Docker containers have given them competition and, in fact, containers are more effective.

Let's find out the basic differences between both and find out the reason behind the popularity of containers:

Virtual machines	Containers
In the virtual machine, we need to install an operating system with the appropriate device drivers; hence, the footprint or size of a virtual machine is huge. A normal VM with Tomcat and Java installed may take up to 10 GB of drive space:	A container shares the operating system and device drivers of the host. Containers are created from images, and for a container with Tomcat installed, the size is less than 500 MB:
There's an overhead of memory management and device drivers. A VM has all the components a normal physical machine has in terms of operation.	Containers are small in size and hence effectively give faster and better performance.
In a VM, the hypervisor abstracts resources.	Containers abstract the operating system.

In a VM, the package includes not only the application but also the necessary binaries and libraries, and an entire guest operating system, for example, CentOS 6.7 and Windows 2003.	A container runs as an isolated user space, with processes and filesystem in the user space on the host operating system itself, and it shares the kernel with other containers. Sharing and resource utilization are at their best in containers, and more resources are available due to less overhead. It works with very few required resources.
Cloud service providers use a hypervisor to provide a standard runtime environment for VMs. Hypervisors come in type 1 and type 2 categories.	Docker makes it efficient and easier to port applications across environments.

In the next section, we will install and configure Docker on a CentOS virtual machine.

Installing and configuring Docker on CentOS

To create a virtual machine using VMware Workstation or VirtualBox, install CentOS 6.6 or 6.7.

Follow these steps to use CentOS 6.7 to run Docker. In CentOS 6.x, there was a minor issue of a package name conflict with a system tray application and its executable, so the Docker RPM package was called docker-io.

1. Let's install docker-io:

```
[root@localhost Desktop]# yum install docker-io
Loaded plugins: fastestmirror, refresh-packagekit, security
Setting up Install Process
Loading mirror speeds from cached hostfile
 * epel: ftp.riken.jp
Resolving Dependencies
--> Running transaction check
---> Package docker-io.x86_64 0:1.7.1-2.el6 will be installed
--> Processing Dependency: lxc for package: docker-
io-1.7.1-2.el6.x86_64
--> Running transaction check
---> Package lxc.x86_64 0:1.0.8-1.el6 will be installed
--> Processing Dependency: lua-lxc(x86-64) = 1.0.8-1.el6 for package:
lxc-1.0.8-1.el6.x86_64
--> Processing Dependency: lua-alt-getopt for package:
lxc-1.0.8-1.el6.x86_64
--> Processing Dependency: liblxc.so.1()(64bit) for package:
```

```
lxc-1.0.8-1.el6.x86_64
    --> Running transaction check
    ---> Package lua-alt-getopt.noarch 0:0.7.0-1.el6 will be installed
    ---> Package lua-lxc.x86_64 0:1.0.8-1.el6 will be installed
    --> Processing Dependency: lua-filesystem for package: lua-
lxc-1.0.8-1.el6.x86_64
    ---> Package lxc-libs.x86_64 0:1.0.8-1.el6 will be installed
    --> Running transaction check
    ---> Package lua-filesystem.x86_64 0:1.4.2-1.el6 will be installed
    --> Finished Dependency Resolution
Dependencies Resolved
Package     Arch      Version      Repository     Size
Installing:
docker-io   x86_64    1.7.1-2.el6     epel      4.6 M
Installing for dependencies:
lua-alt-getopt     noarch    0.7.0-1.el6      epel    6.9 k
lua-filesystem     x86_64    1.4.2-1.el6      epel     24 k
lua-lxc     x86_64    1.0.8-1.el6     epel     16 k
lxc     x86_64     1.0.8-1.el6     epel     122 k
lxc-libs     x86_64     1.0.8-1.el6     epel     255 k
Transaction Summary
================================================================
Install        6 Package(s)
Total download size: 5.0 M
Installed size: 20 M
Is this ok [y/N]: y
Downloading Packages:
(1/6): docker-io-1.7.1-2.el6.x86_64.rpm          | 4.6 MB   04:32
(2/6): lua-alt-getopt-0.7.0-1.el6.noarch.rpm     | 6.9 kB   00:01
(3/6): lua-filesystem-1.4.2-1.el6.x86_64.rpm     |  24 kB   00:01
(4/6): lua-lxc-1.0.8-1.el6.x86_64.rpm            |  16 kB   00:01
(5/6): lxc-1.0.8-1.el6.x86_64.rpm                | 122 kB   00:03
(6/6): lxc-libs-1.0.8-1.el6.x86_64.rpm           | 255 kB   00:11
----------------------------------------------------------------Total
17 kB/s | 5.0 MB      05:02
    Running rpm_check_debug
    Running Transaction Test
    Transaction Test Succeeded
    Running Transaction
      Installing : lxc-libs-1.0.8-1.el6.x86_64                1/6
      Installing : lua-filesystem-1.4.2-1.el6.x86_64          2/6
      Installing : lua-lxc-1.0.8-1.el6.x86_64                 3/6
      Installing : lua-alt-getopt-0.7.0-1.el6.noarch          4/6
      Installing : lxc-1.0.8-1.el6.x86_64                     5/6
      Installing : docker-io-1.7.1-2.el6.x86_64               6/6
      Verifying  : lxc-libs-1.0.8-1.el6.x86_64                1/6
      Verifying  : lua-lxc-1.0.8-1.el6.x86_64                 2/6
      Verifying  : lxc-1.0.8-1.el6.x86_64                     3/6
```

```
    Verifying    : docker-io-1.7.1-2.el6.x86_64                      4/6
    Verifying    : lua-alt-getopt-0.7.0-1.el6.noarch                 5/6
    Verifying    : lua-filesystem-1.4.2-1.el6.x86_64                 6/6
Installed:
   docker-io.x86_64 0:1.7.1-2.el6
Dependency Installed:
   lua-alt-getopt.noarch 0:0.7.0-1.el6          lua-filesystem.x86_64
0:1.4.2-1.el6          lua-lxc.x86_64 0:1.0.8-1.el6          lxc.x86_64
0:1.0.8-1.el6
   lxc-libs.x86_64 0:1.0.8-1.el6
Complete!
You have new mail in /var/spool/mail/root
```

2. Let's try to run the sample `hello-world` image of Docker:

```
[root@localhost Desktop]# docker run hello-world
Post http:///var/run/docker.sock/v1.19/containers/create: dial unix
/var/run/docker.sock: no such file or directory. Are you trying to connect
to a TLS-enabled daemon without TLS?
You have new mail in /var/spool/mail/root
```

3. The sample image execution didn't complete successfully as the Docker service
    wasn't running. Let's verify the Docker installation:

    1. First, start the Docker service:

       ```
       [root@localhost Desktop]# service docker start
       Starting cgconfig service: [  OK  ]
       Starting docker:[  OK  ]
       You have new mail in /var/spool/mail/root
       ```

    2. Verify the status of the Docker service:

       ```
       [root@localhost Desktop]# service docker status
       docker (pid  12340) is running...
       ```

So we have now successfully installed Docker and verified whether its services are running
on a CentOS 6.7 virtual machine.

Creating your first Docker container

Just to get a feel of Docker, let's run a sample `hello-world` container, which we tried to do
earlier without success.

The `hello-world` image is not available locally, so it will be fetched from Docker Hub:

```
[root@localhost Desktop]# docker run hello-world
Unable to find image 'hello-world:latest' locally
latest: Pulling from hello-world
d59cd4c39e50: Pull complete
f1d956dc5945: Pull complete
Digest:
sha256:4f32210e234b4ad5cac92efacc0a3d602b02476c754f13d517e1ada048e5a8ba
Status: Downloaded newer image for hello-world:latest
Hello from Docker.
```

This message shows that your installation appears to be working correctly.

To generate this message, Docker performs the following steps:

1. The Docker client communicates with the Docker daemon.
2. Then Docker daemon pulls the `hello-world` image from Docker Hub.
3. After that, the Docker daemon creates a new container from that image, which runs the executable that produces the output you are currently reading.
4. When the executable gets executed in a newly created container, the Docker daemon streams that output to the Docker client, which sends it to your terminal.

Let's try something more ambitious:

1. You can run an Ubuntu container with this command:

```
$ docker run -it ubuntu bash
You have new mail in /var/spool/mail/root
[root@localhost Desktop]#
```

- Share images, automate workflows, and more with a free Docker Hub account by visiting `https://hub.docker.com`. For more examples and ideas, visit `https://docs.docker.com/engine/userguide/`.

2. Now we have one image available locally. Let's try to create an Ubuntu container and open its `bash` shell directly:

```
[root@localhost Desktop]# docker run -it ubuntu bash
Unable to find image 'ubuntu:latest' locally
 latest: Pulling from ubuntu
 dd25ab30afb3: Pull complete
 a83540abf000: Pull complete
 630aff59a5d5: Pull complete
 cdc870605343: Pull complete
 686477c12982: Pull complete
 Digest:
sha256:5718d664299eb1db14d87db7bfa6945b28879a67b74f36da3e34f5914866b71c
 Status: Downloaded newer image for ubuntu:latest
```

3. Use the `docker images` command to verify that the existing images are available locally:

```
[root@localhost Desktop]# docker images
REPOSITORY    TAG      IMAGE ID    CREATED VIRTUALSIZE
ubuntu        latest   686477c12982  5 weeks ago120.7 MB
hello-worldlatest    f1d956dc5945  6 weeks ago   967 B
```

After these two examples, let's try to understand the client-server architecture of Docker using another example of a Tomcat container.

Understanding the client-server architecture of Docker

Let's recollect our main objective: we want to deploy a sample Spring application named `Pet-clinic` on our Tomcat server. How it is different when we install tomcat in the virtual machine and use containers? In Container environment, host OS is installed and then it is used to host container layer. Container layer is used for provisioning container instances. Container instances are extremely lightweight and efficient as extra libraries or resources are needed for the operating system that is needed in the virtual machine while not in case of containers.

For that, in the rest of the section, we will try to use the existing Tomcat image and also create a sample image with a Tomcat installation:

1. Navigate to `https://hub.docker.com`, and after you login, search for `tomcat` in the search section. Click on **tomcat**, and you will be presented with something like this:

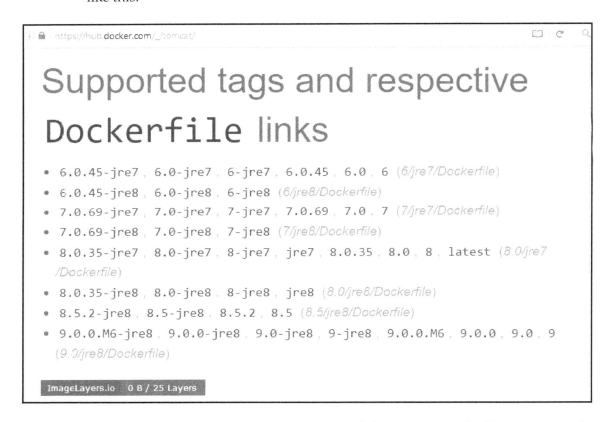

2. Verify the images with `docker images`, and then try to run the Tomcat image. It will take a while.

3. Once image is pulled completely, the container will be created and a bash shell will be available for command execution:

```
[root@localhost Desktop]# docker run  -it tomcat bash
```

```
[root@localhost Desktop]# docker images
REPOSITORY          TAG              IMAGE ID          CREATED          VIRTUAL SIZE
centos              latest           2a332da70fd1      2 weeks ago      196.7 MB
ubuntu              latest           686477c12982      6 weeks ago      120.7 MB
hello-world         latest           f1d956dc5945      7 weeks ago      967 B
[root@localhost Desktop]# docker run -it tomcat bash
Unable to find image 'tomcat:latest' locally
latest: Pulling from tomcat

7d7852532044: Downloading [====================>                        ] 20.97 MB/51.35 MB
435cb21051b6: Download complete
4c76b3c13563: Download complete
35e170305690: Download complete
14fa7ed0654b: Download complete
02dec3806bda: Download complete
b50599b96e33: Download complete
ec7e4967fab4: Download complete
499b5c54f1ed: Download complete
cc5b39d4a8b7: Downloading [===========>                                 ] 18.37 MB/77.64 MB
290876b830ae: Download complete
30167fbc73d4: Download complete
3a80d45737ff: Download complete
d4c89486429f: Download complete
4513ebd4451d: Download complete
4d3f030833b5: Download complete
9b29824628e2: Download complete
91fa6d6b4e7a: Download complete
aa3cd4ef3986: Download complete
1e96877e40eb: Download complete
fa9f8e22fb74: Download complete
```

4. Let's try to install Tomcat 8.0; you'll notice that the image is pulled from Docker Hub. However, most of the parts are already available locally:

```
[root@localhost Desktop]# docker run -it --rm tomcat:8.0
Unable to find image 'tomcat:8.0' locally
8.0: Pulling from tomcat
7d7852532044: Already exists
435cb21051b6: Already exists
.
.
.
5d4577339b14: Already exists
Digest:
sha256:2af935d02022b22717e41768dc523a62d4c78106997ff467d652a506b70bc860
Status: Downloaded newer image for tomcat:8.0
```

```
          Using CATALINA_BASE:   /usr/local/tomcat
          Using CATALINA_HOME:   /usr/local/tomcat
          Using CATALINA_TMPDIR: /usr/local/tomcat/temp
          Using JRE_HOME:        /usr/lib/jvm/java-7-openjdk-amd64/jre
          Using CLASSPATH:
 /usr/local/tomcat/bin/bootstrap.jar:/usr/local/tomcat/bin/tomcat-juli.jar
          19-Jun-2016 10:54:03.230 INFO [main]
 org.apache.catalina.startup.VersionLoggerListener.log Server version:
          Apache Tomcat/8.0.36
     .
     .
     .

          19-Jun-2016 12:05:22.745 INFO [Thread-3]
 org.apache.coyote.AbstractProtocol.destroy Destroying ProtocolHandler
 ["ajp-apr-8009"]
          You have new mail in /var/spool/mail/root
```

5. The container is created successfully. Verify existing containers using the `docker ps` command:

```
[root@localhost Desktop]# docker ps
CONTAINER ID        IMAGE             COMMAND             CREATED
STATUS              PORTS             NAMES
c3fbd72a1b35        tomcat:8.0        "catalina.sh run"   29 minutes ago
Up 29 minutes       8080/tcp          sad_pasteur
```

Once we have the Tomcat container ready, let's try to find out it's IP address so we can access Tomcat using it.

Use `docker inspect` with the container ID to find out the IP address of the container:

```
[root@localhost Desktop]# docker inspect c3fbd72a1b35
[
{
    "Id": "c3fbd72a1b35c6725606df726b5651cbd774b02d55bad6352c0e5205894b8b56",
    "Created": "2016-06-19T10:54:01.330825881Z",
    "Path": "catalina.sh",
    "Args": [
        "run"
    ],
    "State": {
        "Running": true,
        "Paused": false,
        "Restarting": false,
        "OOMKilled": false,
        "Dead": false,
        "Pid": 6293,
        "ExitCode": 0,
        "Error": "",
        "StartedAt": "2016-06-19T10:54:02.250775469Z",
        "FinishedAt": "0001-01-01T00:00:00Z"
    },
    "Image": "5d4577339b146f4e71ddb267812213bdc1a612eeb48a5f3c95f105b7894a4a73",
    "NetworkSettings": {
        "Bridge": "",
        "EndpointID": "a88792ad6a30316dbf8ad50c565d2c2c5951a040f4909f97418405142c7224e8",
        "Gateway": "172.17.42.1",
        "GlobalIPv6Address": "",
        "GlobalIPv6PrefixLen": 0,
        "HairpinMode": false,
        "IPAddress": "172.17.0.3",
```

Docker networking is a different concept itself and is not in the scope of this book, so we are not going to cover it.

However, let's verify whether the Tomcat container is running properly:

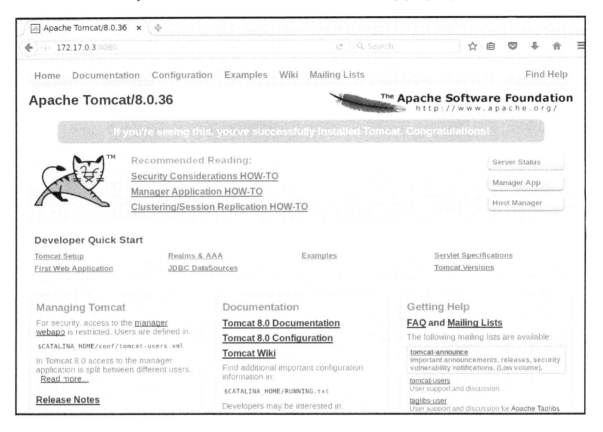

So finally, we are able to run a Tomcat container. In the next section, we will try to cover some basic but useful commands and try to build an image.

Managing containers

Let's try to run the Tomcat container as a background process.

1. It is best practice to run a Docker container as a background process to avoid accidentally stopping containers from the terminal:

2. Use the –d parameter:

```
[root@localhost Desktop]# docker run -d tomcat
```

```
68c6d1f7bc631613813ffb761cc833156a70e2063c2a743dd2729fe73b2873f9
```

3. Verify the container you just created:

```
[root@localhost Desktop]# docker ps
CONTAINER ID          IMAGE             COMMAND
CREATED                         STATUS           PORTS
NAMES
68c6d1f7bc63          tomcat                "catalina.sh run"    15
              seconds ago      Up 11 seconds          8080/tcp
              desperate_hypatia
You have new mail in /var/spool/mail/root
```

4. Get the IP address of the container with the `docker inspect` command along
   with the container ID:

```
[root@localhost Desktop]# docker inspect 68c6d1f7bc63
[
{
"Id":
"68c6d1f7bc631613813ffb761cc833156a70e2063c2a743dd2729fe73b2873f9",
    "Created": "2016-06-21T18:25:20.73708668Z",
    "Path": "catalina.sh",
    "Args": [
    "run"
        ],
    "State": {
    "Running": true,
    "Paused": false,
    "Restarting": false,
    "OOMKilled": false,
    "Dead": false,
    "Pid": 20448,
    "ExitCode": 0,
    "Error": "",
    "StartedAt": "2016-06-21T18:25:23.086757711Z",
    "FinishedAt": "0001-01-01T00:00:00Z"
        },
    "Image":
"5d4577339b146f4e71ddb267812213bdc1a612eeb48a5f3c95f105b7894a4a73",
    "NetworkSettings": {
    "Bridge": "",
    "EndpointID":
```

```
    "7ef4f440a137222ad96c20bd53330875ec8192499419f8d5d9c9a337c6044f9f",
        "Gateway": "172.17.42.1",
        "GlobalIPv6Address": "",
        "GlobalIPv6PrefixLen": 0,
        "HairpinMode": false,
        "IPAddress": "172.17.0.10",
        "IPPrefixLen": 16,
        "IPv6Gateway": "",
        "LinkLocalIPv6Address": "",
        "LinkLocalIPv6PrefixLen": 0,
        "MacAddress": "02:42:ac:11:00:0a",
        "NetworkID":
    "c5d8d33430092901b8f643f96f9d0fee2d70b45db782bd405a10a38b8cb12447",
        "PortMapping": null,
        "Ports": {
        "8080/tcp": null
                },
        "SandboxKey": "/var/run/docker/netns/68c6d1f7bc63",
        "SecondaryIPAddresses": null,
        "SecondaryIPv6Addresses": null
            },
    .
    .
    .

        "Image": "tomcat",
        "Volumes": null,
        "VolumeDriver": "",
        "WorkingDir": "/usr/local/tomcat",
        "Entrypoint": null,
        "NetworkDisabled": false,
        "MacAddress": "",
        "OnBuild": null,
        "Labels": {}
            }
    }
    ]
```

5. Note the IP address `http://172.17.0.10:8080/` and try to access it from the browser:

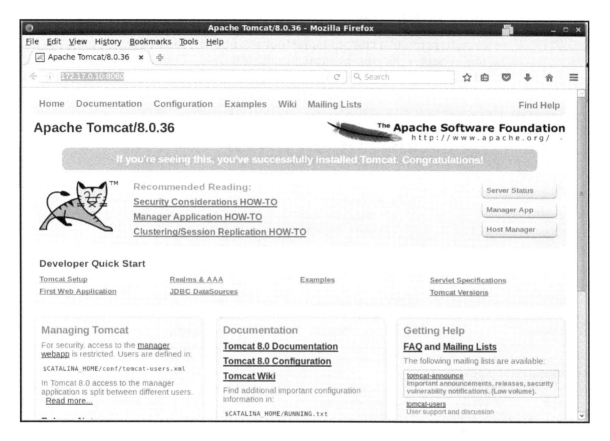

6. Now the obvious question is how to stop containers, right? To obtainthe details of running containers, use `docker ps`.

7. Observe the last column, **Names**; you can see a strange name `desperate_hypatia` being automatically allocated to a container if it is not given a name explicitly:

```
[root@localhost Desktop]# docker ps
CONTAINER ID          IMAGE          COMMAND
CREATED                  STATUS          PORTS             NAMES
68c6d1f7bc63          tomcat          "catalina.sh run"   15
    minutes ago       Up 15 minutes       8080/tcp
                desperate_hypatia
```

8. Let's stop the container using this automatically assigned container name:

```
[root@localhost Desktop]# docker stop desperate_hypatia
desperate_hypatia
```

9. If we want to provide a custom name to the container, then we can rename it using the `--name` operator, as shown in the following command:

```
[root@localhost Desktop]# docker run -d --name devops_tomcat
tomcat
cf2c1d19070fab73b840f94009391ad211f010044a7763fe201a115b0bc6a4b8
You have new mail in /var/spool/mail/root
[root@localhost Desktop]# docker ps
CONTAINER ID          IMAGE                    COMMAND
CREATED                              STATUS              PORTS
NAMES
            cf2c1d19070f        tomcat                "catalina.sh
run"            10 seconds ago      Up 9 seconds          8080/tcp
                    devops_tomcat
```

10. Can we see the list of all containers that have been stopped? Yes: use the `docker ps -a` command, to get the list of stopped containers:

```
[root@localhost Desktop]# docker ps -a
  CONTAINER ID          IMAGE                COMMAND             CREATED
STATUS                    PORTS              NAMES
    68c6d1f7bc63        tomcat              "catalina.sh run"   16 minutes
ago      Exited (143) 47 seconds ago
desperate_hypatia
    51e055a3414b        ubuntu              "ls -l"             43 minutes
ago      Exited (0) 43 minutes ago                sick_meitner
    a6f402e7a2a8        ubuntu              "ls"                43 minutes
ago      Exited (0) 43 minutes ago                naughty_hopper
    a4699613f112        ubuntu              "bash"              47 minutes
ago      Exited (127) 46 minutes ago
backstabbing_bardeen
    66a04d9137d8        ubuntu              "/bin/bash"         47 minutes
ago      Exited (0) 47 minutes ago
hungry_mcclintock
    a27b460778e6        ubuntu              "pwd"               48 minutes
ago      Exited (0) 48 minutes ago                dreamy_yonath
```

• A container's lifetime is limited to the existence of a parent process.

Let's run the container from the image with Tomcat to deploy application in it.

```
[root@localhost Desktop]# docker run -p 8080:9090 -d --name
devops_tomcat9 tomcat
```

```
0f8c251929b2f316bac1d53c5b8d03a155d790dada1ce2fcf94f95844a3acfef
```

11. To get access to a terminal on the container, use the following command after creating the container:

```
[root@localhost Desktop]# docker exec -it devops_tomcat9 bash
```

12. Once you have access to the container console, verify its IP address using `ip addr show eth0`:

```
root@0f8c251929b2:/usr/local/tomcat# ip addr show eth0
57: eth0: <BROADCAST,MULTICAST,UP,LOWER_UP> mtu 1500 qdisc
noqueue state UP
    link/ether 02:42:ac:11:00:14 brd ff:ff:ff:ff:ff:ff
    inet 172.17.0.20/16 scope global eth0
    inet6 fe80::42:acff:fe11:14/64 scope link
        valid_lft forever preferred_lft forever
root@0f8c251929b2:/usr/local/tomcat# ip route
172.17.0.0/16 dev eth0   proto kernel   scope link   src
172.17.0.20
default via 172.17.42.1 dev eth0
root@0f8c251929b2:/usr/local/tomcat#
```

13. Now, let's try to search for the Tomcat images available on Docker Hub. Try `docker search tomcat` command:

```
[root@localhost Desktop]# docker search tomcat
NAME            DESCRIPTION
STARS                 OFFICIAL    AUTOMATED
tomcat                          Apache Tomcat is an open source
            implementa...  750       [OK]
dordoka/tomcat              Ubuntu 14.04, Oracle JDK 8 and
Tomcat 8            ba...   19    [OK]
        .
        .
        .
```

```
davidcaste/debian-tomcat    Yet another Debian Docker image for
    Tomcat...    0    [OK]
```

14. Let's verify the existing images again:

```
[root@localhost Desktop]# docker images
REPOSITORY    TAG    IMAGE IDCREATEDVIRTUAL SIZE
tomcat        8.0    5d4577339b14 7 days ago   359.2 MB
tomcat        latest 5d4577339b14  7 days  ago        359.2 MB
centos        latest 2a332da70fd1  2 weeks ago        196.7 MB
ubuntu        latest 686477c12982  7 weeks ago        120.7 MB
hello-world   latest f1d956dc5945  8 weeks ago        967 B
You have new mail in /var/spool/mail/root
```

Creating a Docker image from Dockerfile

Our next step is to create a sample image file. We can build a Docker image using a Dockerfile. It provides step-by-step instructions to building images.

Let's try with a simple CentOS image:

1. The Dockerfile contains the following two lines:

   ```
   FROM centos
   MAINTAINER mitesh <mitesh.soxxxxxx@xxxxxxxx.com>
   ```

2. Go to the same directory in the terminal and use `docker build` `.` to build an image:

   ```
   [root@localhost Desktop]# docker build .
   Sending build context to Docker daemon 681.6 MB
   Sending build context to Docker daemon
   Step 0 : FROM centos
    ---> 2a332da70fd1
   Step 1 : MAINTAINER mitesh < mitesh.soxxxxxx@xxxxxxxx.com >
    ---> Running in 305e8da05500
    ---> b636e26a333a
   Removing intermediate container 305e8da05500
   Successfully built b636e26a333a
   You have new mail in /var/spool/mail/root
   ```

3. We have successfully built a sample Docker image. Now, let's verify it by executing the following command:

   ```
   [root@localhost Desktop]# docker images
   ```

```
REPOSITORY      TAG IMAGE ID      CREATED    VIRTUAL SIZE
<none><none> b636e26a333a   16 seconds ago      196.7 MB
tomcat     8.0      5d4577339b14   7 days ago         359.2 MB
tomcat     latest 5d4577339b14 7 days ago      359.2 MB
centos    latest    2a332da70fd1   2 weeks ago    196.7 MB
ubuntu    latest686477c12982 7 weeks ago     120.7 MB
hello-worldlatest      f1d956dc5945   8 weeks ago         967 B
```

4. Now, we will create an image with Java 8 and Tomcat 9 to understand how we can create a sample image. Verify whether you a have 32- or 64-bit operating system. Based on that, we will download the respective installable files:

```
[root@localhost Desktop]# uname -m
x86_64
```

We have a 64-bit operating system, so for Java, we will use the 64-bit installer:

1. The download URL for Java is `http://www.oracle.com/technetwork/java/jav ase/downloads/jdk8-downloads-2133151.html`:

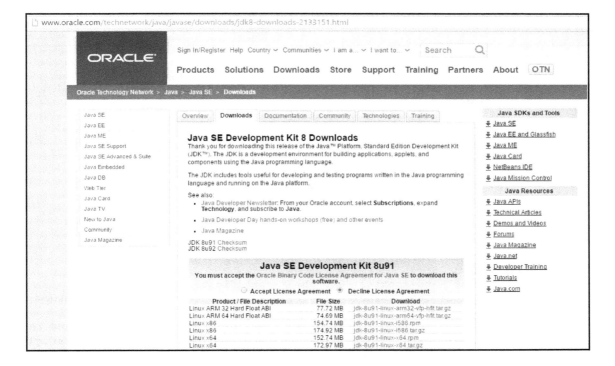

2. Download Tomcat from `http://apache-mirror.rbc.ru/pub/apache/tomcat/`:

```
←  →  C  🗋 apache-mirror.rbc.ru/pub/apache/tomcat/
```

Index of /pub/apache/tomcat

Name	Last modified	Size	Description
Parent Directory		-	
maven-plugin/	2015-02-17 21:55	-	
taglibs/	2015-05-14 16:48	-	
tomcat-6/	2016-04-12 10:39	-	
tomcat-7/	2016-06-21 11:32	-	
tomcat-8/	2016-06-13 18:53	-	
tomcat-9/	2016-06-13 18:31	-	
tomcat-connectors/	2015-02-17 21:55	-	

3. For a Java and Tomcat installation, we have the following Dockerfile:

```
FROM centos
MAINTAINER mitesh <mixxxx.xxxx@xxxxx.com>
RUN yum -y update && yum -y install wget && yum -y install tar

# Set Environment Variables
ENV JAVA_HOME /usr/java
ENV CATALINA_HOME /usr/tomcat
ENV PATH $PATH:$JAVA_HOME/bin:$CATALINA_HOME/bin

# Download and Install Java 8 :
```

```
http://www.oracle.com/technetwork/java/javase/downloads/jdk8-downloads-
   2133151.html
      RUN wget --no-cookies --no-check-certificate --header "Cookie:
gpw_e24=http%3A%2F%2Fwww.oracle.com%2F; oraclelicense=accept-securebackup-
cookie"
"http://download.oracle.com/otn-pub/java/jdk/8u92-b14/jdk-8u92-linux-x64.ta
r.gz" && tar -xvf jdk-8u92-linux-x64.tar.gz && rm jdk-8u92-linux-x64.tar.gz
&& mv jdk*           ${JAVA_HOME}

# Download and Install Tomcat 9 :
```

```
http://apache-mirror.rbc.ru/pub/apache/tomcat/
RUN wget
http://apache-mirror.rbc.ru/pub/apache/tomcat/tomcat-9/v9.0.0.M8/bin/apache
-tomcat-9.0.0.M8.tar.gz && tar -xvf apache-tomcat-9.0.0.M8.tar.gz && rm
apache-tomcat-9.0.0.M8.tar.gz && mv apache-tomcat*
${CATALINA_HOME}

         WORKDIR /usr/tomcat

         EXPOSE 8080
         EXPOSE 8009
```

4. Let's run the Dockerfile and build an image out of it:

```
         [root@localhost Desktop]# docker build -t devopstomcat .
         Sending build context to Docker daemon 681.6 MB
         Sending build context to Docker daemon
         Step 0 : FROM centos
          ---> 2a332da70fd1
         Step 1 : MAINTAINER mitesh <mitesh.soni@outlook.com>
          ---> Using cache
          ---> b636e26a333a
         Step 2 : RUN yum -y update && yum -y install wget && yum -y
install            tar
          ---> Using cache
          ---> 665ffbc90cba
         Step 3 : ENV JAVA_HOME /usr/java
          ---> Using cache
          ---> 0be3176a4b86
         Step 4 : ENV CATALINA_HOME /usr/tomcat
          ---> Using cache
          ---> 9c8ccd332f45
         Step 5 : ENV PATH $PATH:$JAVA_HOME/bin:$CATALINA_HOME/bin
          ---> Using cache
          ---> 64f697c88093
         Step 6 : RUN wget --no-cookies --no-check-certificate --header
"Cookie: gpw_e24=http%3A%2F%2Fwww.oracle.com%2F; oraclelicense=accept-
securebackup-
cookie""http://download.oracle.com/otn-pub/java/jdk/8u92-b14/jdk-8u92-linux
-x64.tar.gz"&& tar -xvf jdk-8u92-linux-x64.tar.gz && rm jdk-8u92-linux-
x64.tar.gz && mv jdk* ${JAVA_HOME}
          ---> Running in 116b0e860348
          --2016-06-23 19:48:41--
http://download.oracle.com/otn-pub/java/jdk/8u92-b14/jdk-8u92-linux-x64.tar
.gz
         Resolving download.oracle.com (download.oracle.com)...
203.192.223.200, 203.192.223.202
         Connecting to download.oracle.com
```

```
(download.oracle.com)|203.192.223.200|:80... connected.
           HTTP request sent, awaiting response... 302 Moved Temporarily
           Location:
https://edelivery.oracle.com/otn-pub/java/jdk/8u92-b14/jdk-8u92-linux-x64.t
ar.gz [following]
    .
    .
    .
           Connecting to download.oracle.com
(download.oracle.com)|203.192.223.200|:80... connected.
           HTTP request sent, awaiting response... 200 OK
           Length: 181389058 (173M) [application/x-gzip]
           Saving to: 'jdk-8u92-linux-x64.tar.gz'
               OK .......... .......... .......... .......... ..........
0%                      1.12M 2m35s
             50K .......... .......... .......... .......... ..........
0%                      4.88M 95s
                 .
                 .
                 .
           177100K .......... .......... .......... .......
100%                    397K=3m22s
           2016-06-23 19:52:06 (878 KB/s) - 'jdk-8u92-linux-x64.tar.gz'
saved                   [181389058/181389058]
           jdk1.8.0_92/
           jdk1.8.0_92/javafx-src.zip
           jdk1.8.0_92/bin/
           jdk1.8.0_92/bin/jmc
           jdk1.8.0_92/bin/serialver
           .
           .
           .
           jdk1.8.0_92/README.html
            ---> b025a8495f67
           Removing intermediate container 116b0e860348
           Step 7 : RUN wget
http://apache-mirror.rbc.ru/pub/apache/tomcat/tomcat-9/v9.0.0.M8/bin/apache
-tomcat-9.0.0.M8.tar.gz && tar -xvf apache-tomcat-9.0.0.M8.tar.gz && rm
apache-tomcat-9.0.0.M8.tar.gz && mv apache-tomcat* ${CATALINA_HOME}
            ---> Running in 485e2f6059b0
            --2016-06-23 19:53:18--
http://apache-mirror.rbc.ru/pub/apache/tomcat/tomcat-9/v9.0.0.M8/bin/apache
-tomcat-9.0.0.M8.tar.gz
           Resolving apache-mirror.rbc.ru (apache-mirror.rbc.ru)...
80.68.250.217
           Connecting to apache-mirror.rbc.ru (apache-
mirror.rbc.ru)|80.68.250.217|:80... connected.
```

```
HTTP request sent, awaiting response... 200 OK
Length: 9320099 (8.9M) [application/octet-stream]
Saving to: 'apache-tomcat-9.0.0.M8.tar.gz'
           OK ..........  ..........  ..........  .........
0%                 87.5K 1m43s
           50K ..........  ..........  ..........  .........
1%                 45.1K 2m31s
        9100K .
100%         3165G=5m55s
2016-06-23 19:59:19 (25.7 KB/s) - 'apache-
tomcat-9.0.0.M8.tar.gz'                saved [9320099/9320099]
apache-tomcat-9.0.0.M8/conf/
apache-tomcat-9.0.0.M8/conf/catalina.policy
           .
           .
           .
           .
           .
apache-tomcat-9.0.0.M8/bin/version.sh
 ---> 2cfaa947f591
Removing intermediate container 485e2f6059b0
Step 8 : WORKDIR /usr/tomcat
 ---> Running in 6d162a187968
 ---> 8edc567dda6a
Removing intermediate container 6d162a187968
Step 9 : EXPOSE 8080
 ---> Running in 6be43c6c3e35
 ---> aa0fe5cee557
Removing intermediate container 6be43c6c3e35
Step 10 : EXPOSE 8009
 ---> Running in c497dd2387c7
 ---> 400f097677e9
Removing intermediate container c497dd2387c7
Successfully built 400f097677e9
You have new mail in /var/spool/mail/root
```

So, we have successfully built a sample image using a Dockerfile.

This was just a quick example to get started and familiar with Docker and its concepts.

Self-test questions

State whether the following statements are true or false:

1. Has Docker a client-server architecture?
2. Docker has two main components: the Docker host and Docker Hub?
3. While creating a container, the image has to be available locally or the operation fails?
4. Is Docker Hub used to store and manage containers?
5. The overhead of memory management and device drivers is extremely high in Docker containers?
6. For CentOS6, the Docker RPM package is called `docker-io`?
7. The `docker ps -a` command is used to see the list of stopped containers?

Summary

In this chapter, we had an overview of Docker containers, architecture details, and details of the main components of Docker, including a quick overview of Docker Hub. Based on the overview, we tried to compare virtual machines with Docker containers to gain a clear picture of why containers have recently been gaining traction.

After gaining some understanding of virtual machines and containers, we covered the process of installing Docker on a CentOS 6.x virtual machine. We created a `hello-world` container and Ubuntu and CentOS containers from the images available on Docker Hub.

Our main aim is to use a Tomcat container for deploying a sample Spring application, so we used a Tomcat image and created a container from it for verification. To gain more understanding, we used a Dockerfile to build an image with Java and Tomcat.

On the subject of containers, this quote by Ted Engstrom is quite suitable:

> *"Anything that is wasted effort represents wasted time. The best management of our time thus becomes linked inseparably with the best utilization of our efforts."*

In the next chapter, we will see how to use Chef to create a virtual machine in Amazon Web Services and Microsoft Azure and set up a runtime environment.

6

Cloud Provisioning and Configuration Management with Chef

"You may delay, but time will not."

-Benjamin Franklin

Let's revisit what we have covered till now and what our goal was in the first chapter. Our main objective is to create an end-to-end automated pipeline for application deployment. We considered source code repositories, build tools, continuous integration, configuration management to setup runtime environment, resource provisioning in the cloud and containers, continuous delivery, continuous deployment, continuous monitoring, continuous feedback, continuous improvement, and continuous innovation. We want to use an end-to-end pipeline for our sample Spring application, PetClinic. In Chapter 4, *Installing and Configuring Chef* and Chapter 5, *Installing and Configuring Docker*, we covered the configuration management tool Chef and Docker containers in brief. Both could be topics for book on their own. Now we are at the stage where we understand the basics of configuration management and containers, so we can start with resource provisioning in a cloud environment using Chef and install the runtime environment required to run PetClinic. In this scenario, it will be an installation of Java and Tomcat.

This chapter describes in detail how to install knife plugins used to manage cloud resources using Chef. It will cover creating instances in AWS and Azure using the **knife EC2** and **knife Azure** plugins. It will also cover how Chef is used to manage Docker containers.

We will explore the following topics:

- Chef and cloud provisioning
- Installing knife plugins for Amazon EC2 and Microsoft Azure
- Creating and configuring a virtual machine in Amazon Web Services
- Creating and configuring a virtual machine in Microsoft Azure
- Managing Docker containers with Chef

Chef and cloud provisioning

Chef is not only used for setting up runtime environments or configuration management, but it is also used for resource provisioning in cloud environments. It supports cloud service providers such as Microsoft Azure, Amazon Web Services, VMware, OpenStack, HP Cloud, and Google Compute Engine. Chef provides more flexibility to the concept of infrastructure as a code and brings configuration management into the picture as well. Knife plugins are used to manage or use different cloud service providers. With knife plugins, it is easier to provision and deprovision resources along with controlled and centralized configuration management. In this chapter we will focus on infrastructure provisioning in Cloud environment and setting up runtime environment as shown in below diagram:

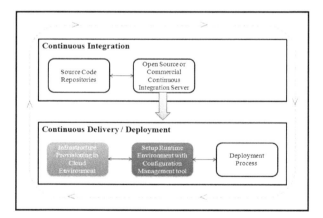

We will specifically focus on infrastructure provisioning in a cloud environment and setting up a runtime environment with a configuration management tool:

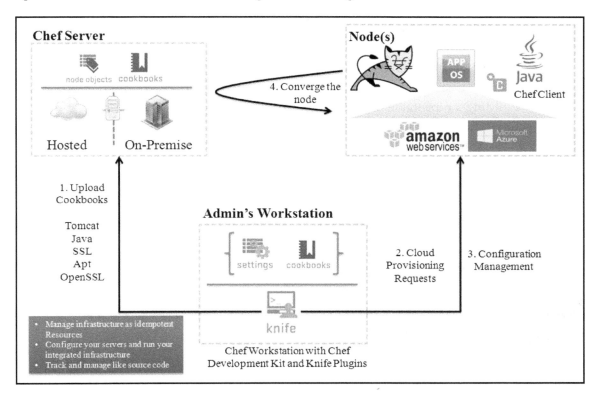

We will provision resources in a public cloud environment using knife plugins using a Chef workstation. We configured a Chef workstation in Chapter 4, *Installing and Configuring Chef*. From the Chef workstation, we can execute knife commands to create instances (Chef nodes) in different cloud environments. In our case, we will provision resources in Amazon EC2 and Microsoft Azure. This is how the process will work:

1. Chef workstation to CSP: Create a new instance in your cloud environment.
2. CSP: OK...done! The new instance is up and running (the Chef node is available).
3. Chef node to Chef server: Hello!
4. Chef server to Chef node: Here is your task-download the Chef client.
5. Chef server <-> Chef node: A secure handshake is made; the Chef server generates a security certificate. The security certificate is used to authenticate the new node's upcoming requests.

6. Chef server to Chef node: Here is the list of recipes you need to install.

7. Chef node to Chef server: Thank you; I've been updated!

Some of the major benefits we get through using Chef with different cloud platforms are as follows:

- Easy policy enforcement with centralized control
- Setup of a consistent runtime environment
- Building a repeatable infrastructure to avoid manual effort and errors
- Rapid deployment of new applications
- Easy restoration of environments
- Disaster recovery and business continuity
- Community-based cookbooks and recipes
- Faster time to market to remain in competition
- Support for major cloud service providers through plugins

In the next section, we will install knife plugins for some popular cloud platforms.

Installing knife plugins for Amazon Web Services and Microsoft Azure

The **Chef Development Kit** (**ChefDK**) comes with development tools built by the Chef community. It makes the task of installing knife plugins easier.

Go to `https://downloads.chef.io/chef-dk/` and download the ChefDK for your platform. For our purposes, select **Red Hat Enterprise Linux** and select the version. Click on the Red Hat Enterprise Linux 6 **Download** button as it works on 64 bit (x86_64) versions of Red Hat Enterprise Linux and CentOS 6:

```
[root@localhost Desktop]# sudo rpm -ivh chefdk-0.13.21-1.el6.x86_64.rpm
Preparing...                ###########################################
[100%]
    1:chefdk                ###########################################
[100%]
    Thank you for installing Chef Development Kit!
```

Once we have the ChefDK installed, we can use `chef gem install knife-ec2` to create, bootstrap, and manage EC2 instances. It is available at `https://github.com/chef/knife-ec2`.

```
[root@localhost Desktop]# chef gem install knife-ec2
Fetching: knife-ec2-0.13.0.gem (100%)
WARNING:  You don't have /root/.chefdk/gem/ruby/2.1.0/bin in your PATH,
  gem executables will not run.
Successfully installed knife-ec2-0.13.0
1 gem installed
```

Once `knife-ec2` has been installed successfully, we should verify the available EC2 commands:

```
[root@localhost Desktop]# knife ec2 --help
** EC2 COMMANDS **
knife ec2 amis ubuntu DISTRO [TYPE] (options)
knife ec2 flavor list (options)
knife ec2 server create (options)
knife ec2 server delete SERVER [SERVER] (options)
knife ec2 server list (options)
```

We can configure Amazon EC2 credentials for `knife ec2` in the `knife.rb` file using `knife[:aws_access_key_id]` and `knife[:aws_secret_access_key]`, like this:

```
knife[:aws_access_key_id] = "Your AWS Access Key ID"
knife[:aws_secret_access_key] = "Your AWS Secret Access Key"
```

Once we have the ChefDK installed, we can use the `chef gem install knife-azure` plugin, which is used to create, delete, and enumerate Microsoft Azure resources to be managed by Chef. The Chef knife plugin for Microsoft Azure is available at `https://github.com/chef/knife-azure`.

```
[root@localhost Desktop]# chef gem install knife-azure -v 1.5.2
Fetching: knife-azure-1.5.2.gem (100%)
WARNING:  You don't have /root/.chefdk/gem/ruby/2.1.0/bin in your PATH,
  gem executables will not run.
Successfully installed knife-azure-1.5.2
1 gem installed
```

Once `knife-azure` has been installed successfully, we should verify the available Azure commands:

```
[root@localhost Desktop]# knife azure --help
** AZURE COMMANDS **
knife azure ag create (options)
knife azure ag list (options)
```

```
knife azure image list (options)
knife azure internal lb create (options)
knife azure internal lb list (options)
knife azure server create (options)
knife azure server delete SERVER [SERVER] (options)
knife azure server list (options)
knife azure server show SERVER [SERVER]
knife azure vnet create (options)
knife azure vnet list (options)
```

Chef knife has support for VMware Workstation and allows deployments against a workstation. It is available at `https://github.com/chipx86/knife-wsfusion`:

```
[root@localhost Desktop]# chef gem install knife-wsfusion
Fetching: knife-wsfusion-0.1.1.gem (100%)
WARNING:  You don't have /root/.chefdk/gem/ruby/2.1.0/bin in your PATH,
   gem executables will not run.
Successfully installed knife-wsfusion-0.1.1
1 gem installed
You have new mail in /var/spool/mail/root
```

Once `knife-wsfusion` has been installed successfully, verify its available commands:

```
[root@localhost Desktop]# knife wsfusion --help
** WSFUSION COMMANDS **
knife wsfusion create (options)
```

Thus, we have installed the knife plugins required for AWS and Microsoft Azure.

In the next section, we will try to create a virtual machine using Amazon EC2.

Creating and configuring a virtual machine in Amazon EC2

Before creating and configuring a virtual machine in Amazon EC2, let's verify the existing nodes converged by Chef. Local virtual machines are only configured using Chef:

```
[root@devops1 Desktop]# knife node list
tomcatserver
```

1. After installing knife EC2 plugin, we can use `knife ec2 server create` command with following parameters to create new virtual machine:

Parameter	Value	Description
`-I`	`ami-1ecae776`	ID of the Amazon machine image
`-f`	`t2.micro`	Type of virtual machine
`-N`	DevOpsVMonAWS	Name of the Chef node
`--aws-access-key-id`	Your access key ID	AWS account access key ID
`--aws-secret-access-key`	Your secret access key	AWS account secret access key
`-S`	Book	SSH key
`--identity-file`	`book.pem`	PEM file
`--ssh-user`	`ec2-user`	User for AWS instance
`-r`	`role[v-tomcat]`	Chef role

```
[root@devops1 Desktop]# knife ec2 server create -I ami-1ecae776 -f
t2.micro -N DevOpsVMonAWS --aws-access-key-id '< Your Access Key ID >' --
aws-secret-access-key '< Your Secret Access Key >' -S book --identity-file
book.pem --ssh-user ec2-user -r role[v-tomcat]
    Instance ID: i-640d2de3
    Flavor: t2.micro
    Image: ami-1ecae776
    Region: us-east-1
    Availability Zone: us-east-1a
    Security Groups: default
    Tags: Name: DevOpsVMonAWS
    SSH Key: book
    Waiting for EC2 to create the instance......
    Public DNS Name: ec2-52-90-219-205.compute-1.amazonaws.com
    Public IP Address: 52.90.219.205
    Private DNS Name: ip-172-31-1-27.ec2.internal
    Private IP Address: 172.31.1.27
```

2. At this stage, the AWS EC2 instance has beencreated and is waiting for `sshd` access to become available:

```
Waiting for sshd access to become available...................done
Creating new client for DevOpsVMonAWS
Creating new node for DevOpsVMonAWS
Connecting to ec2-52-90-219-205.compute-1.amazonaws.com
    ec2-52-90-219-205.compute-1.amazonaws.com -----> Installing Chef
Omnibus (-v 12)
```

```
    .
    .
    .
    ec2-52-90-219-205.compute-1.amazonaws.com version12.9.41
    ec2-52-90-219-205.compute-1.amazonaws.com downloaded metadata file
looks valid...
    ec2-52-90-219-205.compute-1.amazonaws.com downloading
https://packages.chef.io/stable/el/6/chef-12.9.41-1.el6.x86_64.rpm
    ec2-52-90-219-205.compute-1.amazonaws.com    1:chef-12.9.41-1.el6
################################## [100%]
    ec2-52-90-219-205.compute-1.amazonaws.com Thank you for installing
Chef!
```

3. At this stage, the Chef client has been installed on the AWS instance. It is ready for the initial Chef Client run with version 12.9.41:

```
    ec2-52-90-219-205.compute-1.amazonaws.com Starting the first Chef
Client run...
    ec2-52-90-219-205.compute-1.amazonaws.com Starting Chef Client, version
12.9.41
```

4. It is now ready to resolve cookbooks based on the role and install runtime environments:

```
    ec2-52-90-219-205.compute-1.amazonaws.com resolving cookbooks for run
list: ["tomcat"]
    ec2-52-90-219-205.compute-1.amazonaws.com Synchronizing Cookbooks:
    ec2-52-90-219-205.compute-1.amazonaws.com    - tomcat (0.17.0)
    ec2-52-90-219-205.compute-1.amazonaws.com    - java (1.39.0)
    ec2-52-90-219-205.compute-1.amazonaws.com    - apt (3.0.0)
    ec2-52-90-219-205.compute-1.amazonaws.com    - openssl (4.4.0)
    ec2-52-90-219-205.compute-1.amazonaws.com    - chef-sugar (3.3.0)
    ec2-52-90-219-205.compute-1.amazonaws.com Installing Cookbook Gems:
    ec2-52-90-219-205.compute-1.amazonaws.com Compiling Cookbooks...
    ec2-52-90-219-205.compute-1.amazonaws.com Converging 3 resources
    ec2-52-90-219-205.compute-1.amazonaws.com Recipe: tomcat::default
    ec2-52-90-219-205.compute-1.amazonaws.com    * yum_package[tomcat6]
action install
    ec2-52-90-219-205.compute-1.amazonaws.com    - install version
6.0.45-1.4.amzn1 of package tomcat6
    ec2-52-90-219-205.compute-1.amazonaws.com    * yum_package[tomcat6-
admin-webapps] action install
    ec2-52-90-219-205.compute-1.amazonaws.com    - install version
6.0.45-1.4.amzn1 of package tomcat6-admin-webapps
    ec2-52-90-219-205.compute-1.amazonaws.com    * tomcat_instance[base]
action configure (up to date)
```

5. Our runtime environment is setup, and now it is time to start Tomcat services in our AWS instance:

```
ec2-52-90-219-205.compute-1.amazonaws.com
ec2-52-90-219-205.compute-1.amazonaws.com   * service[tomcat6] action
start
    .

    .
ec2-52-90-219-205.compute-1.amazonaws.com Chef Client finished, 13/15
resources updated in 01 minutes 13 seconds
```

6. Here are the details of the newly created AWS instance:

```
Instance ID: i-640d2de3
Flavor: t2.micro
Image: ami-1ecae776
Region: us-east-1
Availability Zone: us-east-1a
Security Groups: default
Security Group Ids: default
Tags: Name: DevOpsVMonAWS
SSH Key: book
Root Device Type: ebs
Root Volume ID: vol-1e0e83b5
Root Device Name: /dev/xvda
Root Device Delete on Terminate: true
Block devices
===========================
Device Name: /dev/xvda
Volume ID: vol-1e0e83b5
Delete on Terminate: true
===========================
Public DNS Name: ec2-52-90-219-205.compute-1.amazonaws.com
Public IP Address: 52.90.219.205
Private DNS Name: ip-172-31-1-27.ec2.internal
Private IP Address: 172.31.1.27
Environment: _default
Run List: role[v-tomcat]
You have new mail in /var/spool/mail/root
[root@devops1 Desktop]#
```

7. Go to `https://aws.amazon.com/`, and log in with admin or **Identity and Access Management (IAM)** credentials:

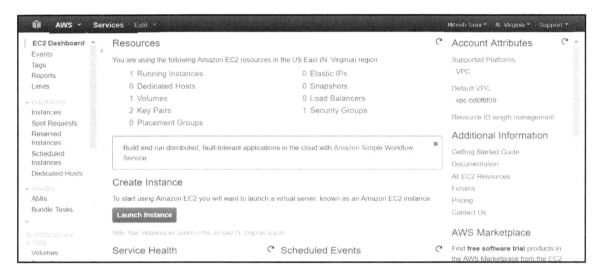

8. Click on **Instances** in the left-hand sidebar or on **Running Instances** on the **Resources** page get to the details about AWS instances. Verify the**Name**, **Tags**, **Public DNS**, and other details that we get in the Chef client run:

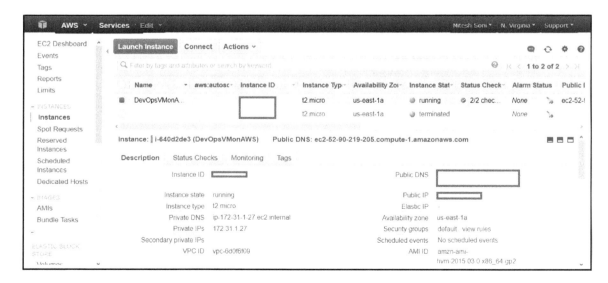

9. Now, let's go to the hosted Chef dashboard and log in. Click on **Nodes** and verify the newly created/converged node:

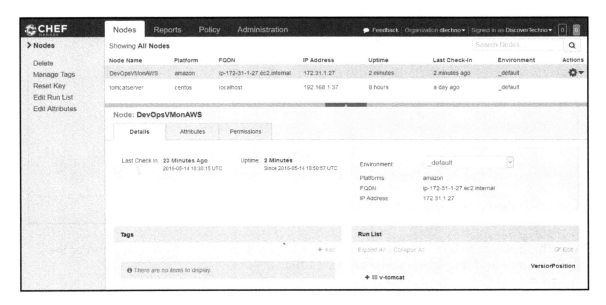

10. Verify the **Instance** details and **Run List**:

11. Check the **Attributes** section in the hosted Chef dashboard:

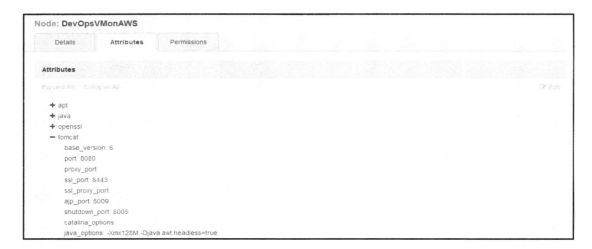

Everything seems to be nicely done with regard to the creation and configuration of the AWS instance and its registration on hosted Chef.

Let's try to access the Tomcat server installed on our newly created AWS instance:

1. You'll see that **The connection has timed out**:

2. The reason for this is the restriction of security groups in AWS. Verify the **Security groups** the AWS instance belongs to:

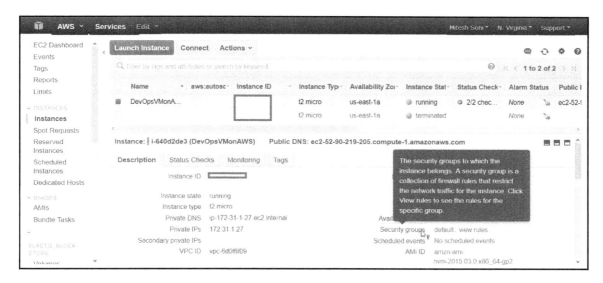

3. Go to the **Security groups** section from the AWS dashboard. Select the default security group and verify the **Inbound** rules. We can see only the **SSH** rule available:

4. Let's create a new custom rule with port `8080`:

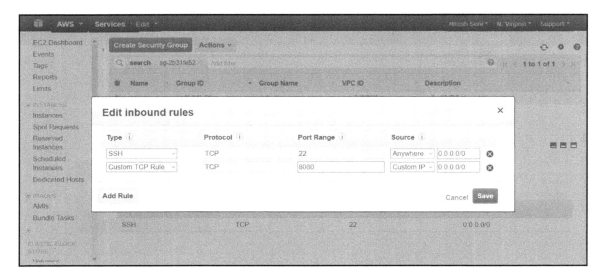

5. Now, let's verify the URL, and we will get the Tomcat page on our AWS instance.

In the next section, we will see how to create and configure a virtual machine in Microsoft Azure.

Creating and configuring a virtual machine in Microsoft Azure

For the `knife azure` plugin to communicate with Azure's REST API, we need to provide information to knife regarding our Azure account and credentials:

1. Sign in into the Azure portal and download a publish-settings file by visiting `htt ps://manage.windowsazure.com/publishsettings/index?client=xplat`.

2. Store it on a Chef workstation on the a local filesystem and refer to this local file by creating an entry in `knife.rb`:

```
knife[:azure_publish_settings_file] = "~/<name>.publishsettings"
```

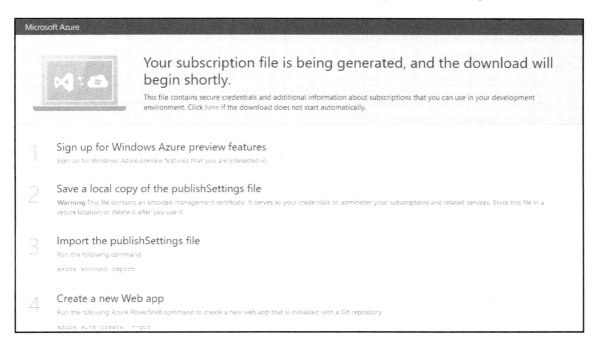

3. Here are the parameters used to create a virtual machine in Microsoft Azure:

Parameter	Value	Description
`--azure-dns-name`	`distechnodemo`	DNS name
`--azure-vm-name`	`dtserver02`	Virtual machine name
`--azure-vm-size`	Small	Virtual machine size
`-N`	`DevOpsVMonAzure2`	Name of the Chef node
`--azure-storage-account`	`classicstorage9883`	Azure storage account
`--bootstrap-protocol`	`cloud-api`	Bootstrap protocol

`--azure-source-image`	`5112500ae3b842c8b9c604889f8753c3__OpenLogic-CentOS-67-20160310`	Name of the Azure source image
`--azure-service-location`	Central US	Azure location to host virtual machine
`--ssh-user`	dtechno	SSH user
`--ssh-password`	<YOUR PASSWORD>	SSH password
`-r`	role[v-tomcat]	Role
`--ssh-port`	22	SSH port

After installing knife azure plugin, let's create virtual machine in Microsoft Azure:

```
[root@devops1 Desktop]# knife azure server create --azure-dns-name
'distechnodemo' --azure-vm-name 'dtserver02' --azure-vm-size 'Small' -N
DevOpsVMonAzure2 --azure-storage-account 'classicstorage9883' --bootstrap-
protocol 'cloud-api' --azure-source-image
'5112500ae3b842c8b9c604889f8753c3__OpenLogic-CentOS-67-20160310' --azure-
service-location 'Central US' --ssh-user 'dtechno' --ssh-password
'cloud@321' -r role[v-tomcat] --ssh-port 22
     .....Creating new client for DevOpsVMonAzure2
     Creating new node for DevOpsVMonAzure2
     .........
     Waiting for virtual machine to reach status
'provisioning'..............vm state 'provisioning' reached after 2.47
minutes.
     ..
     DNS Name: distechnodemo.cloudapp.net
     VM Name: dtserver02
     Size: Small
     Azure Source Image: 5112500ae3b842c8b9c604889f8753c3__OpenLogic-
CentOS-67-20160310
     Azure Service Location: Central US
     Private Ip Address: 100.73.210.70
     Environment: _default
     Runlist: ["role[v-tomcat]"]
     Resource provisioning is going to start.
     Waiting for Resource Extension to reach status 'wagent
provisioning'.....Resource extension state 'wagent provisioning' reached
after 0.17 minutes.
     Waiting for Resource Extension to reach status
'installing'...................Resource extension state 'installing'
reached after 2.21 minutes.
     Waiting for Resource Extension to reach status
```

```
'provisioning'.....Resource extension state 'provisioning' reached after
0.19 minutes.
    ..
    DNS Name: distechnodemo.cloudapp.net
    VM Name: dtserver02
    Size: Small
    Azure Source Image: 5112500ae3b842c8b9c604889f8753c3__OpenLogic-
CentOS-67-20160310
    Azure Service Location: Central US
    Private Ip Address: 100.73.210.70
    Environment: _default
    Runlist: ["role[v-tomcat]"]
    [root@devops1 Desktop]#
```

1. Go to the hosted Chef portal and click on **Nodes** to check whether the new node has been registered on the hosted Chef server:

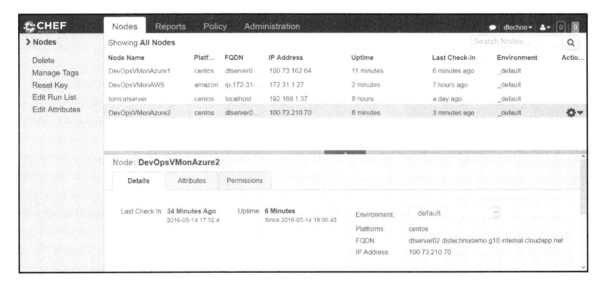

2. Click on the **Reports** section on the hosted Chef server and verify the graphs for **Runs Summary**, **Run Durations**, and **Run Counts**:

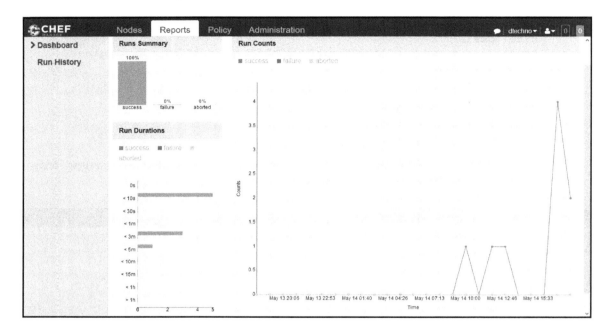

3. Now, let's go to the **classic Azure portal** and verify the newly created virtual machine:

4. Click on **VIRTUAL MACHINES** in Microsoft Azure, and you'll get details about it:

5. At the bottom of the page, verify the extensions section and check whether it shows **chef-server enabled**:

Verify the Tomcat installation and virtual machine creation in VMware Workstation as an exercise, the way we did for the AWS instance.

> For VMware Workstation, use `https://github.com/chipx86/knife-wsf`
> `usion` for reference.

Just to reiterate, we are now close to our main objective, that is, the end-to-end automation of the application deployment pipeline. We have covered continuous integration, cloud provisioning, containers, and configuration management. What's left is the actual deployment, monitoring, and orchestration of all the activities involved in the end-to-end automation.

Docker containers

Docker containers are extremely lightweight. We are going to use Tomcat as a web application server to deploy the PetClinic application. Docker Hub already has the Tomcat image, so we are not going to configure too many things except users for accessing the Tomcat manager app:

1. To `Tomcat-users.xml`, an add role and user, as follows:

```
<?xml version='1.0' encoding='utf-8'?>
<tomcat-users xmlns="http://tomcat.apache.org/xml"
              xmlns:xsi="http://www.w3.org/2001/XMLSchema-instance"
              xsi:schemaLocation="http://tomcat.apache.org/xml tomcat-
users.xsd"
              version="1.0">

<role rolename="manager-gui"/>
<user username="admin" password="admin@123" roles="manager-gui"/>

</tomcat-users>
```

2. Now, we are going to use the image available in Docker Hub and add `tomcat-sers.xml` to `/usr/local/tomcat/conf/tomcat-users.xml`. Create a Dockerfile, as shown here:

```
FROM tomcat:8.0
MAINTAINER Mitesh <mitesh.xxxx @xxxxx.com>
COPY tomcat-users.xml /usr/local/tomcat/conf/tomcat-users.xml
```

3. Once everything is ready, use `docker build` to build a new image:

```
[root@localhost mitesh]# docker build -t devopstomcatnew .
Sending build context to Docker daemon 8.192 kB
Sending build context to Docker daemon
Step 0 : FROM tomcat:8.0
 ---> 5d4577339b14
Step 1 : MAINTAINER Mitesh <YourEmailID@xyz.com>
 ---> Running in 9430cac12c4c
 ---> c63f90db4c14
Removing intermediate container 9430cac12c4c
Step 2 : COPY tomcat-users.xml /usr/local/tomcat/conf/tomcat-users.xml
 ---> eb50c4ceefb5
Removing intermediate container 7f31aed05097
Successfully built eb50c4ceefb5
You have new mail in /var/spool/mail/root
```

4. The image has been successfully built. Let's verify using `docker images`:

```
[root@localhost mitesh]# docker images
REPOSITORY              TAG           IMAGE ID          CREATED
VIRTUAL SIZE
    devopstomcatnew     latest        eb50c4ceefb5      10 seconds
ago        359.2 MB
    devopstomcat8       latest        f3537165ebe7      10 minutes
ago        344.6 MB
    devopstomcat        latest        400f097677e9      9 days ago
658.4 MB
    tomcat6             latest        400f097677e9      9 days ago
658.4 MB
    tomcat              9.0           ce07000625c6      2 weeks ago
344.6 MB
    centos              latest        2a332da70fd1      4 weeks ago
196.7 MB
    ubuntu              latest        686477c12982      8 weeks ago
120.7 MB
    hello-world         latest        f1d956dc5945      9 weeks ago
967 B
```

5. Create a container from the newly created Tomcat image. Verify existing
   containers using `docker ps` and `docker ps -a`:

```
[root@localhost mitesh]# docker ps
CONTAINER ID          IMAGE            COMMAND             CREATED
STATUS                PORTS            NAMES
    You have new mail in /var/spool/mail/root
    [root@localhost mitesh]# docker ps -a
CONTAINER ID          IMAGE            COMMAND             CREATED
STATUS                PORTS            NAMES
    [root@localhost mitesh]# docker run -p 8180:8080 -d --name
devopstomcat1 devopstomcatnew
    b5f054ee4ac36d67279db10497fe7a780aecf2a72a7f52fa31ee80c618d98e4a
```

6. Verify existing containers using `docker ps` and `docker ps -a`:

```
[root@localhost mitesh]# docker ps
CONTAINER ID          IMAGE            COMMAND             CREATED
STATUS                PORTS            NAMES
    b5f054ee4ac3        devopstomcatnew      "catalina.sh run"   21 seconds
ago      Up 20 seconds        0.0.0.0:8180->8080/tcp   devopstomcat1
```

7. Use `docker inspect b5f054ee4ac3` to obtain the IP address, and browse the Tomcat web server using the IP address and port:

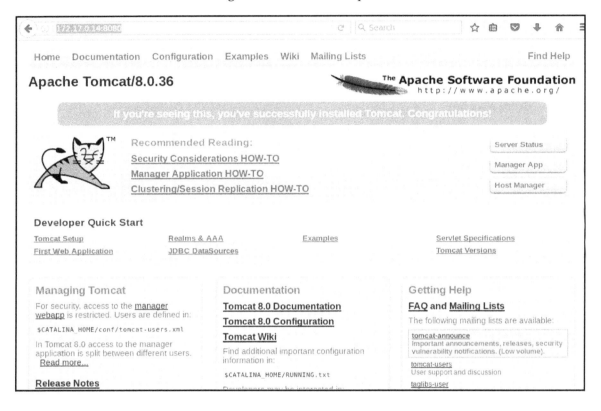

8. Click on the **Manager App** button. It will ask for a **User Name** and **Password**. Type them in and click on **OK**:

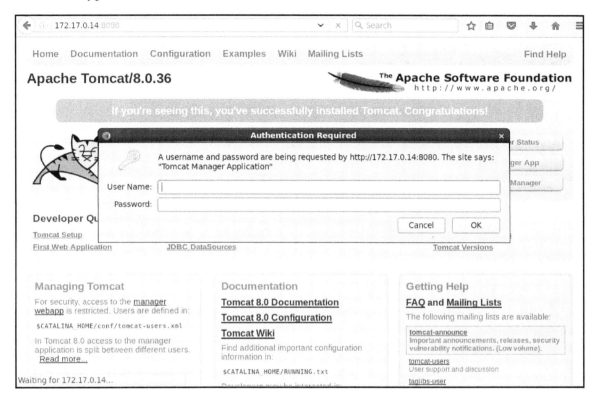

9. Now. we can access the Tomcat manager application:

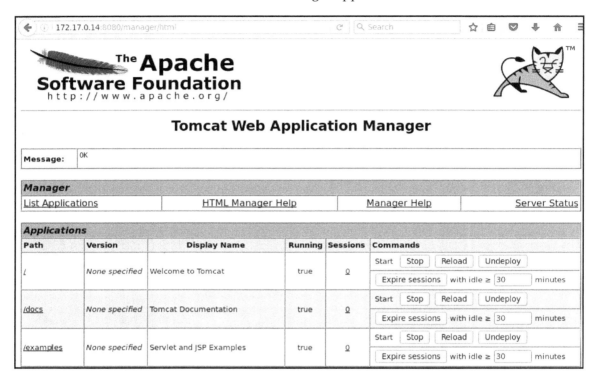

We can use Tomcat manager application to deploy applications. Until now, we have looked at continuous integration, configuration management, containers, and cloud provisioning. Next, we will cover application deployment using different methods, monitoring, and end-to-end automation pipeline using **orchestration**.

Self-test questions

1. Which of the following are benefits of Chef?

   - Easy policy enforcement with centralized control
   - Enables setup of consistent runtime environment
   - Enables easy restoration of environments
   - Enables disaster recovery and business continuity
   - Community-based cookbooks and recipes
   - All of these

2. Which two parameters are configured for Amazon EC2 credentials for `knife-ec2` in the `knife.rb` file?

   - `knife[:aws_access_key_id]` ="your AWS access key ID"
   - `knife[:aws_secret_access_key]` ="your AWS secret access key"
   - Both

3. Which of the following are `knife ec2` commands?

   - `knife ec2 flavor list` (options)
   - `knife ec2 server create` (options)
   - `knife ec2 server delete SERVER [SERVER]` (options)
   - `knife ec2 server list` (options)
   - All of the Above

4. True or false: The `rvm use` command is used to set the Ruby version.

   - True
   - False

5. Which of the following are `knife azure` commands?

   - `knife azure server create` (options)
   - `knife azure server delete SERVER [SERVER]` (options)
   - `knife azure server list` (options)
   - `knife azure image list` (options)
   - All of these

6. True or false: In the `knife ec2 server create` command, the `-I` parameter is used for the type of virtual machine.

- True
- False

7. True or false: In the `knife ec2 server create` command, the `-N` parameter is used for the name of the Chef Node.

- True
- False

Summary

In this chapter, we covered how to provision resources in the cloud and configure them. We used the knife EC2 and knife Azure plugins to create virtual machines in AWS and Microsoft Azure, respectively. We used the Docker Hub Tomcat image to build a new image with the `tomcat-users.xml` file, which has roles and users configured to access the Tomcat manager web app.

In the next chapter, we will cover different methods to deploy an application in a Tomcat web container. Let's again reiterate the goal of the book: end-to-end automation using an application deployment pipeline.

7
Deploying Application in AWS, Azure, and Docker

"Ultimate automation...will make our modern industry as primitive and outdated as the Stone Age man looks to us today."

-Albert Einstein

Finally, we are at the business end of the book, and our focus is on deployment, automation, monitoring, and orchestration.

Why?

It's because we want to achieve end-to-end application lifecycle automation or end-to-end deployment automation.

First, we will go step by step to deploy our PetClinic application to a remote Tomcat server. Once that is done, it can be used as common practice for all instances. This chapter describes in detail all the steps required to deploy our sample application to a different environment once the configuration management tool prepares it for the final deployment. We will also learn how to deploy the application in different environments, such as cloud or container-based ones.

This chapter will also cover on how to deploy an application on a PaaS model. We will deploy the application on AWS Elastic Beanstalk.

We will cover the following topics:

- Prerequisite – deploying our application on a remote server
- Deploying the application on AWS
- Deploying the application on Microsoft Azure
- Deploying the application in a Docker container

Prerequisites – deploying our application on Remote Server

Our main objective is to deploy application in a web server. Web server and application server can be on local environment or remote environment. We will first deploy on a remote server. We will try to use Windows Agent for compilation and deployment to see how Agent-based architecture can be utilized. Follow these steps to deploy an application on a remote server:

1. First, let's start an agent on a Windows machine. Open command prompt and run the following command, given in the **Manage Nodes** section of the Jenkins dashboard. Change the URL accordingly:

```
java -jar slave.jar -jnlpUrl
http://192.168.0.100:8080/computer/TestServer/slave-agent.jnlp -secret
65464e02c58c85b192883f7848ad2758408220bed2f3af715c01c9b01cb72f9b
 .
 .
INFO: Trying protocol: JNLP2-connect
Jul 06, 2016 8:57:16 PM hudson.remoting.jnlp.Main$CuiListener status
INFO: Connected
```

2. Our agent is now connected to the **master**. Let's verify the status of the agent on the **master** node, where Jenkins is running:

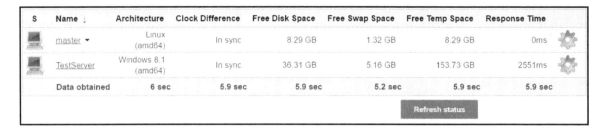

S	Name ↓	Architecture	Clock Difference	Free Disk Space	Free Swap Space	Free Temp Space	Response Time	
	master ▾	Linux (amd64)	In sync	8.29 GB	1.32 GB	8.29 GB	0ms	
	TestServer	Windows 8.1 (amd64)	In sync	36.31 GB	5.16 GB	153.73 GB	2551ms	
	Data obtained	6 sec	5.9 sec	5.9 sec	5.2 sec	5.9 sec	5.9 sec	
							Refresh status	

3. Click on the **TestServer** agent, and you'll get all the details regarding projects tied to it, as shown in this screenshot:

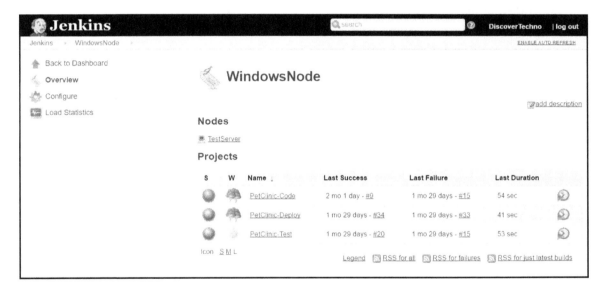

Now that we have the **agent** node ready, let's prepare a remote server by downloading and setting up Tomcat.

Setting up Tomcat server

In our case, we need not to do it for cloud instances as they will be configured using Chef. The following is a more involved perspective on how we did it earlier and how all of the installation and other activities can be automated using Chef. Let's take a step-by-step tour:

1. Download Tomcat 7 from `https://tomcat.apache.org/download-7.cgi`. We are going to use the **Deploy** plugin from Jenkins, and it requires specific versions of Tomcat for deployment:

7.0.70

Please see the README file for packaging information. It explains what every distribution contains.

Binary Distributions

- Core:
  - zip (pgp, md5, sha1)
  - tar.gz (pgp, md5, sha1)
  - 32-bit Windows zip (pgp, md5, sha1)
  - 64-bit Windows zip (pgp, md5, sha1)
  - 32-bit/64-bit Windows Service Installer (pgp, md5, sha1)
- Full documentation:
  - tar.gz (pgp, md5, sha1)
- Deployer:
  - zip (pgp, md5, sha1)
  - tar.gz (pgp, md5, sha1)
- Extras:
  - JMX Remote jar (pgp, md5, sha1)
  - Web services jar (pgp, md5, sha1)
  - JULI adapters jar (pgp, md5, sha1)
  - JULI log4j jar (pgp, md5, sha1)
- Embedded:
  - tar.gz (pgp, md5, sha1)
  - zip (pgp, md5, sha1)

---

2. Extract the Tomcat installation files:

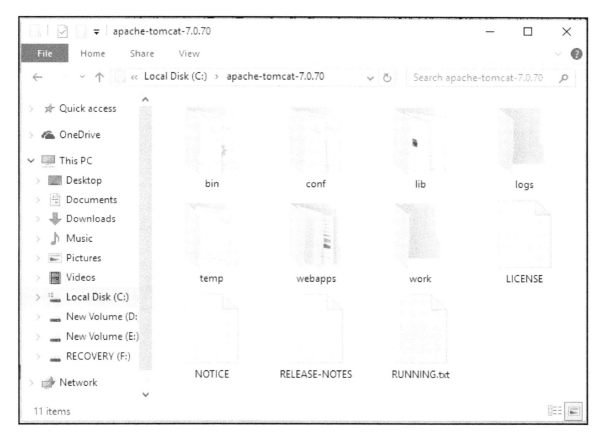

3. Open command prompt and go to the `bin` directory to start Tomcat:

`C:\>cd apache-tomcat-7.0.70\bin`

4. Run `startup.bat` from command prompt:

`C:\apache-tomcat-7.0.70\bin>startup.bat`

> Neither the JAVA_HOME nor the JRE_HOME environment variable is defined. At least one of these environment variable is needed to run this program.

5. Oops! We need to set environment variables. Go to **Control Panel** | **All Control Panel Items** | **System**.

6. Click on **Advanced system settings**:

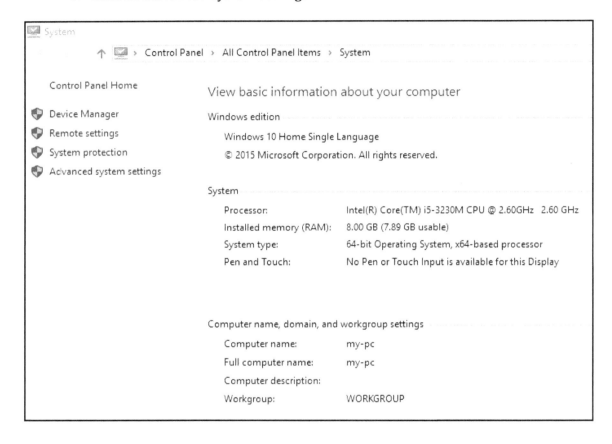

7. Click on **Environment Variables…** to set JAVA_ HOME:

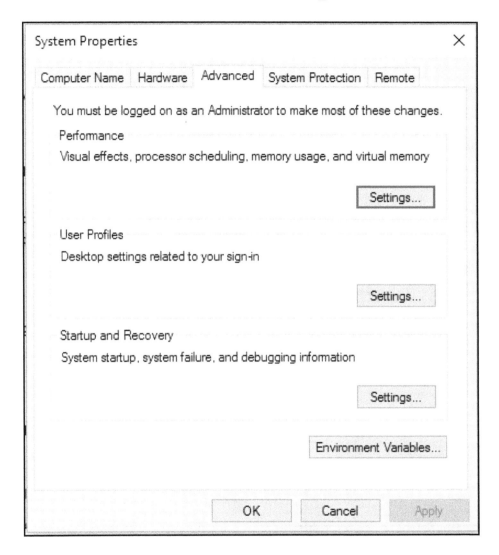

8. Click on **New...** and create a new variable for JAVA_HOME with the value C:\Program Files\Java\jdk1.8.0, and click on **OK**:

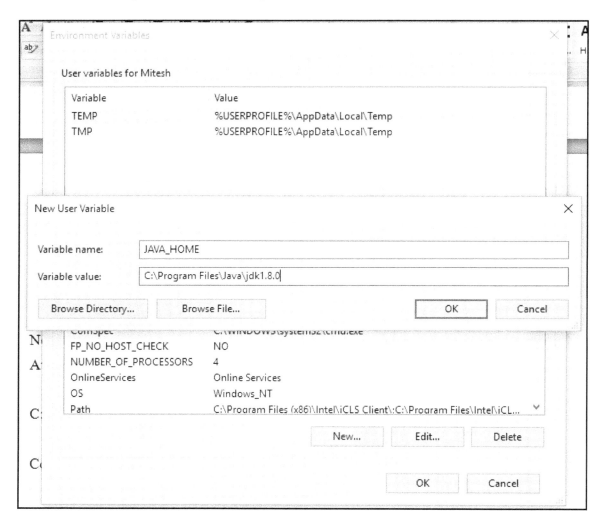

9. Click on **OK** once again to complete the process:

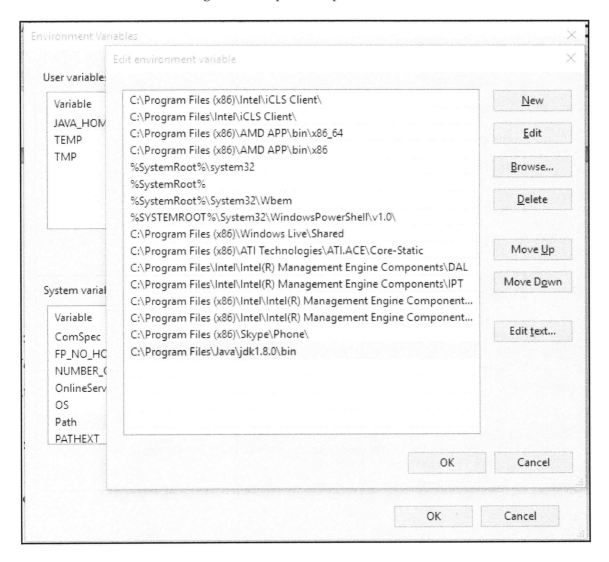

10. Open a new command prompt windows and verify the Java version by executing the following command:

```
C:\>java -version
java version "1.8.0-ea"
Java(TM) SE Runtime Environment (build 1.8.0-ea-b115)
Java HotSpot(TM) 64-Bit Server VM (build 25.0-b57, mixed mode)
```

11. Now, go to `tomcat\bin` and execute `startup.bat`:

```
C:\apache-tomcat-7.0.70\bin>startup.bat
Using CATALINA_BASE:   "C:\apache-tomcat-7.0.70"
Using CATALINA_HOME:   "C:\apache-tomcat-7.0.70"
Using CATALINA_TMPDIR: "C:\apache-tomcat-7.0.70\temp"
Using JRE_HOME:        "C:\Program Files\Java\jdk1.8.0"
Using CLASSPATH:       "C:\apache-
tomcat-7.0.70\bin\bootstrap.jar;C:\apache-tomcat-7.0.70\bin\tomcat-
juli.jar"
C:\apache-tomcat-7.0.70\bin>
```

12. Our Tomcat server is now running. It will have output similar to the following. Verify the server startup message:

```
INFO: Starting Servlet Engine: Apache Tomcat/7.0.70
Jul 06, 2016 9:29:07 PM
org.apache.catalina.startup.HostConfigdeployDirectory
    INFO: Deploying web application directory C:\apache-
tomcat-7.0.70\webapps\docs
    .

    .
Jul 06, 2016 9:29:11 PM org.apache.coyote.AbstractProtocol start
INFO: Starting ProtocolHandler ["ajp-apr-8009"]
Jul 06, 2016 9:29:11 PM org.apache.catalina.startup.Catalina start
INFO: Server startup in 5172 ms
```

13. Use the proper IP address and port number combination to navigate to the Tomcat**Home** page, which looks like this:

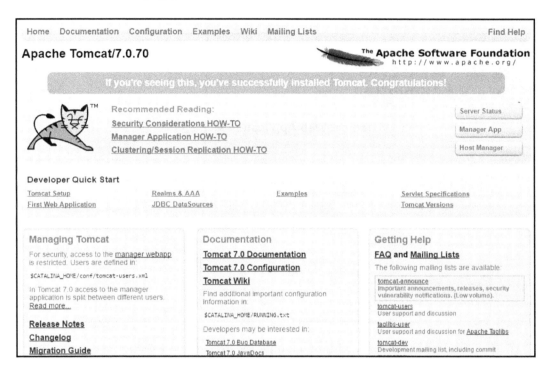

14. Go to `conf` and then open `tomcat-users.xml` in your Tomcat installation directory and *uncomment* the `role` and `user` lines or rewrite them. Set `manager-gui` as the `rolename` for testing purposes. We need `manager-script` for deployment via the Deploy plugin:

```xml
<?xml version='1.0' encoding='utf-8'?>
<!--
<tomcat-users>
<!--
<!--
    NOTE:  The sample user and role entries below are intended for use with the
    examples web application. They are wrapped in a comment and thus are ignored
    when reading this file. If you wish to configure these users for use with the
    examples web application, do not forget to remove the <!.. ..> that surrounds
    them. You will also need to set the passwords to something appropriate.
-->
    <role rolename="manager-script"/>
    <user username="admin" password="admin@123" roles="manager-script"/>
</tomcat-users>
```

15. Click on the manager application link on the Tomcat **Home** page and enter the username and password you set in `tomcat-users.xml`. Now, we can access the management application:

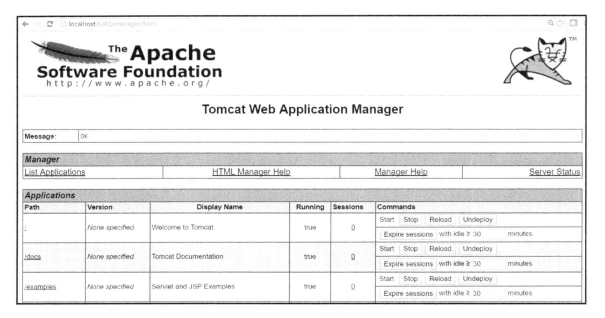

16. For the Jenkins Deploy plugin, change the `rolename` to `manager-script`.

17. Restart Tomcat and visit `http://<IP Address>:8080/manager/text/list`. You should see this output:

```
OK - Listed applications for virtual host localhost
/:running:0:ROOT
/petclinic:running:1:petclinic
/examples:running:0:examples
/host-manager:running:0:host-manager
/manager:running:0:manager
/docs:running:0:docs
```

18. Go to the Jenkins job build page and click on **Configure**. Select the proper **JDK** configuration for the Jenkins agent:

19. Under **Post-build Actions**, select **Deploy war/ear to a container**. Provide the location of the WAR file in the Jenkins workspace, the Tomcat manager credentials, and the **Tomcat URL** with the port:

20. Click on **Apply** and **Save**. Click on **Build now** on the Jenkins build's page. Verify the console output as showing a fresh deployment:

```
Results :

Tests run: 59, Failures: 0, Errors: 0, Skipped: 0

[INFO]
[INFO] --- maven-war-plugin:2.3:war (default-war) @ spring-petclinic ---
[INFO] Packaging webapp
[INFO] Assembling webapp [spring-petclinic] in [d:\jenkins\workspace\PetClinic-Test\target\spring-
petclinic-4.2.5-SNAPSHOT]
[INFO] Processing war project
[INFO] Copying webapp resources [d:\jenkins\workspace\PetClinic-Test\src\main\webapp]
[INFO] Webapp assembled in [1669 msecs]
[INFO] Building war: d:\jenkins\workspace\PetClinic-Test\target\spring-petclinic-4.2.5-SNAPSHOT.war
[INFO] ------------------------------------------------------------------------
[INFO] BUILD SUCCESS
[INFO] ------------------------------------------------------------------------
[INFO] Total time: 28.772 s
[INFO] Finished at: 2016-07-06T22:59:37+05:30
[INFO] Final Memory: 29M/261M
[INFO] ------------------------------------------------------------------------
Deploying d:\jenkins\workspace\PetClinic-Test\target\spring-petclinic-4.2.5-SNAPSHOT.war to container
Tomcat 7.x Remote
  [d:\jenkins\workspace\PetClinic-Test\target\spring-petclinic-4.2.5-SNAPSHOT.war] is not deployed.
Doing a fresh deployment.
  Deploying [d:\jenkins\workspace\PetClinic-Test\target\spring-petclinic-4.2.5-SNAPSHOT.war]
Finished: SUCCESS
```

21. Once the build is successful, visit the URL from your browser and notice the context. It is similar to name of the application:

22. In **Post-build Actions**, provide a **Context path** and click on **Save**. Click on **Build now** again:

23. Verify the application URL by providing a new **Context path**.

For deployments where we can access the tomcat-users.xml file in cases where we use Tomcat as the application container, we will use the same method for deployment. If we don't have direct access to the Tomcat directory or can't change tomcat-users.xml, another approach can be to SSH the remote host and copy the file into the remote host's webapps file in the Tomcat directory. All SSH commands can be used directly from the build job.

Deploying application in Docker container

We have already covered how to use Tomcat with Docker containers in Chapter 5, *Installing and Configuring Docker*. To deploy an application with the Deploy plugin of Jenkins, we will modify tomcat-users.xml. Let's take it step by step:

1. Change rolename to manager-script in tomcat-users.xml:

```
<?xml version='1.0' encoding='utf-8'?>
<tomcat-users xmlns="http://tomcat.apache.org/xml"
xmlns:xsi="http://www.w3.org/2001/XMLSchema-instance"
xsi:schemaLocation="http://tomcat.apache.org/xml tomcat-users.xsd"
              version="1.0">
<!--
  NOTE:  The sample user and role entries below are intended for use with
the
  examples web application. They are wrapped in a comment and thus are
ignored
  when reading this file. If you wish to configure these users for use with
the
  examples web application, do not forget to remove the <!....> that
surrounds
  them. You will also need to set the passwords to something appropriate.
-->

<role rolename="manager-script"/>
<user username="admin" password="admin@123" roles="manager-script"/>
</tomcat-users>
```

2. In the Dockerfile, we will copy tomcat-users.xml to the /usr/local/tomcat/conf/ directory:

```
FROM tomcat:8.0
MAINTAINER Mitesh<mitesh.soni@outlook.com>
COPY tomcat-users.xml /usr/local/tomcat/conf/tomcat-users.xml
```

3. Execute the docker build command to create an image:

```
[root@localhostmitesh]#docker build -t devops_tomcat_sc .
Sending build context to Docker daemon 8.192 kB
Sending build context to Docker daemon
Step 0 : FROM tomcat:8.0
 ---> 5d4577339b14
Step 1 : MAINTAINER Mitesh<mitesh.soni@outlook.com>
 ---> Using cache
 ---> c63f90db4c14
```

```
Step 2 : COPY tomcat-users.xml /usr/local/tomcat/conf/tomcat-users.xml
 ---> aebbcf634f64
Removing intermediate container 7a528d1c8e3b
Successfully built aebbcf634f64
You have new mail in /var/spool/mail/root
```

4. Verify the newly created image using the `docker images` command:

```
[root@localhostmitesh]#docker images
REPOSITORY            TAG          IMAGE ID      CREATED            VIRTUAL SIZE
devops_tomcat_sc      latest       aebbcf634f64  2 minutes ago
359.2 MB
devopstomcatnew       latest       eb50c4ceefb5  5 days ago
359.2 MB
devopstomcat8         latest       f3537165ebe7  5 days ago
344.6 MB
tomcat6               latest       400f097677e9  2 weeks ago
658.4 MB
devopstomcat          latest       400f097677e9  2 weeks ago
658.4 MB
centos                latest       2a332da70fd1  5 weeks ago
196.7 MB
ubuntu                latest       686477c12982  9 weeks ago
120.7 MB
hello-world           latest       f1d956dc5945  10 weeks ago
967 B
```

5. Execute `docker run` to create a container:

```
[root@localhostmitesh]#docker run -p 8180:8080 -d --name
devopstomcatscdevops_tomcat_sc
771bb7cb809dabe9323d65579e98077eaec146db4fc38d2ace1d75577144002d
You have new mail in /var/spool/mail/root
```

6. Verified the new container with the `dockerps` command:

```
[root@localhostmitesh]#dockerps
CONTAINER ID         IMAGE              COMMAND              CREATED
STATUS               PORTS              NAMES
771bb7cb809ddevops_tomcat_sc       "catalina.sh run"   7 seconds ago
Up 6 seconds         0.0.0.0:8180->8080/tcpdevopstomcatsc
```

7. Use `docker inspect 771bb7cb809d<container ID>` to get an IP address.

8. Stop the `iptables` service for verification or opening ports in IP tables:

```
[root@localhostmitesh]# service iptables stop
iptables: Setting chains to policy ACCEPT: nat filter         [  OK  ]
```

```
iptables: Flushing firewall rules:                    [  OK  ]
iptables: Unloading modules:                          [  OK  ]
You have new mail in /var/spool/mail/root
```

9. Use the IP address to access the **Manager App** URL. Verify whether it is successful:

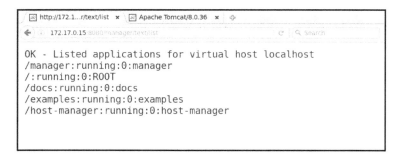

10. As we have mapped the port, use the host's IP address and verify your Tomcat installation:

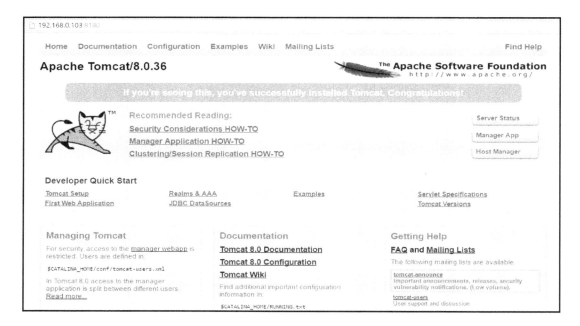

11. Use the IP address of the host, and access the **Manager App** URL. Provide a **User Name** and **Password**:

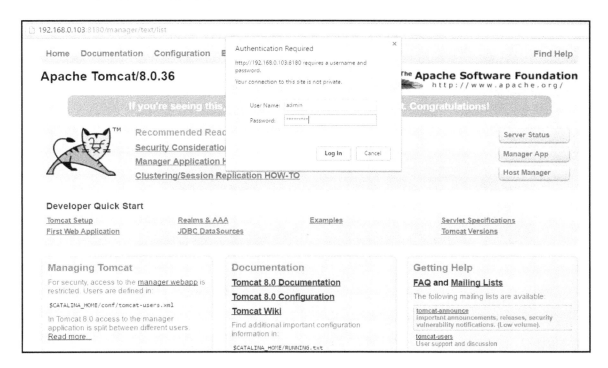

12. Check whether it is successful:

13. Once everything is working fine, use the Deploy plugin to deploy an application in a Docker container.

Deploying Application in AWS

AWS Elastic Beanstalk is a **Platform as a Service** (**PaaS**) offering from Amazon. We will use it to deploy the PetClinic application on the AWS platform. The good part is we need not to manage infrastructure or even platform as it is a PaaS offering. We can configure scaling and other details.

These are the steps to deploy an application on AWS Elastic Beanstalk:

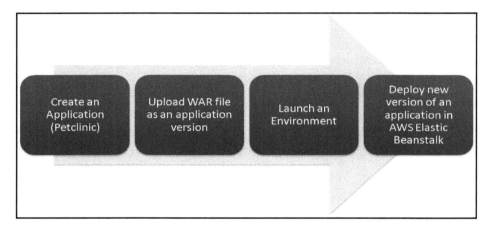

Elastic Beanstalk supports the following programming languages and platforms:

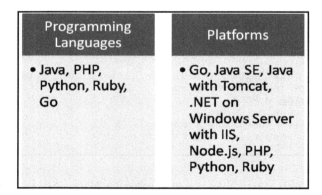

Programming Languages	Platforms
• Java, PHP, Python, Ruby, Go	• Go, Java SE, Java with Tomcat, .NET on Windows Server with IIS, Node.js, PHP, Python, Ruby

Let's create a sample application to understand how Elastic Beanstalk works and then use the Jenkins plugin to deploy an application:

1. Go to the AWS management console and verify whether we have a default **Virtual Private Cloud** (**VPC**). If you've deleted the default VPC and subnet by accident, send a request to AWS customer support to recreate it:

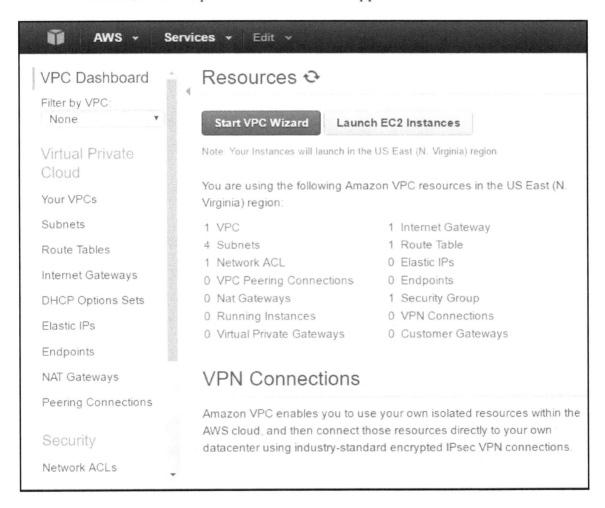

2. Click on **Services** in the AWS management console and select **AWS Elastic Beanstalk**. Create a new application named `petclinic`. Select **Tomcat** as a **Platform** and select the **Sample application** radio button:

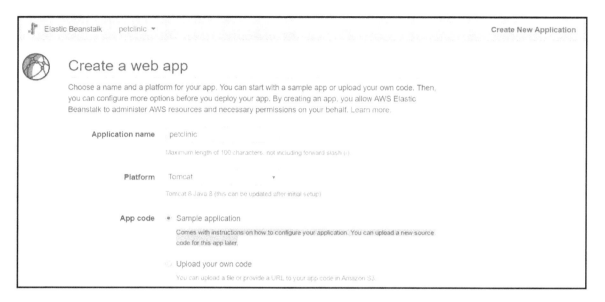

3. Verify the sequence of events for the creation of a sample application:

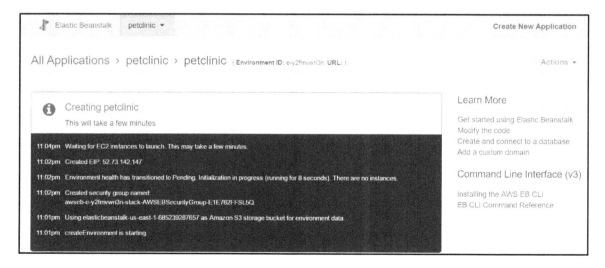

4. It will take a while, and once the environment has been created, it will be highlighted in green, as shown here:

5. Click on the **petclinic** environment and verify the **Health** and **Running Version** in the dashboard:

6. Verify the environment ID and URL. Click on the URL and verify the default page:

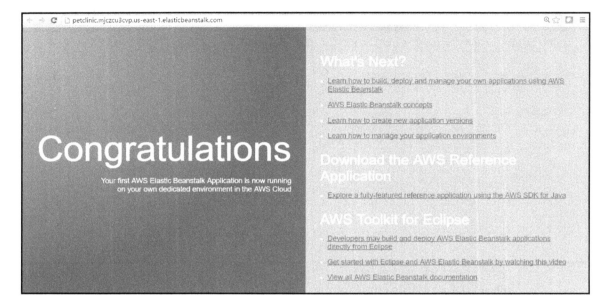

7. Install **AWS Elastic Beanstalk Publisher** plugin.

For more details, visit `https://wiki.jenkins-ci.org/display/JENKINS` `/AWS+Beanstalk+Publisher+Plugin`.

8. Open the Jenkins dashboard and go to **Build job**. Click on **Post-build Actions** and select **Deploy into AWS Elastic Beanstalk**.

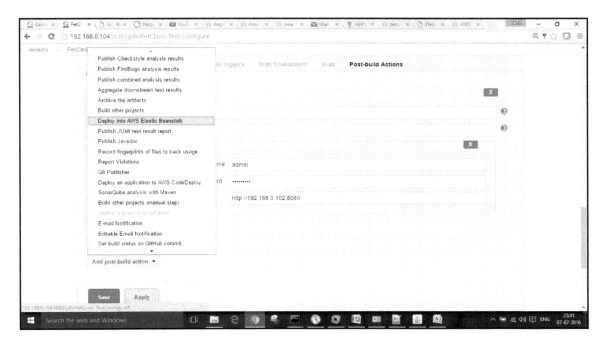

9. A new section will come up in **Post-build Actions** for Elastic Beanstalk:

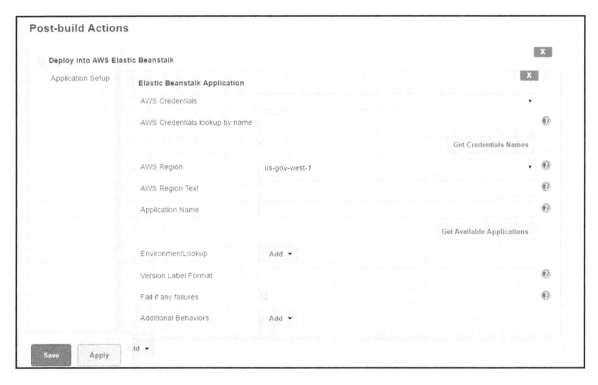

10. Click on the Jenkins dashboard and select **Credentials**; add your AWS credentials:

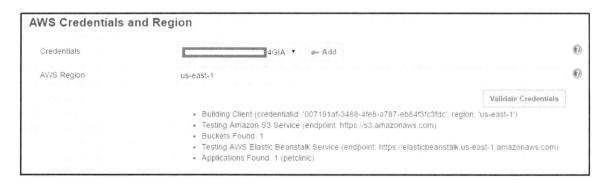

11. Go to your Jenkins build and select an **AWS Credential** that is set in the global configuration:

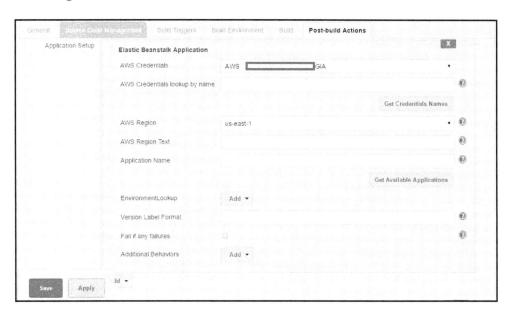

12. Select **AWS Region** from the list and click on **Get Available Applications**. As we have created a sample application, it will show up like this:

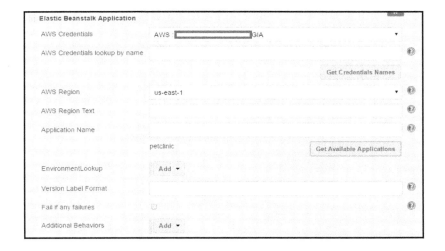

13. In **EnvironmentLookup**, provide an environment ID in the **Get Environments By Name** box and click on **Get Available Environments**:

14. Save the configuration and click on **Build now**.

Let's verify the AWS management console whether WAR file is being copied in Amazon S3 or not:

1. Go to **S3 Services** and check the available buckets:

2. Verify the build job's execution status in Jenkins. Some sections of the expected output follow:

3. Since the WAR file is large, it will take a while to upload to **Amazon S3**. Once it is uploaded, it will be available in the Amazon S3 bucket.

4. The test case execution and WAR file creation are successful:

```
Tests run: 59, Failures: 0, Errors: 0, Skipped: 0
[INFO]
[INFO] --- maven-war-plugin:2.3:war (default-war) @ spring-petclinic ---
[INFO] Packaging webapp
[INFO] Assembling webapp [spring-petclinic] in
[d:\jenkins\workspace\PetClinic-Test\target\spring-petclinic-4.2.5-
SNAPSHOT]
[INFO] Processing war project
[INFO] Copying webapp resources [d:\jenkins\workspace\PetClinic-
Test\src\main\webapp]
[INFO] Webapp assembled in [1539 msecs]
[INFO] Building war: d:\jenkins\workspace\PetClinic-Test\target\spring-
petclinic-4.2.5-SNAPSHOT.war
[INFO] ------------------------------------------------------------------
---------
[INFO] BUILD SUCCESS
[INFO] ------------------------------------------------------------------
---------
[INFO] Total time: 30.469 s
[INFO] Finished at: 2016-07-08T00:51:52+05:30
[INFO] Final Memory: 29M/258M
[INFO] ------------------------------------------------------------------
---------
```

5. The execution of **AWSEB Deployment** plugin – post build action has been started:

```
AWSEB Deployment Plugin Version 0.3.10
Root File Object is a file. We assume its a zip file, which is okay.
bucketName not set. Calling createStorageLocation
Using s3 Bucket 'elasticbeanstalk-us-east-1-685239287657'
Uploading file awseb-5081374840514488317.zip as s3://elasticbeanstalk-
us-east-1-685239287657/petclinic-jenkins-PetClinic-Test-39.zip
```

6. The deployment activity with the new version label starts:

```
Creating application version jenkins-PetClinic-Test-39 for application
petclinic for path s3://elasticbeanstalk-us-east-1-685239287657/petclinic-
jenkins-PetClinic-Test-39.zip
```

```
Created version: jenkins-PetClinic-Test-39
Using environmentId 'e-y2fmvwri3n'
No pending Environment Updates. Proceeding.
Checking health/status of environmentId e-y2fmvwri3n attempt 1/30
Environment Status is 'Ready'. Moving on.
Updating environmentId 'e-y2fmvwri3n' with Version Label set to
'jenkins-PetClinic-Test-39'
```

7. The environment and health statuses are updated along with the deployment status:

```
Fri Jul 08 01:03:10 IST 2016 [INFO] Environment update is starting.
Checking health/status of environmentId e-y2fmvwri3n attempt 1/30
Versions reported: (current=jenkins-PetClinic-Test-39, underDeployment:
jenkins-PetClinic-Test-39). Should I move on? false
Environment Status is 'Ready' and Health is 'Green'. Moving on.
Deployment marked as 'successful'. Starting post-deployment cleanup.
Cleaning up temporary file
C:\Users\Mitesh\AppData\Local\Temp\awseb-5081374840514488317.zip
Finished: SUCCESS
```

8. The build is successful. Now, check the AWS management console:

9. Go to **Services**, click on AWS **Elastic Beanstalk**, and verify the environment. The previous version was **Sample Application**. Now, the version is updated as given in **Version Label Format** in the Jenkins build job configuration:

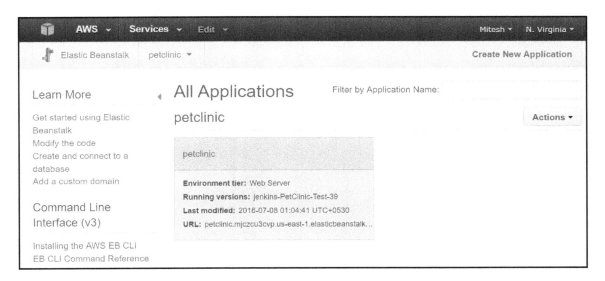

10. Go to the dashboard and verify **Health** and **Running Version** again:

11. Click on the **Configuration** link on the **Elastic Beanstalk** dashboard and verify **Scaling, Instances, Notifications, Software Configuration, Updates and Deployments, Health,** and so on:

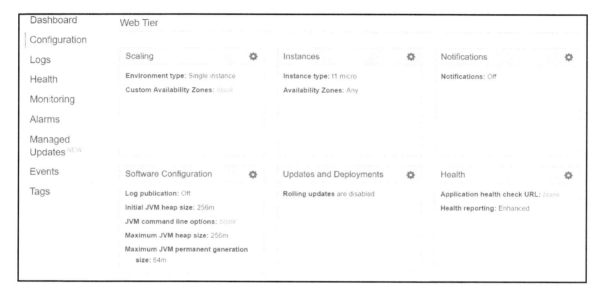

12. Click on **Logs** to download the log files for Elastic Beanstalk:

13. Go to the **Enhanced Health Overview** and check the **Status**:

14. Click on **Monitoring** for extensive monitoring details in the form of CPU utilization and health of an application:

15. Click on **Events** to get list of all the events of the Elastic Beanstalk application lifecycle:

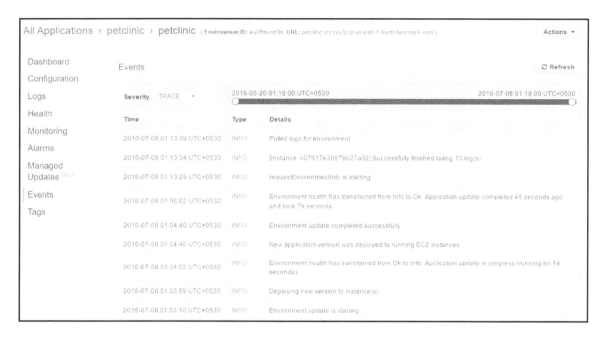

16. Once everything has been verified, click on the URL for the environment, and our PetClinic application is live:

17. Once the application deployment is successful, terminate the environment:

We have thus successfully deployed our application on Elastic Beanstalk.

Deploying application in Microsoft Azure

Microsoft Azure app services is a PaaS. In this section, we will look at the Azure web app and how we can deploy our PetClinic application:

1. Let's install the **Publish Over FTP** plugin in Jenkins. We will use the Azure web app's FTP details to publish the PetClinic WAR file:

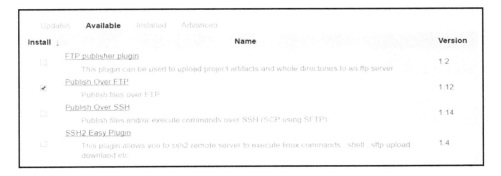

2. Once the plugin has been installed successfully, restart Jenkins:

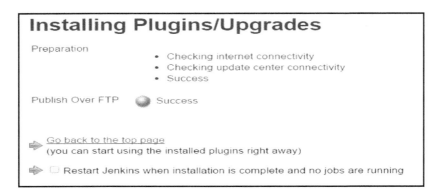

3. Go to Microsoft Azure portal at `https://portal.azure.com`. Click on **App Services** and then on **Add**. Provide values for**App Name**, **Subscription**, **Resource Group**, and **App Service plan/Location**. Click on **Create**:

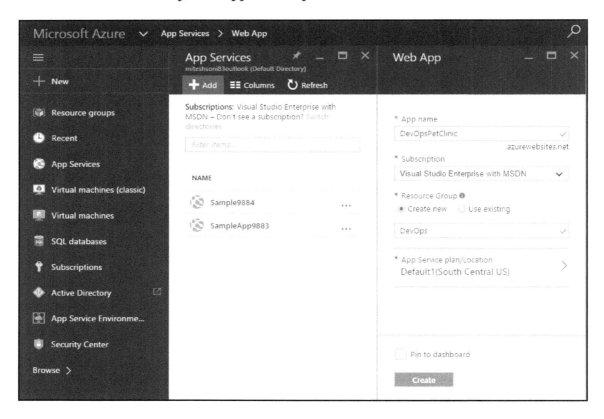

4. Once the Azure web app is created, see whether it shows up in Azure portal:

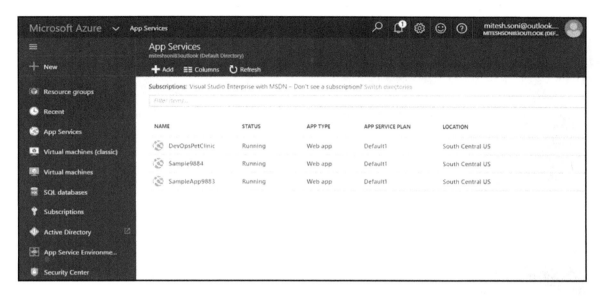

5. Click on **DevOpsPetClinic** to obtain details related to the **URL**, **Status**, **Location**, and so on:

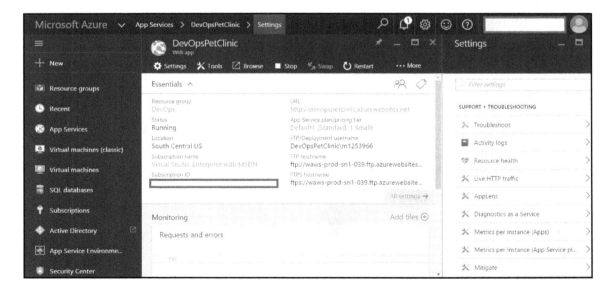

6. Click on **All Settings**, go to the **GENERAL** section, and click on **Application settings** to configure the Azure web app for Java web application hosting. Select the **Java version**, **Java Minor version**, **Web container**, and **Platform**, and click on **Always On**:

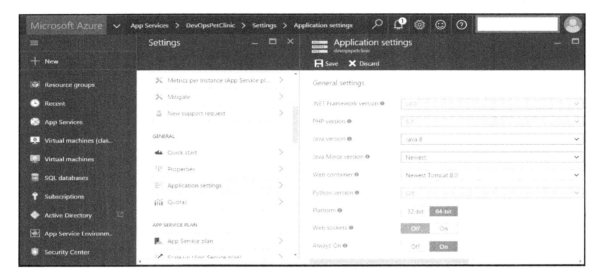

7. Visit the URL of an Azure web app from your browser and verify that it is ready for hosting our sample Spring application, **PetClinic**:

8. Let's go to the Jenkins dashboard. Click on **New Item** and select **Freestyle project**:

9. Copy the general configuration from another build so we don't need to repeat the configuration work in the newly created job:

10. Click on **All Settings**, and go to **Deployment credentials** in the **PUBLISHING** section. Provide a username and password, and save your changes:

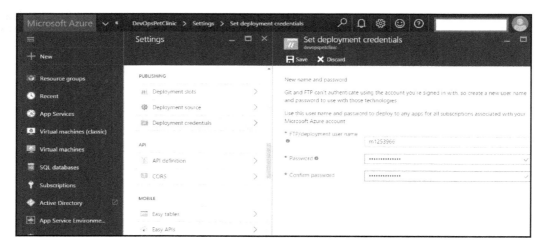

11. In Jenkins, go to **Manage Jenkins** and click on **Configure** | **Configure FTP settings**. Provide a **Hostname**, **Username**, and **Password**, available in Azure portal.

12. Go to `devopspetclinic.scm.azurewebsites.net` and download the **Kudu console**. Navigate to the different options and find the `site directory` and `webapps` directory. Click on **Test Configuration**, and once you get a **Success** message, you are ready to deploy the PetClinic application:

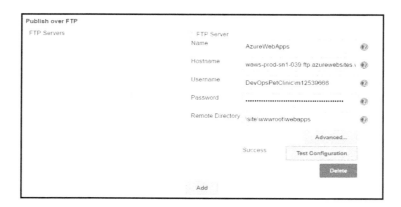

13. In the build job we created, go to the **Build** section and configure **Copy artifacts from another project**. We will copy the WAR file to a specific location on a virtual machine:

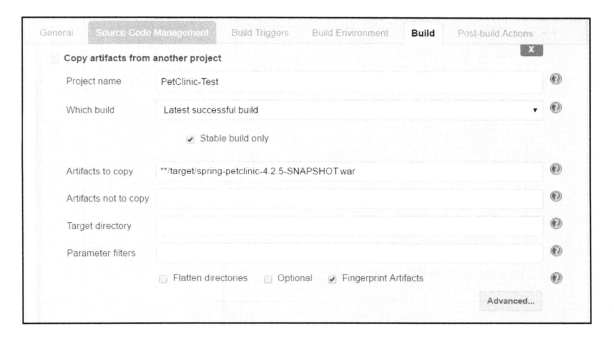

14. In **Post-build Actions**, click on **Send build artifacts over FTP**. Select the FTP server name configured in Jenkins. Configure **Source files** and the **Remove prefix** accordingly for deployment of an Azure web app:

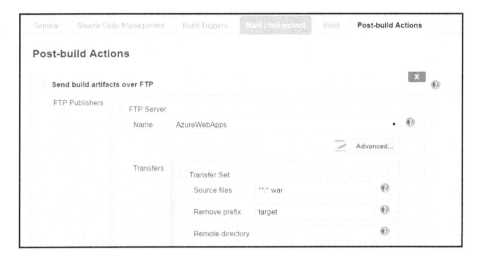

15. Tick **Verbose output in console**:

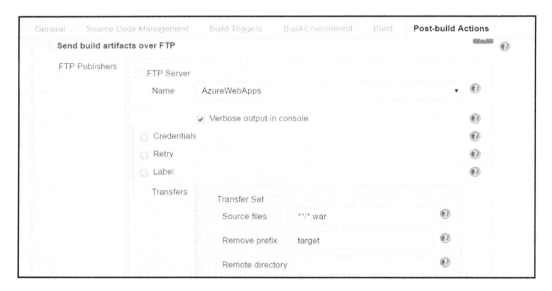

16. Click on **Build now** and see what happens behind the scene:

```
Started by user DiscoverTechno
Building on master in workspace /home/mitesh/.jenkins/workspace/PetClinic-Deploy-Azure
Copied 1 artifact from "PetClinic-Test" build number 55
FTP: Connecting from host [devops1]
FTP: Connecting with configuration [AzureWebApps] ...
220 Microsoft FTP Service
FTP: Logging in, command printing disabled
FTP: Logged in, command printing enabled
CWD \site\wwwroot\webapps
250 CWD command successful.
TYPE I
200 Type set to I.
CWD \site\wwwroot\webapps
250 CWD command successful.
PASV
227 Entering Passive Mode (104,210,159,39,39,189).
STOR spring-petclinic-4.2.5-SNAPSHOT.war
125 Data connection already open; Transfer starting.
FTP: Disconnecting configuration [AzureWebApps] ...
```

17. Go to the **Kudu** console, click on **Debug console**, and go to **Powershell**. Go to site | wwwroot | webapps. Check whether the WAR file has been copied:

18. Visit the Azure web app URL in the browser with the context of an application:

Now we have an application deployed on Azure web apps.

 It is important to note that the FTP username has to be with the domain. In our case, it can be `Sample9888\m1253966`. Using the username without the web app name won't work.

All these different ways of deployment to AWS IaaS, AWS PaaS, Microsoft Azure PaaS, and Docker container can be used in the final end-to-end automation:

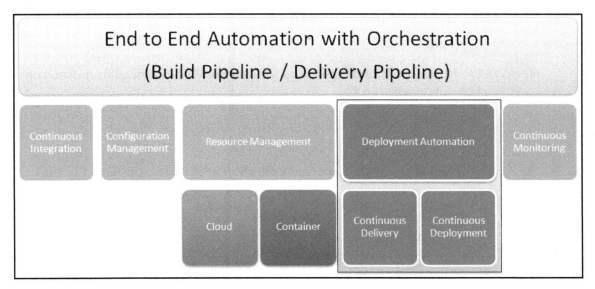

We have covered four phases so far, and we will next discuss about continuous monitoring. In the final chapter, we will manage the entire end-to-end automation with pipeline or orchestration.

Self-test questions

State whether the following statements are true or false:

1. Role and users in Tomcat can be created in `tomcat-users.xml` to access Manager web app?

   - True
   - False

2. To access the **Tomcat Manager** app, the `manager-script` role is required?

   - True
   - False

3. To deploy application in Tomcat container using the Deploy plugin in Jenkins, the `manager-script` role is required?

   - True
   - False

4. AWS Elastic Beanstalk and Azure app services are PaaS offerings from Amazon and Microsoft respectively?

   - True
   - False

5. Which of the following are steps for application deployment on AWS Elastic Beanstalk?

   - Create an application (PetClinic)
   - Upload WAR file as an application version
   - Launch an environment
   - Deploy the new version of the application on AWS Elastic Beanstalk
   - All of these

Summary

In this chapter, we have covered how to deploy an application in Tomcat using **Tomcat Manager Application** by setting `role` and `users` in `tomcat-users.xml`. We can use same deployment method where we can configure or edit `tomcat-users.xml`. Same approach was used for PetClinic application deployment in the Docker container.

It is a suitable approach in **Infrastructure as a Service**. We have also deployed PetClinic application in **Platform as a Service** such as AWS Elastic Beanstalk and Microsoft Azure web app.

We have also verified what topics we have covered till now for end to end deployment for PetClinic application.

In the next chapter, we will discuss about continuous monitoring for infrastructure and application.

8

Monitoring Infrastructure and Applications

"A lot of times, people don't know what they want until you show it to them."
- Steve Jobs

Cloud provides agility, scalability, pay as you go resources, and so on. Based on the Cloud service models, roles and responsibilities of Cloud-service providers and Cloud consumers are different. Having said that, it is equally important to know the status of the cloud resources irrespective of the Cloud deployment model including Private Cloud or Public Cloud. It is advisable to have detailed perspective of cloud resources to maintain and manage high availability and reputation.

An important thing to note here is that all resources are interdependent and if one resource is not in the sync of overall picture than main objective of providing good service and high availability is difficult to achieve. This is a scenario irrespective of the type of environment including physical, virtualized, or cloud.

This chapter describes the need of continuous monitoring and its significance in the end to end automation process in the context of DevOps culture development. It covers different aspects of monitoring such as cloud resources, application server and application monitoring to increase services, and application availability.

In this chapter, we will cover the following topics:

- Getting started-monitoring
- Installation and configuration open source monitoring tools
- Monitoring AWS, Azure resources
- Monitoring web application and Tomcat server with New Relic

Getting started – monitoring

Let's start with a simple definition of monitoring and then we will gradually move towards cloud monitoring. It is about observing progress of some operation or activities performed and to make sure that end goal or performance objectives are achieved as desired. It expands its area from observing to analysis, from analysis to detection, and from detection to notifications to respective stakeholders for corrective measures.

In general, what kind of monitoring we do in traditional environment? Let's start considering component of Cloud service Model to understand it in a better perspective. In Cloud computing, there are three service models:

1. Infrastructure as a Service
2. Platform as a Service
3. Software as a Service

To get a clue from it, it is extremely important to monitor Infrastructure as well as platform running web application. Let's take a case of AWS EC2 instance that can be used to deploy our sample Spring Application – PetClinic. We need to ensure that Instance is running properly, tomcat server is performing well, memory consumption, CPU utilization, and so on. The next level is to monitor application itself. Application security monitoring and performance monitoring is extremely critical to make an application highly available and avoid failures.

Monitoring strategy has to be end to end to be effective. It should be in place at the time of design and not the afterthought. Prevention is always better than cure and it avoids cost implications, rollback to last successful builds, and last minute headaches.

Overview of Monitoring tools and Techniques

In this section, we will cover Nagios monitoring tool, Azure Web Apps Monitoring, and AWS Elastic Beanstalk.

Nagios

Nagios Core is an open source application written in C and PHP to monitor servers, networks, and infrastructure.

Below are some important features of Nagios:

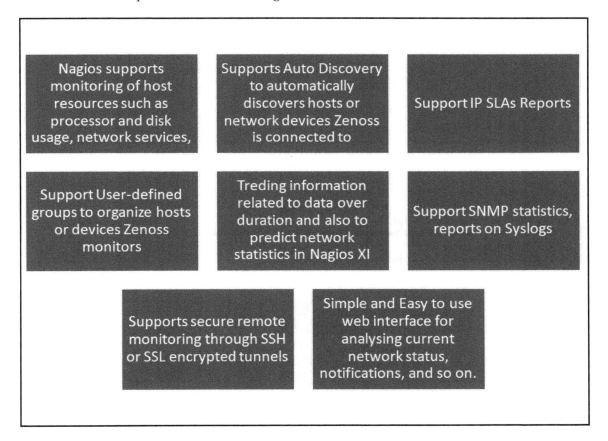

Nagios XI uses Nagios Core as the back-end and provides an extended interface for monitoring resources. Nagios XI is supported in CentOS and RedHat. Let's have a quick tour of Nagios XI.

Quick start with Nagios

1. Go to `https://www.nagios.com/downloads/nagios-xi/` and download VMware 64 bit virtual machine so we can use the image in VMware workstation. Open the OVF in the VMware workstation:

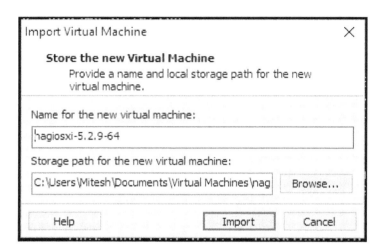

2. Importing Nagios OVF will take some time:

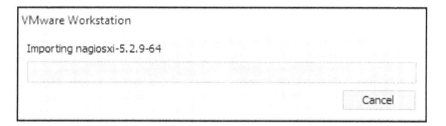

3. Wait for the completion of the process:

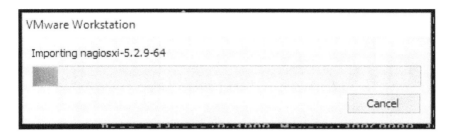

4. Once importing process is completed, click on the **Power on this virtual Machine**:

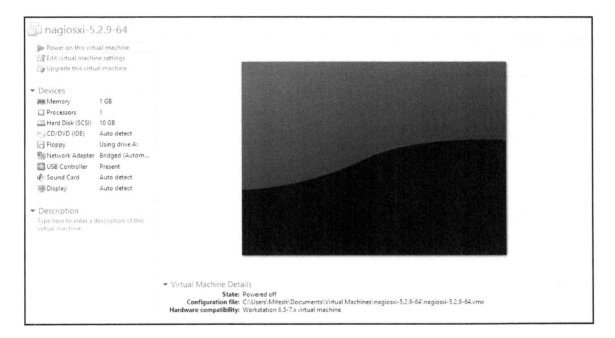

5. Once the virtual machine is ready, login as root with password `nagiosxi`. Note the URL to access Nagios dashboard:

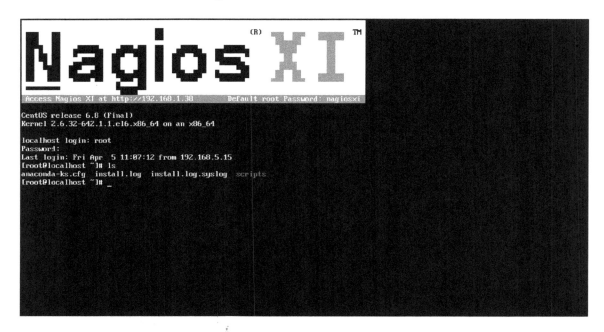

6. Open the Nagios URL from the browser. Click on the **Access Nagios XI**:

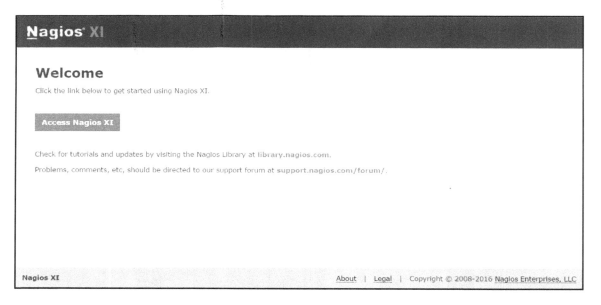

7. Note the username and password with other details, select the **timezone** and click on **Install**:

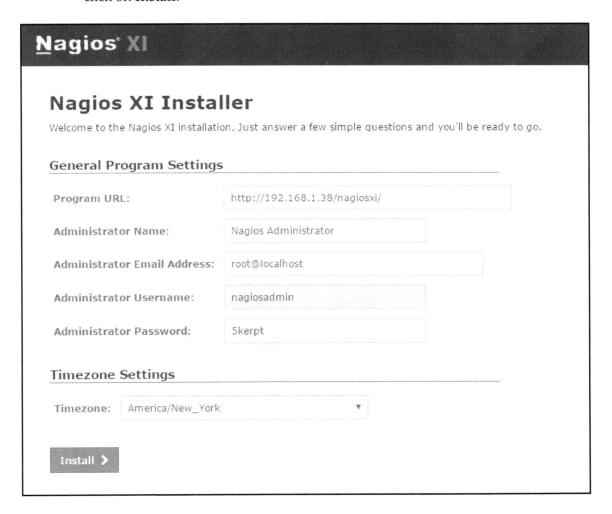

8. Once installation is complete, click on the **Login to Nagios XI**:

Now, we have installed Nagios. Next step will be to configure Nagios to monitor resources from Cloud platforms.

Now, to monitor Cloud resources with Nagios, we will a simple scenario to monitor an AWS instance using Nagios:

1. Login to Nagios dashboard using admin credentials:

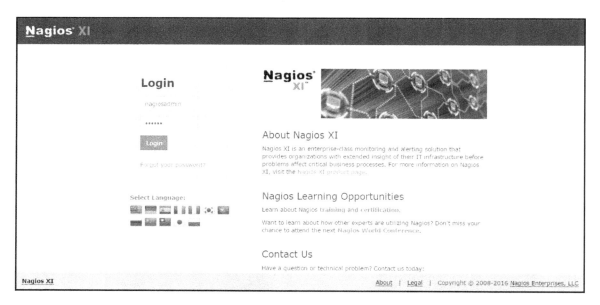

2. Accept **License Agreement**:

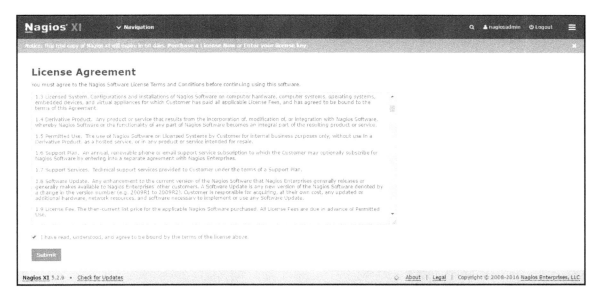

3. Here is the Nagios dashboard and we can configure our AWS instance to monitor with it:

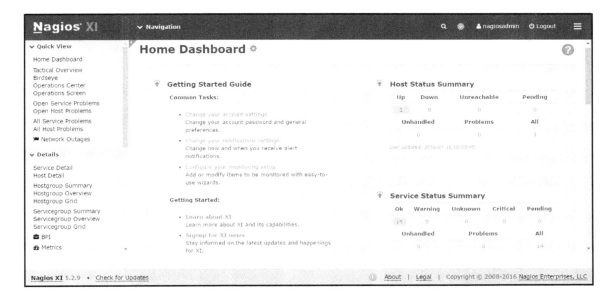

4. From the **Navigation** menu, got to **Configure** section for **Auto Discovery** Job:

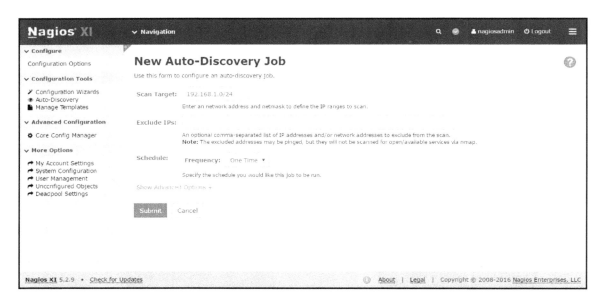

5. There are different options also available to monitor in the configure section:

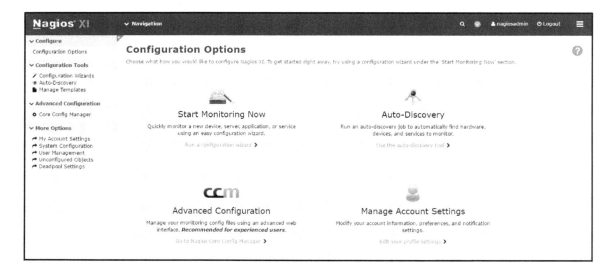

6. We can also configure monitoring using **Configuration wizards**:

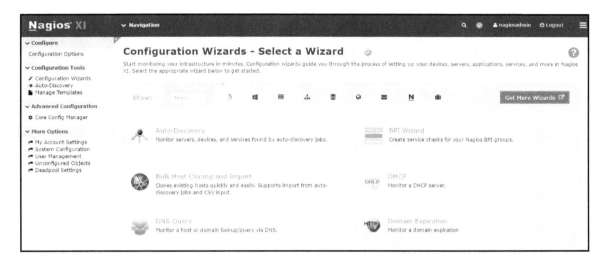

7. We have created AWS Linux instance and we would like to monitor it using Nagios. Select a **Linux Server**:

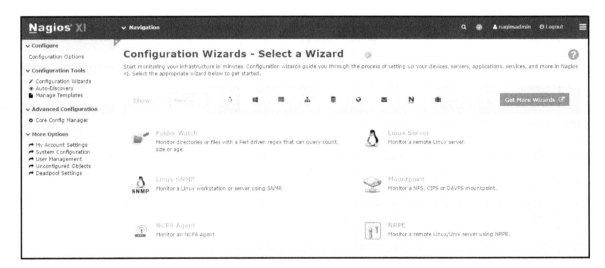

8. Get the **IP address** of AWS instance and input it here. Select the Linux Distribution as `Other`. Click on **Next**:

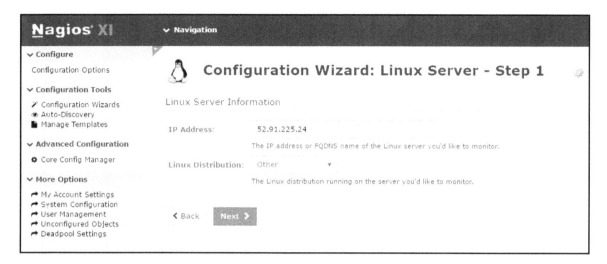

9. Verify the IP address in the next step:

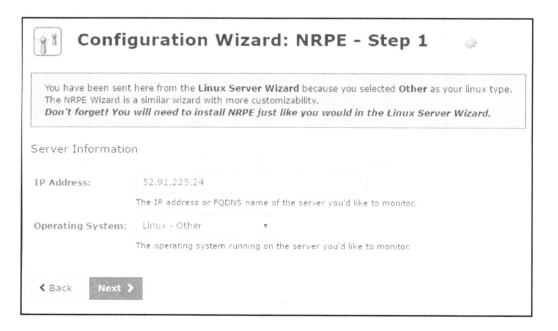

10. Provide Host name for the EC2 instance:

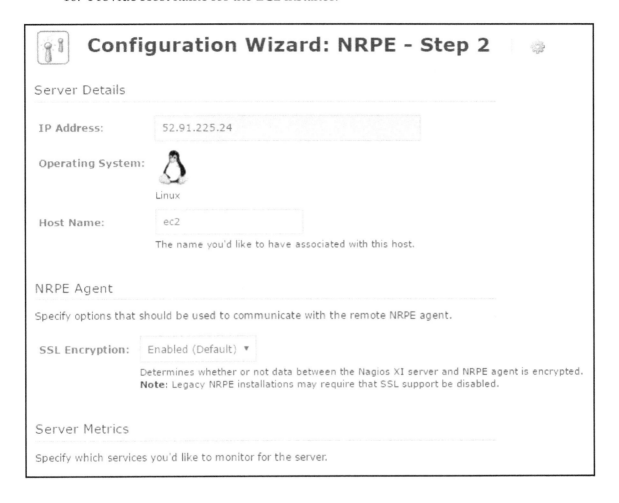

11. Configure the basic parameters for monitoring. Click on **Next**:

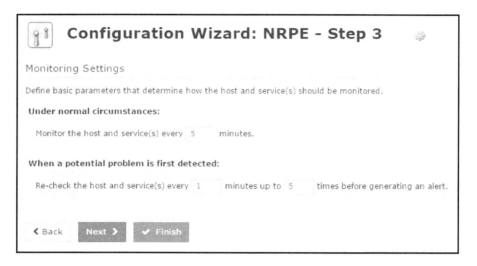

12. Configure **Notification Settings**:

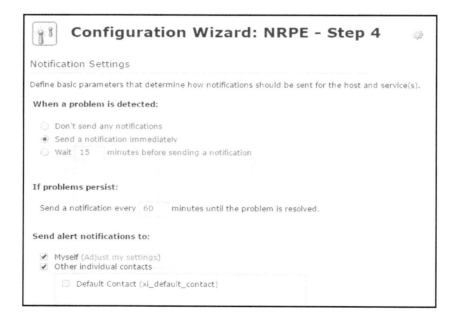

13. Configure the **Host Groups**:

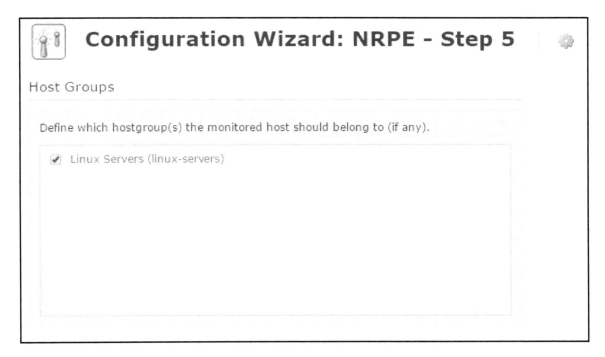

14. Click **Apply** to finish the configuration:

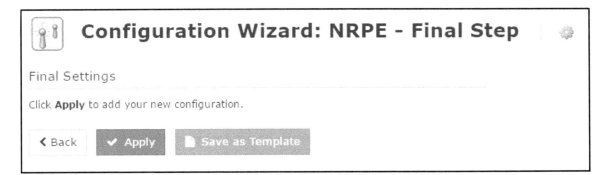

15. Within few minutes, monitoring of EC2 instance will start:

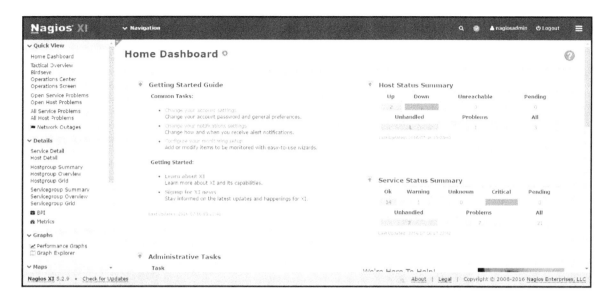

16. Click on the EC2 instance in Nagios dashboard. It is showing the status as **Down**:

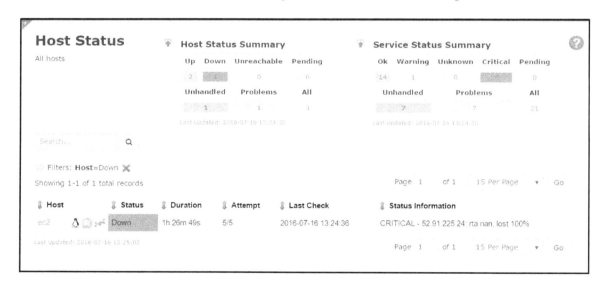

17. Verify the Host status in detail. Click on the **Ping this host**:

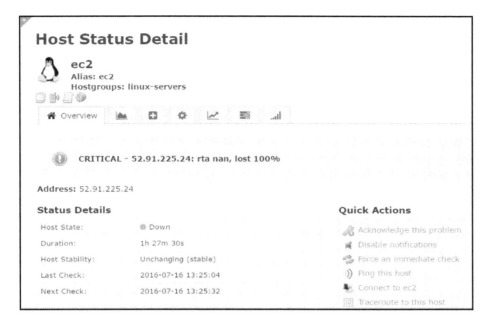

18. We will get packet loss message:

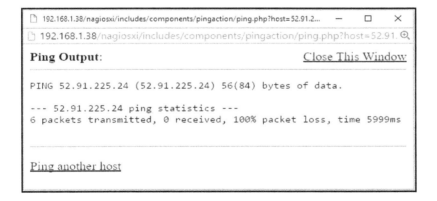

19. Go to AWS Management console and change in the Inbound rules of security group assigned to EC2 instance to all ICMP traffic. Verify Ping this Host again and we can see Ping requests are successful:

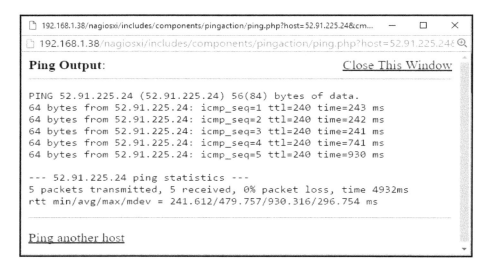

20. Verify the **Host Availability**:

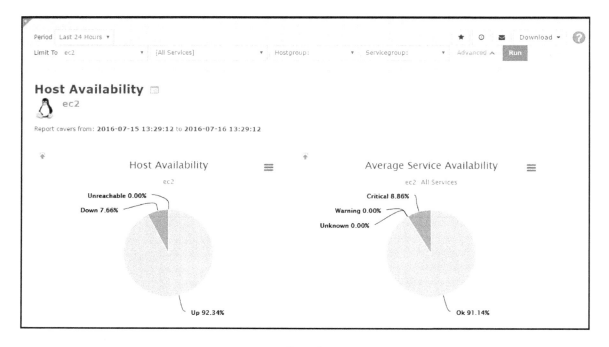

21. Click on the graph and get details on **Host Data** and **Service Data**:

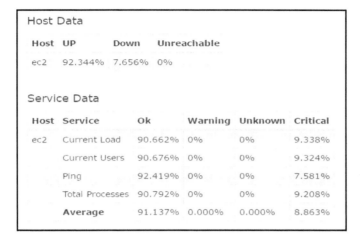

22. Verify the Nagios dashboard and all three configured instances are **Up**:

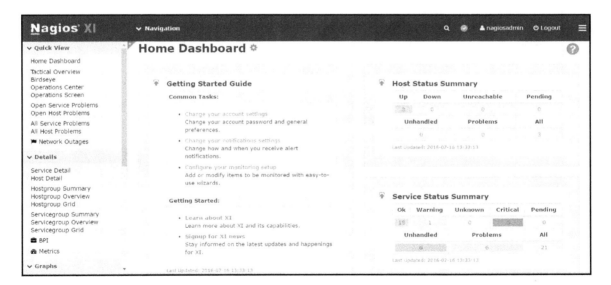

23. Verify the **Host Status Detail** again:

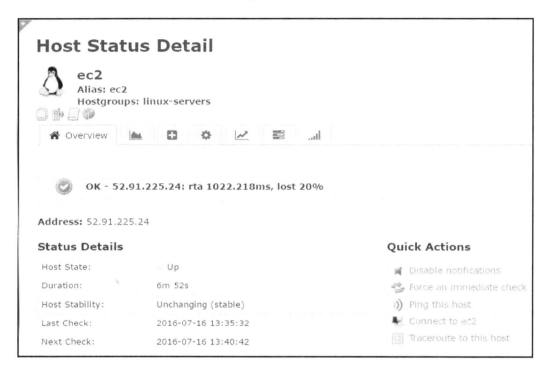

24. From the **Incident Management** section, click on the **Latest Alerts** to get details on latest notifications or alerts:

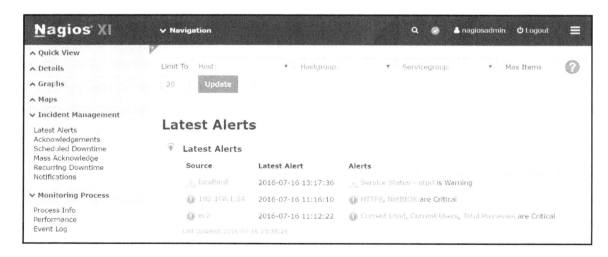

25. Click on the **ec2**, and get all the notification for EC2 instance:

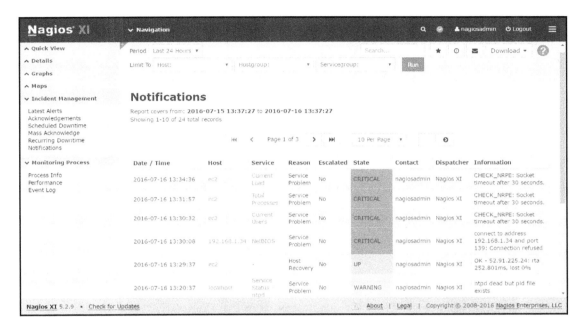

26. We can verify **Service Status** from Nagios Dashboard:

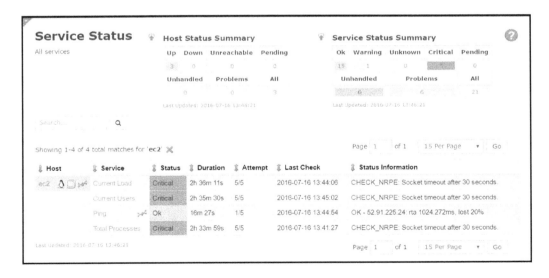

27. Verify all hosts' status from Nagios dashboard.

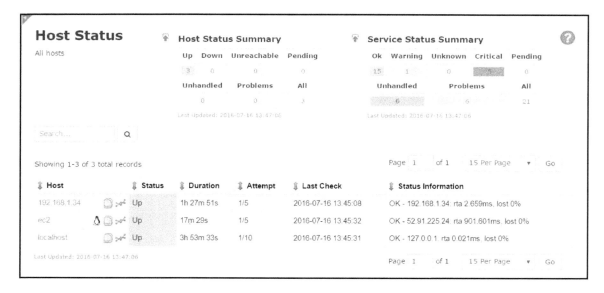

28. We can also verify **Host Group Status** from the Nagios Dashboard:

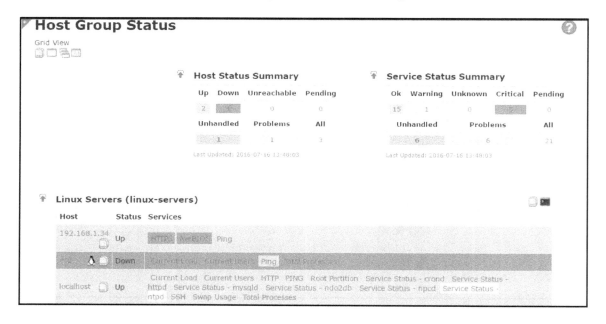

29. In the **Graphs** section, click on **Graph Explorer** to get graphical details on top alerts produced in the last 24 hours:

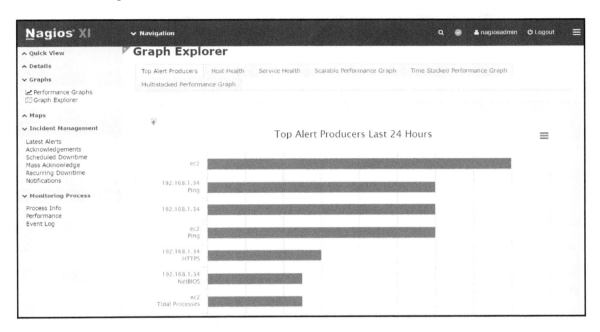

In the next section we will use Nagios to monitor Tomcat instance.

Monitoring AWS Elastic Beanstalk

We have deployed PetClinic Application in to AWS Elastic Beanstalk as well with the use of Jenkins plugin. In AWS Elastic Beanstalk, health status of an environment is determined by Grey, Green, Yellow, and Red color. Grey indicates that environment is in the process of updation. Green indicates successful health check status in recent times. Yellow indicates that environment has failure of one or more Health checks. Red indicates that environment has failure of three or more Health checks.

Health status is based on the response of an application running in the **Environments**:

On the Environment dashboard in AWS Elastic Beanstalk, we get basic details such as **Health** as well as configuration of instances:

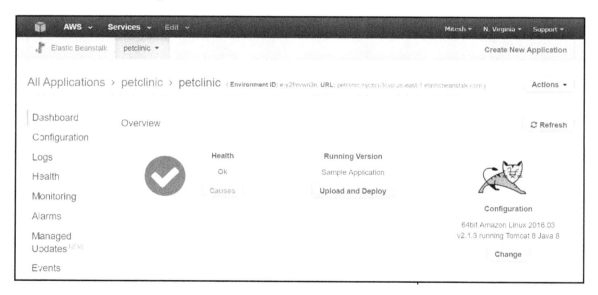

Click on the **Monitoring** for extensive monitoring details in form of **CPU Utilization** and Health of an application. We can change **Time Range** to get more details on **Monitoring**:

For more information on monitoring AWS Elastic Beanstalk, visit `http://docs.aws.amazon.com/elasticbeanstalk/latest/dg/environments-health.html`

Monitoring Microsoft Azure Web App Service

In Chapter 6, *Cloud Provisioning and Configuration Management* we deployed PetClinic Application in the Azure Web Apps. Once deployment is successful, monitoring Web App is an essential activity and Azure Portal itself provide many ways to monitor it.

1. In Azure web app find **Monitoring** section below Application details. Click on **edit** to change the time range and chart type:

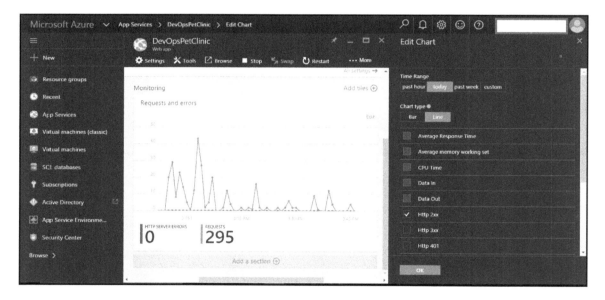

2. Verify the updated graph with more details based on selection:

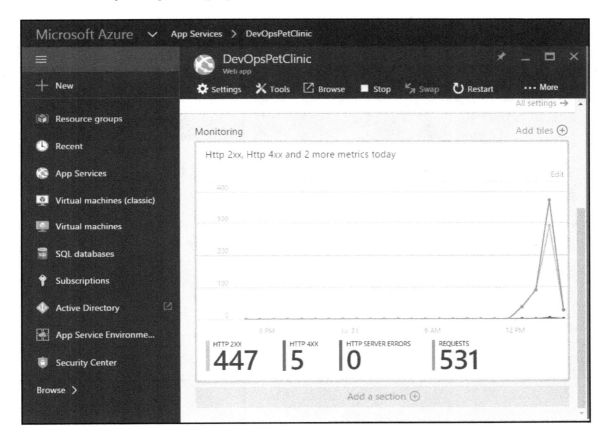

3. In Application, go to **Settings** and navigate to Features section. Click on **Diagnostics logs**. Here we can select **Application Logging (Filesystem)**, **Level**, **Application Logging (Blob)**, **Web server logging**, **Detailed error messages**, and **failed request tracing**:

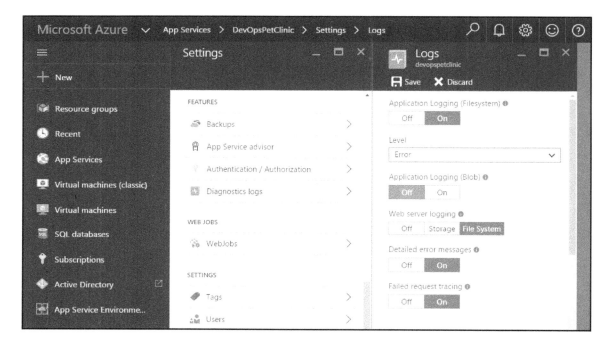

4. In Application, go to **Settings** and navigate to **SUPPORT + TROUBLESHOOTING** section. Click on **Troubleshoot**, verify **RESOURCEHEALTH**. There are common solutions available here in case common problems such **5xx errors**:

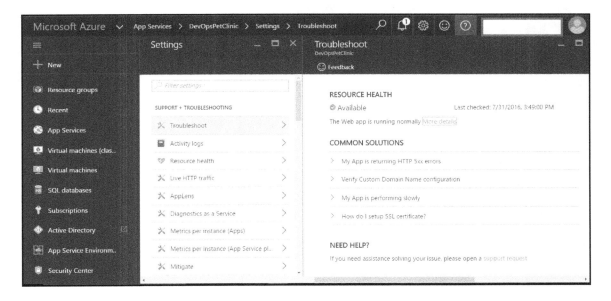

5. In case application is not accessible, we can restart the application or also do
   Advanced Application restart:

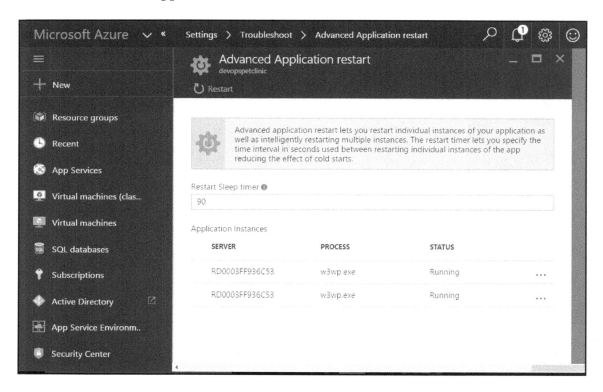

6. We can also verify activities performed on an application by filtering **Audit logs** from **Settings**:

7. To automatically fix the issues in Azure Web App, go to **Settings** and navigate to **SUPPORT + TROUBLESHOOTING** section. Click on **Mitigate**:

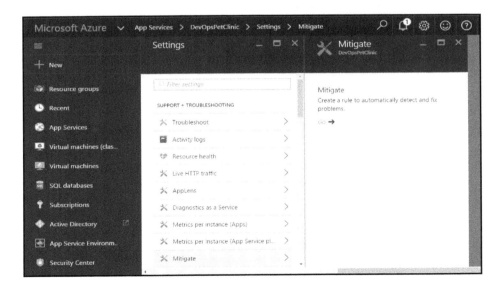

8. Select the Web App and enable **Autoheal**. Here we can configure settings to recover from application issues:

9. We can configure Max Requests per specific Interval:

10. Status Code related monitoring. For example, when 5xx errors occur multiple times:

11. Verify newly added details of the Rule:

Once, everything is configured, click on **Action**. Here we can configure actions on the specific situation we have configured earlier. We can set recycle to auto recover from the issues.

1. Click on the **Update** button to set the rules for your web app:

2. You'll see the following message:

Go to KUDU Console by visiting
`https://<application_name>.scm.azurewebsites.net/`. In our case,
it will be `https://devopspetclinic.scm.azurewebsites.net`:

3. Click on **Debug console** and from drop down menu, select **CMD**. Click on **LogFiles**:

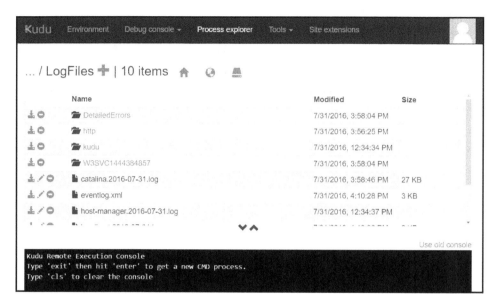

4. Go to `DetailedErrors` folder and verify what kind of errors have occurred:

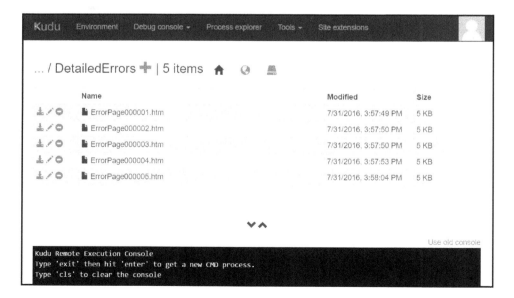

5. We can also Detailed Error logs from **FREB logs** in the portal itself:

6. Open the Error Page in browser and we will get more details about the error:

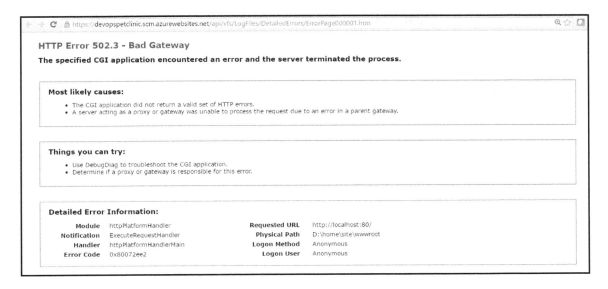

7. Go to **http** | **RawLogs** | **Open log files** to monitor all logs related to HTTP:

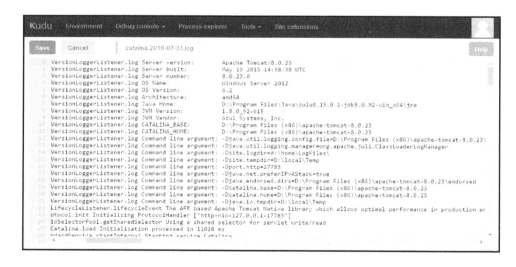

8. Catalina logs are also available and we can get all details about tomcat server and execution in it:

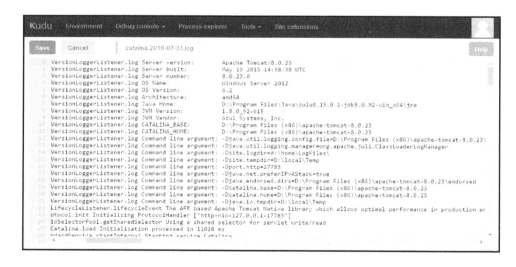

9. In Azure Web App, go to Application blade and click on **Tools**. In **DEVELOP** section, we get the feature to test the performance of an application. We need to have VSTS account for this feature. Click on **New**:

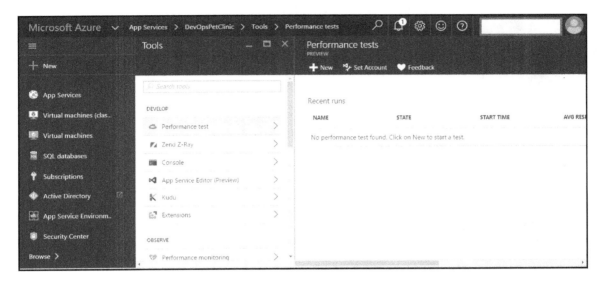

10. Configure test using **TEST TYPE**, **URL**, **USER LOAD**, Duration of Test:

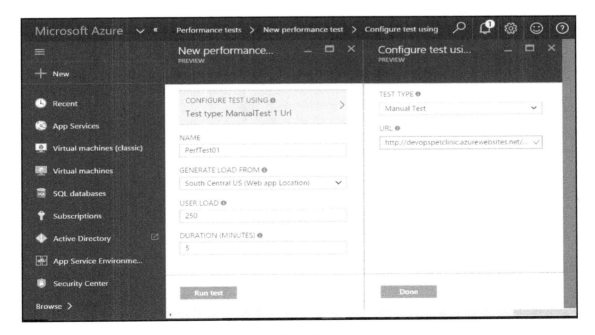

11. It will take around 15 minutes to acquire resources:

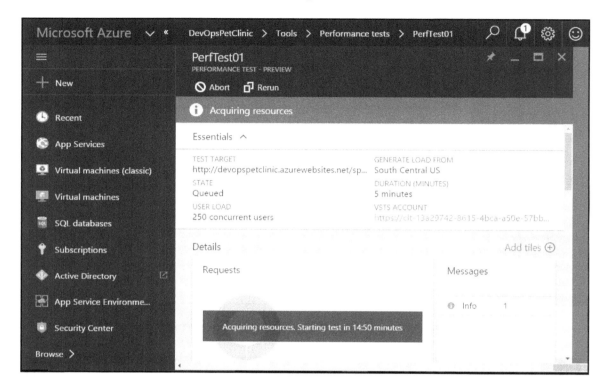

12. Once performance test is over, verify the details in Azure Portal:

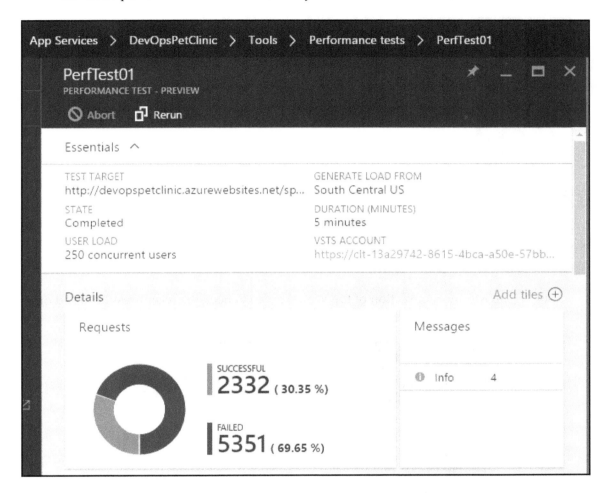

13. Verify the **Request Failures**:

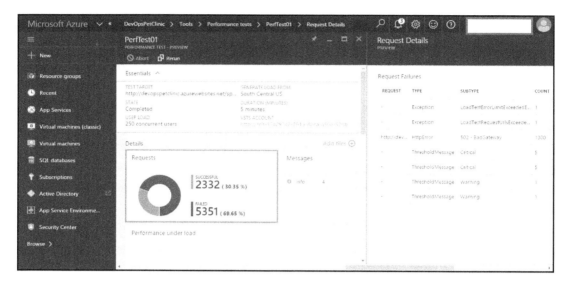

14. Go to Monitoring section of the Web App and check the recent results based on customized parameters:

15. Visual Studio Application Insights is in PREVIEW version and it has a capacity to Detect and diagnose issues in web apps and services. Click on **Browse** in Azure Portal and select **Application Insights**:

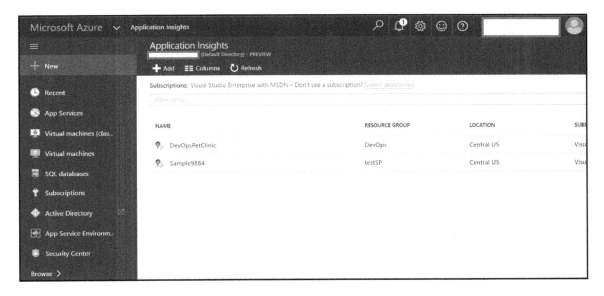

16. Select the application we have created and **Enable Application Insights to start collecting telemetry**:

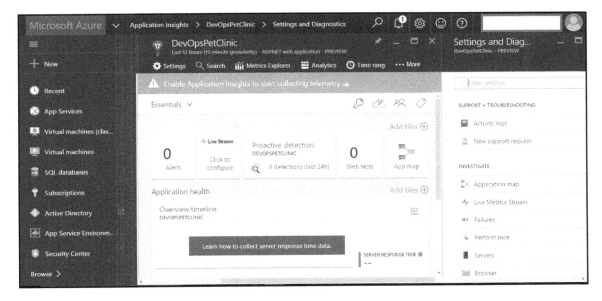

17. Click on **Start monitoring**:

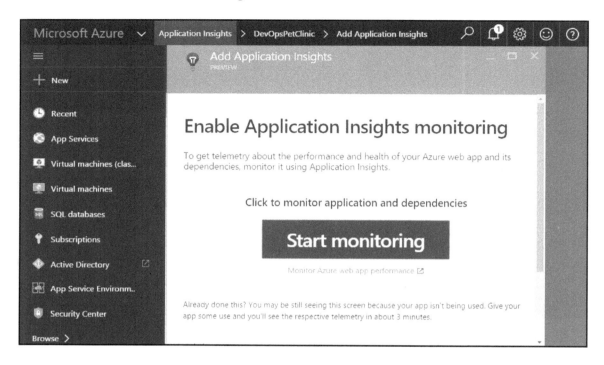

18. Wait till installation is completed.

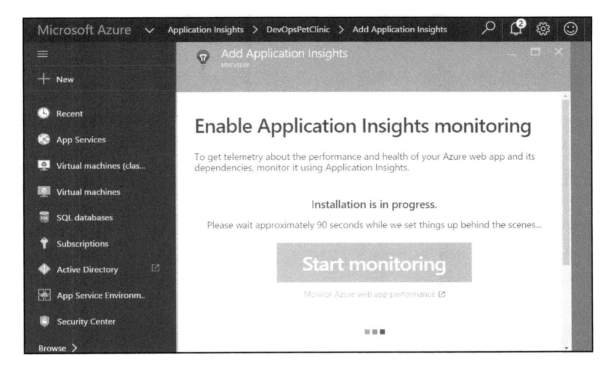

19. Verify the successful installation in portal:

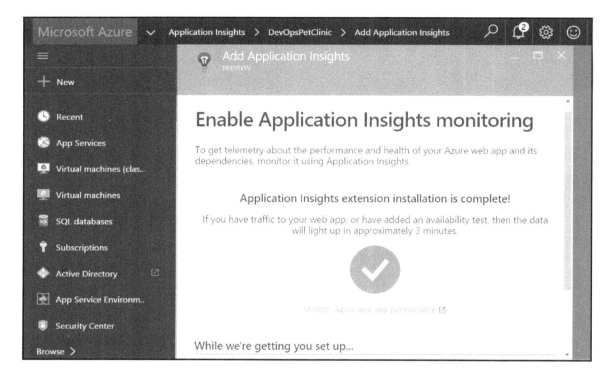

20. In **Application Insights**, we can also monitor**Application map** as shown in below figure:

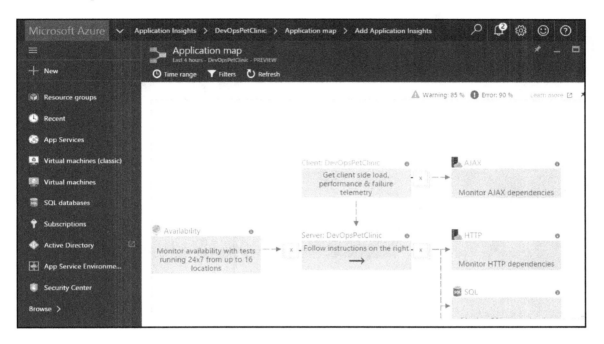

21. In Application Insights, We can configure Web tests to check availability of an application from different locations.

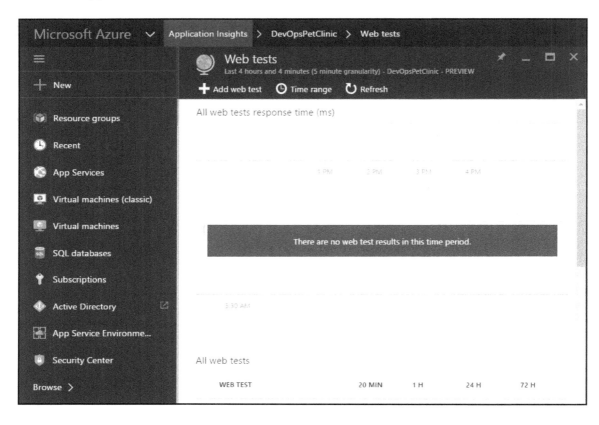

22. We can configure Availability tests from different regions to verify whether it is available or not. Configure regions based on priority:

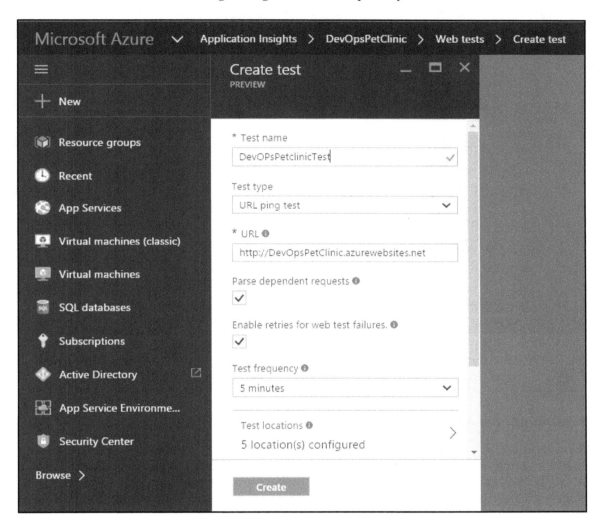

23. Create a Web test and within some time we will get results on Azure Portal:

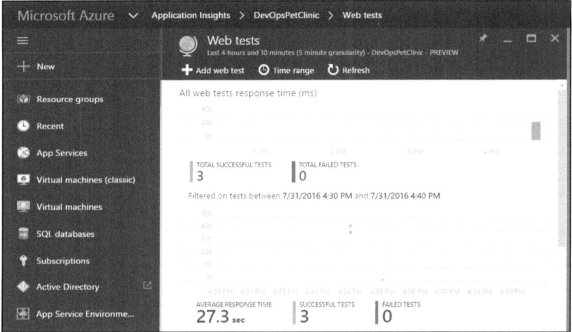

We have covered most of the monitoring features available with Azure Web Apps. In the next section, we will cover how to use New Relic tool to monitor PetClinic Spring Application.

Monitoring Web Application and Tomcat Server with New Relic

New Relic is a Software as a Service in the context of Cloud service models. New Relic monitors applications in real time and that also in any environment such as on premise or in cloud. We can install New Relic in the Application server's root directory and within minutes it starts providing monitoring and it reflects in the New Relic portal. It allows free trial.

New Relic supports monitoring for web applications developed in Java, .Net, PHP, Python, Node.js, Ruby and so on.

1. Create an account in New Relic. New Relic has Java installer for JBoss, Tomcat, Jetty, and Glassfish.
2. Login to New Relic.
3. Go to Account Settings and Download the Agent for the specific platform. In our case, we will install a Java Agent.

4. In the downloaded zip file, there will be two important files that are needed for monitoring:

   - `newrelic.jar`: that contains agent class files and
     - `newrelic.yml`: to configure license details that will be available on New Relic dashboard even for a free trial.

5. Extract the files from the zip folder and put the directory into Tomcat installation directory.
6. Open `newrelic.yml` in notepad and find the placeholder for License key and replace it with actual license key.
7. It will be in `common: &default_settings` as shown below:

```
common: &default_settings
# ================LICENSE KEY ==================
# You must specify the license key associated with your New Relic
# account. For example, if your license key is 12345 use this:
# license_key: '12345'
# The key binds your Agent's data to your account in the New Relic service.
license_key: '12345'
```

8. Run Tomcat. Once Tomcat is up and running, open a command prompt and go to the Directory of New Relic in the Tomcat root directory.
9. Execute java -jar newrelic.jar install in the command prompt.

- We are trying to monitor an application that is deployed on a local environment in Tomcat 7. We can do similar installation and monitoring for virtual machine available in cloud or virtualized environment.

```
Microsoft Windows [Version 10.0.10586]
(c) 2015 Microsoft Corporation. All rights reserved.

C:\Users\Mitesh>cd \

C:\>cd apache-tomcat-7.0.70\newrelic

C:\apache-tomcat-7.0.70\newrelic>java -jar newrelic.jar install
***** ( ( o))  New Relic Java Agent Installer

***** Installing version 3.30.1 ...

* Backed up start script to C:\apache-tomcat-7.0.70\bin\catalina.bat.20160724_180719

* Added agent switch to start script C:\apache-tomcat-7.0.70\bin\catalina.bat

* No need to create New Relic configuration file because:
 A config file already exists: C:\apache-tomcat-7.0.70\newrelic\newrelic.yml

***** Install successful

***** Next steps:
You're almost done! To see performance data for your app:

1) Restart your app server
2) Exercise your app
3) Log into http://rpm.newrelic.com

Within two minutes, your app should show up, ready to monitor and troubleshoot.
If app data doesn't appear, check newrelic/logs/newrelic_agent.log for errors.

C:\apache-tomcat-7.0.70\newrelic>
```

10. Once the installation is successful, restart the Tomcat server.

11. Verify the `newrelic` directory under Tomcat installation directory. New log folder will be created as shown in the following screenshot:

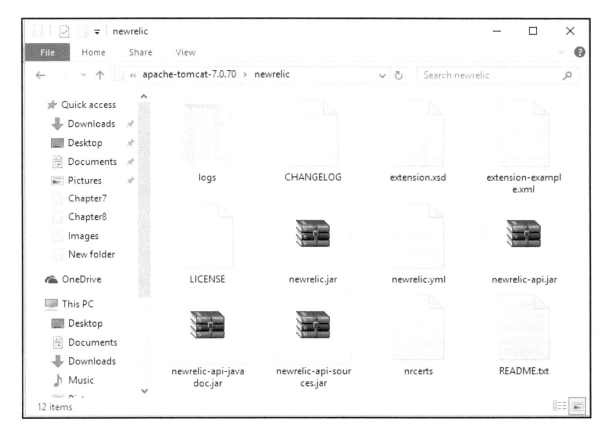

12. Open `newrelic_agent.log` file in notepad.

13. Verify the reporting to line:

Jul 24, 2016 18:14:50 +0530 [6920 27] com.newrelic INFO: Reporting to:
https://rpm.newrelic.com/accounts/64925/applications/20830005

```
Jul 24, 2016 18:14:17 +0530 [6920 7] com.newrelic INFO: Instrumentation
com.newrelic.instrumentation.hibernate-3.5 is enabled. Loading.
Jul 24, 2016 18:14:19 +0530 [6920 1] com.newrelic.agent.RPMServiceManagerImpl INFO: Configured
to connect to New Relic at collector.newrelic.com:443
Jul 24, 2016 18:14:20 +0530 [6920 1] com.newrelic INFO: Setting audit_mode to false
Jul 24, 2016 18:14:20 +0530 [6920 1] com.newrelic INFO: Setting protocol to "https"
Jul 24, 2016 18:14:21 +0530 [6920 1] com.newrelic.agent.config.ConfigServiceImpl INFO:
Configuration file is C:\apache-tomcat-7.0.70\newrelic\.\newrelic.yml
Jul 24, 2016 18:14:21 +0530 [6920 1] com.newrelic INFO: New Relic Agent v3.30.1 has started
Jul 24, 2016 18:14:21 +0530 [6920 1] com.newrelic INFO: Agent class loader:
sun.misc.Launcher$AppClassLoader@58644d46
Jul 24, 2016 18:14:21 +0530 [6920 1] com.newrelic INFO: Premain startup complete in 6,381ms
Jul 24, 2016 18:14:25 +0530 [6920 1] com.newrelic INFO: Server Info: Apache Tomcat/7.0.70
Jul 24, 2016 18:14:46 +0530 [6920 27] com.newrelic INFO: Display host name is my-pc for
application My Application
Jul 24, 2016 18:14:49 +0530 [6920 27] com.newrelic INFO: Collector redirection to
collector-216.newrelic.com:443
Jul 24, 2016 18:14:50 +0530 [6920 27] com.newrelic INFO: Agent run id: 89464200178842674
Jul 24, 2016 18:14:50 +0530 [6920 27] com.newrelic INFO: Agent 6920@my-pc/My Application
connected to collector.newrelic.com:443
Jul 24, 2016 18:14:50 +0530 [6920 27] com.newrelic INFO: Reporting to:
https://rpm.newrelic.com/accounts/64925/applications/20830005
Jul 24, 2016 18:14:50 +0530 [6920 27] com.newrelic INFO: Using RUM version 963 for application
"My Application"
Jul 24, 2016 18:14:50 +0530 [6920 27] com.newrelic INFO: Real user monitoring is enabled with
auto instrumentation for application "My Application"
```

14. Copy the URL and open it in browser and observe the **Overview** section with graphs:

15. Click on the Applications link to get list of Applications:

16. **Service maps** provides view of relationships between different components:

17. In the **MONITORING** Section of left sidebar, click on the **Databases** to get details of top database operations based on the time:

18. Click on **JVMs** to get details on the JVM and Tomcat:

19. Verify the **Apache Tomcat** Section for details related to **Memory**, **Threads**, and **Http Sessions**:

20. In the same page Garbage Collection and Class count related details are also available:

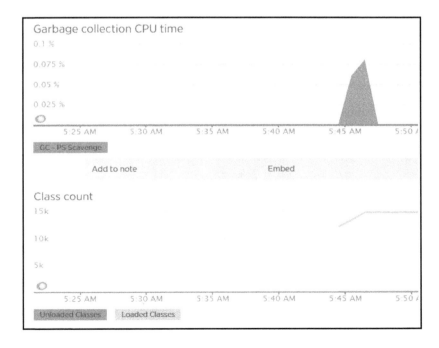

21. **Errors** section will display graph of errors per request:

This is just a simple overview of New Relic for our PetClinic application deployed on premise.

So till now we have covered Overview of installation and configuration of Nagios; monitoring of AWS Elastic Beanstalk environment, monitoring of Azure Web Apps, and Application monitoring with New Relic.

Monitoring itself is a huge topic and to cover things in detail is out of scope of this book so we have only covered some portion to give a glimpse of Monitoring of resources.

We have covered five phases till now and now we will discuss about end to end automation with pipeline and orchestration:

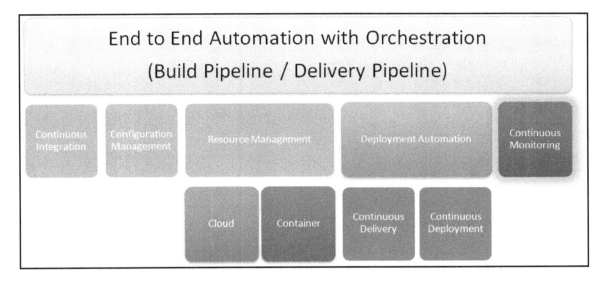

Self-test questions

State true or false:

1. Nagios Core, is an open source application written in C and PHP to monitor servers, networks, and infrastructure.

    - True
    - False

2. Nagios XI is supported in CentOS and RedHat.
    - True
    - False

3. In AWS Elastic Beanstalk, health status of an environment is determined by Grey, Green, Yellow, and Red color.
    - True
    - False

4. In AWS Elastic Beanstalk, Yellow color of health status indicates that environment has failure of one or more Health checks.
   - True
   - False

5. New Relic supports monitoring for web applications developed in Java, .Net, PHP, Python, Node.js, and Ruby
   - True
   - False

Summary

In this chapter, we have seen quick overview of instance monitoring with Nagios, basic monitoring with AWS Elastic Beanstalk, Azure Web Apps monitoring, and Java web application monitoring with New Relic.

The constant monitoring of each event and interaction may look like very complex and not required but it is a need of an hour in the competitive environment where users are more demanding and hence availability of an application is extremely important.

In the next chapter we will see end to end automation with orchestration of activities such as Continuous Integration, Cloud Provisioning, Configuration Management, Continuous Delivery or Continuous Deployment.

9
Orchestrating Application Deployment

"Success is a lousy teacher. It seduces smart people into thinking they can't lose. It's fine to celebrate success but it is more important to heed the lessons of failure"

This chapter describes in detail how to orchestrate different build jobs for continuous integration, configuration management, continuous delivery, and so on. It will cover how the build pipeline plugin and pipeline feature of Jenkins 2.0 can be used to orchestrate an end-to-end automation process for application deployment.

Until now, we have covered continuous integration, cloud provisioning using Chef, configuration management, and continuous delivery. Each was configured in a unique build job. Now we are only going to manage all those build jobs in a manner that the checkout or execution of the build pipeline will result in the checkout, compilation, unit test execution, installation of the Linux instance on Amazon EC2, installation of the runtime environment, configuration of permissions in the newly created instance, and deployment of the WAR file.

In this chapter, we will cover the following topics:

- Creating parameterized build jobs for end-to-end automation
- Configuring a build pipeline for the orchestration of a build job
- Executing the build pipeline for application deployment automation

Creating build jobs for end-to-end automation

Before we configure end-to-end automation for build job execution, let's understand it graphically:

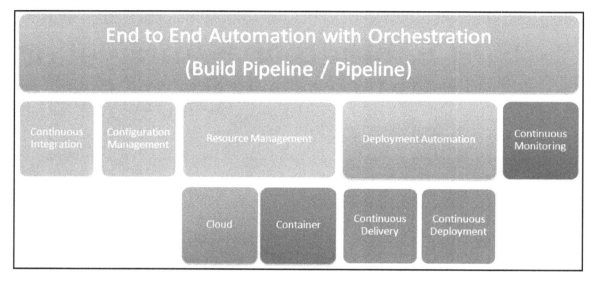

We will configure it using upstream and downstream job configuration in the case of the Build Pipeline plugin, while in the case of the Jenkins 2.0 pipeline, we will use a script.

Configuration management depends on the environment we use for deployment. We have covered the following deployment environments in this book:

- PetClinic Spring application deployment on a Tomcat server (on-premise environment/personal laptop or desktop)
- PetClinic Spring application deployment on a Tomcat server on Amazon EC2 (IaaS)
- PetClinic Spring application deployment on a Tomcat server on a Microsoft Azure virtual machine (IaaS)

- PetClinic Spring application deployment on a Tomcat server in a Docker image (container)
- PetClinic Spring application deployment on a Tomcat server on Amazon Elastic Beanstalk (PaaS)
- PetClinic Spring application deployment on a Tomcat server in Microsoft Azure web apps (PaaS)

Based on the deployment environment, we need configuration management. In IaaS, we need to install a runtime environment, while in the case of PaaS and Docker containers, we only need minor modifications of the addition of a file or similar types of smaller changes.

Considering the deployment environment, we need to introduce build jobs for end-to-end automation.

In the case of the PetClinic Spring application deployment on a Tomcat server on Amazon EC2 (IaaS), we need the following flow:

Build Job 1: Continuous Integration	Build Job 2: Cloud Provisioning and Configuration Management	Build Job 3: Continuous Delivery & Continuous Deployment
• Code Chekout • Compile • Junit Test Case Execution • Code Ananlysis (Optional)	• Knife EC2 plugin • Tomcat & Java Cookbooks with dependencies	• Permissions • Stop and Start Tomcat Server • Deploy WAR file

Let's try to implement previous steps in Jenkins to achieve end-to-end automation that includes in the previously mentioned steps.

1. Let's visit the Jenkins dashboard. Click on **Manage Jenkins**. In the following screenshot, we can see that a new version of Jenkins is available. Click on **Or Upgrade Automatically** to update the application:

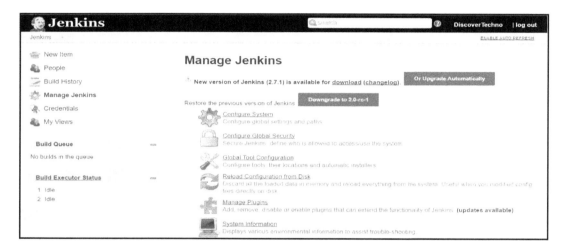

2. It will start installing `jenkins.war`:

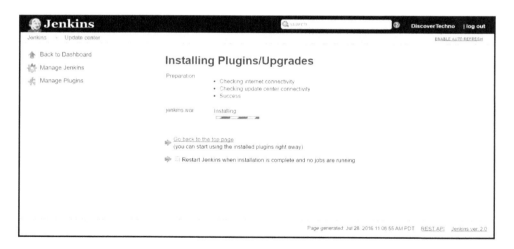

3. Once installation is successful, restart Jenkins from the terminal:

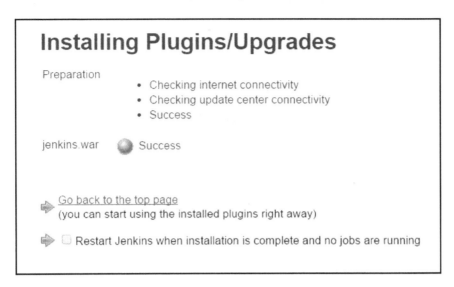

4. Refresh the Jenkins dashboard and check whether the new version has been installed properly:

5. Verify the version number in the status bar:

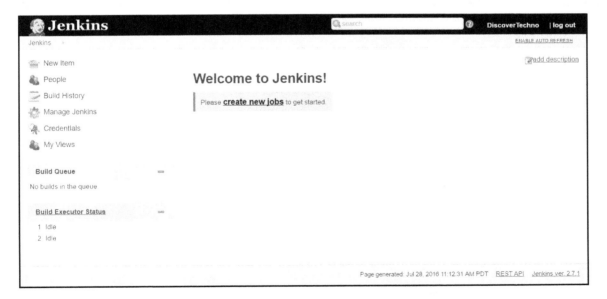

Configuring SSH authentication using a key

Before starting with end-to-end automation and orchestration, we need to configure SSH authentication using a key. The objective behind it is to allow the Jenkins VM to connect to the Chef workstation. Then, we can issue SSH commands from the Jenkins dashboard on the Chef workstation VM to create an instance in AWS or Azure cloud and install a runtime environment on it to deploy the PetClinic application:

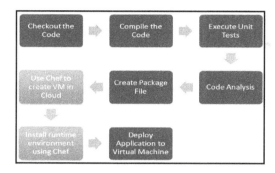

If we try to access the SSH Chef workstation from Jenkins, it won't work as we still need to configure password less configuration for security:

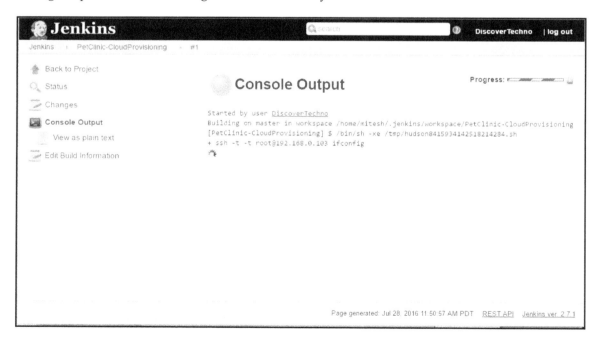

Let's configure virtual machine where Jenkins is installed to access virtual machine where Chef Workstation is installed.

1. Open a terminal in Jenkins. Use `ssh-keygen` to create a new key:

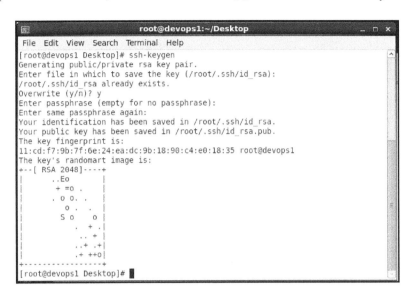

2. Verify the newly generated key on the local filesystem:

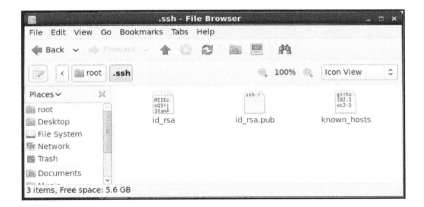

3. Copy the key to the remote host using `ssh-copy-id`:

```
File  Edit  View  Search  Terminal  Help
[root@devops1 Desktop]# ssh-copy-id -i ~/.ssh/id_rsa.pub 192.168.0.106
Agent admitted failure to sign using the key.
root@192.168.0.106's password:
Now try logging into the machine, with "ssh '192.168.0.106'", and check in:

  .ssh/authorized_keys

to make sure we haven't added extra keys that you weren't expecting.

[root@devops1 Desktop]# ssh-copy-id -i ~/.ssh/id_rsa.pub mitesh@192.168.0.106
mitesh@192.168.0.106's password:
Now try logging into the machine, with "ssh 'mitesh@192.168.0.106'", and check i
n:

  .ssh/authorized_keys

to make sure we haven't added extra keys that you weren't expecting.
```

4. Now try to access the Chef workstation using the Jenkins build job:

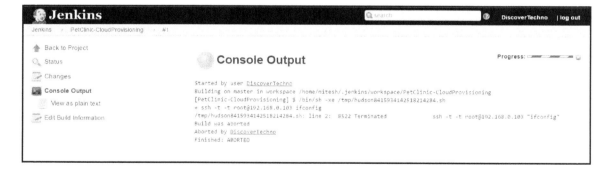

5. If it fails, then try to access it from the Jenkins VM using a terminal. If you get the `Agent admitted failure to sign in using key` message, then use `ssh-add` to fix the issue:

```
[mitesh@devops1 Desktop]$ ssh-copy-id -i ~/.ssh/id_rsa.pub root@192.168.0.103
root@192.168.0.103's password:
Now try logging into the machine, with "ssh 'root@192.168.0.103'", and check in:

  .ssh/authorized_keys

to make sure we haven't added extra keys that you weren't expecting.

[mitesh@devops1 Desktop]$ ssh -t root@192.168.0.103
Agent admitted failure to sign using the key.
root@192.168.0.103's password:

[mitesh@devops1 Desktop]$ ssh-add
Identity added: /home/mitesh/.ssh/id_rsa (/home/mitesh/.ssh/id_rsa)
[mitesh@devops1 Desktop]$ ssh -t root@192.168.0.103
Last login: Thu Jul 28 12:21:56 2016 from 192.168.0.106
[root@devops1 ~]# ifconfig
eth5      Link encap:Ethernet  HWaddr 00:0C:29:91:3F:2F
          inet addr:192.168.0.103  Bcast:192.168.0.255  Mask:255.255.255.0
          inet6 addr: fe80::20c:29ff:fe91:3f2f/64 Scope:Link
          UP BROADCAST RUNNING MULTICAST  MTU:1500  Metric:1
          RX packets:2664 errors:0 dropped:0 overruns:0 frame:0
          TX packets:1727 errors:0 dropped:0 overruns:0 carrier:0
          collisions:0 txqueuelen:1000
          RX bytes:716002 (699.2 KiB)  TX bytes:197090 (192.4 KiB)

lo        Link encap:Local Loopback
          inet addr:127.0.0.1  Mask:255.0.0.0
          inet6 addr: ::1/128 Scope:Host
          UP LOOPBACK RUNNING  MTU:65536  Metric:1
          RX packets:50663 errors:0 dropped:0 overruns:0 frame:0
          TX packets:50663 errors:0 dropped:0 overruns:0 carrier:0
          collisions:0 txqueuelen:0
```

6. Now, our SSH connection is successful using not a password but a key:

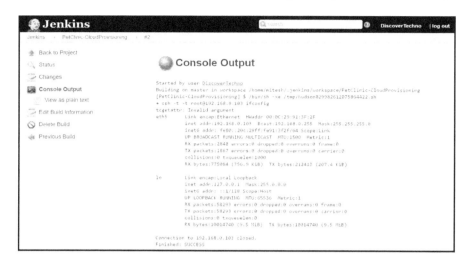

7. Let's try to create an instance in AWS using the Jenkins build job and Chef workstation:

8. Add a **Build** step, select **Execute shell**, and add paste the command mentioned here. We have already discussed `knife ec2` commands in `Chapter 6`, *Cloud Provisioning and Configuration Management with Chef*.

```
ssh -t -t root@192.168.1.36 "ifconfig; rvm use 2.1.0; knife ec2 server
create -I ami-1ecae776 -f t2.micro -N DevOpsVMonAWS1 --aws-access-key-id
'<YOUR ACCESS KEY ID>' --aws-secret-access-key '<YOUR SECRET ACCESS KEY>' -
S book --identity-file book.pem --ssh-user ec2-user -r role[v-tomcat]"
```

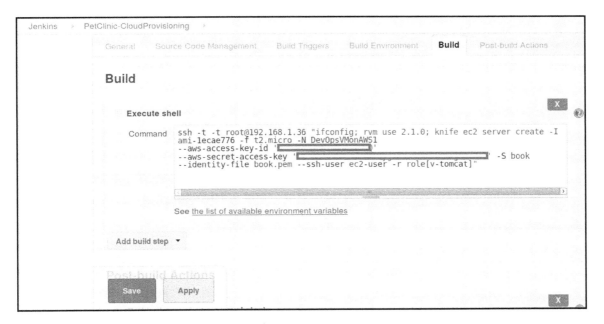

9. Click on **Save**. Click on the **Build Now** link to execute the build job.

10. Go to **Console Output** to check the progress:

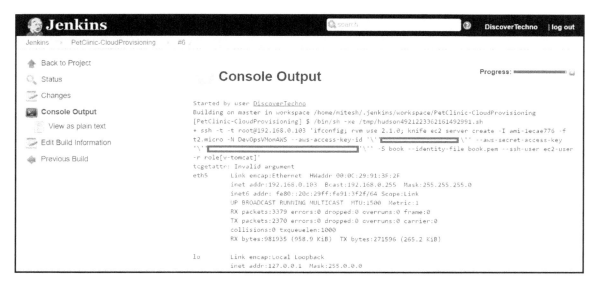

11. AWS instance creation has started:

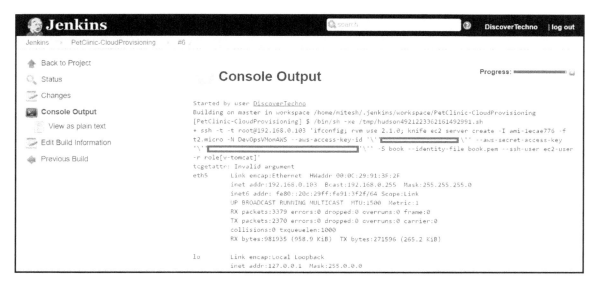

12. Verify it in the AWS management console:

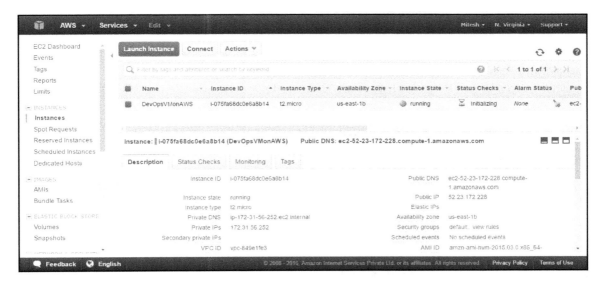

13. Before its execution can go further, check whether the AWS security group has an entry for SSH access:

14. Once SSH access is available, it will start Chef client installations:

```
[32mUsing /usr/local/rvm/gems/ruby-2.1.0[0m
[36mInstance ID[0m: i-024d3bf83022b89e4
[36mFlavor[0m: t2.micro
[36mImage[0m: ami-1ecae776
[36mRegion[0m: us-east-1
[36mAvailability Zone[0m: us-east-1d
[36mSecurity Groups[0m: default
[36mTags[0m: Name: DevOpsVMonAWS
[36mSSH Key[0m: book

[35mWaiting for EC2 to create the instance[0m.....
[36mPublic DNS Name[0m: ec2-52-23-215-193.compute-1.amazonaws.com
[36mPublic IP Address[0m: 52.23.215.193
[36mPrivate DNS Name[0m: ip-172-31-31-133.ec2.internal
[36mPrivate IP Address[0m: 172.31.31.133

[35mWaiting for sshd access to become available[0m................................done
Creating new client for DevOpsVMonAWS
Creating new node for DevOpsVMonAWS
Connecting to [1mec2-52-23-215-193.compute-1.amazonaws.com[0m
[36mec2-52-23-215-193.compute-1.amazonaws.com[0m -----> Installing Chef Omnibus (-v 12)

[36mec2-52-23-215-193.compute-1.amazonaws.com[0m downloading https://omnitruck-direct.chef.io/chef/install.sh

[36mec2-52-23-215-193.compute-1.amazonaws.com[0m   to file /tmp/install.sh.2313/install.sh

[36mec2-52-23-215-193.compute-1.amazonaws.com[0m trying wget...

[36mec2-52-23-215-193.compute-1.amazonaws.com[0m el 6 x86_64
```

15. In our case, it will start downloading the Chef client and installing it on the AWS instance:

```
[36mec2-52-23-215-193.compute-1.amazonaws.com[0m Getting information for chef stable 12 for el...

[36mec2-52-23-215-193.compute-1.amazonaws.com[0m downloading https://omnitruck-direct.chef.io/stable/chef/metadata?
v=12&p=el&pv=6&m=x86_64

[36mec2-52-23-215-193.compute-1.amazonaws.com[0m   to file /tmp/install.sh.2318/metadata.txt

[36mec2-52-23-215-193.compute-1.amazonaws.com[0m trying wget...

[36mec2-52-23-215-193.compute-1.amazonaws.com[0m sha1   67b7e152fc8440ceb2a9f027e3b2edc93d3759db

[36mec2-52-23-215-193.compute-1.amazonaws.com[0m sha256
9c6455bd30568c639e19485837bacbd07972c8e9f5cc3831fba4bc415bed24ad

[36mec2-52-23-215-193.compute-1.amazonaws.com[0m url    https://packages.chef.io/stable/el/6/chef-12.12.15-
1.el6.x86_64.rpm

[36mec2-52-23-215-193.compute-1.amazonaws.com[0m version       12.12.15

[36mec2-52-23-215-193.compute-1.amazonaws.com[0m downloaded metadata file looks valid...

[36mec2-52-23-215-193.compute-1.amazonaws.com[0m downloading https://packages.chef.io/stable/el/6/chef-12.12.15-
1.el6.x86_64.rpm

[36mec2-52-23-215-193.compute-1.amazonaws.com[0m   to file /tmp/install.sh.2318/chef-12.12.15-1.el6.x86_64.rpm

[36mec2-52-23-215-193.compute-1.amazonaws.com[0m trying wget...

[36mec2-52-23-215-193.compute-1.amazonaws.com[0m Comparing checksum with sha256sum...

[36mec2-52-23-215-193.compute-1.amazonaws.com[0m Installing chef 12
```

16. Verify the Chef installation process on the console:

```
[36mec2-52-23-215-193.compute-1.amazonaws.com[0m Installing chef 12

[36mec2-52-23-215-193.compute-1.amazonaws.com[0m installing with rpm...

[36mec2-52-23-215-193.compute-1.amazonaws.com[0m warning: /tmp/install.sh.2318/chef-12.12.15-1.el6.x86_64.rpm: Header
V4 DSA/SHA1 Signature, key ID 83ef826a: NOKEY

[36mec2-52-23-215-193.compute-1.amazonaws.com[0m Preparing...
(100%)#                            (100%)##                            (100%)###
(100%)####                         (100%)#####                         (100%)######
(100%)#######                      (100%)########                      (100%)#########
(100%)##########                   (100%)###########                   (100%)############
(100%)#############                (100%)##############                (100%)###############
(100%)################             (100%)#################             (100%)##################
(100%)###################          (100%)####################          (100%)#####################
(100%)######################       (100%)#######################       (100%)########################
(100%)#########################    (100%)##########################    (100%)###########################
(100%)############################ (100%)#############################
(100%)############################### (100%)############################### [100%]

[36mec2-52-23-215-193.compute-1.amazonaws.com[0m Updating / installing...

[36mec2-52-23-215-193.compute-1.amazonaws.com[0m    1:chef-12.12.15-1.el6
(   1%)#                       (   4%)##                       (   7%)###
(  10%)####                    (  13%)#####                    (  16%)######
(  19%)#######                 (  22%)########                 (  25%)#########
(  28%)##########              (  31%)###########              (  34%)############
(  37%)#############           (  40%)##############           (  43%)###############
(  46%)################        (  49%)#################        (  51%)##################
(  54%)###################     (  57%)####################     (  60%)#####################
(  63%)######################  (  66%)#######################  (  69%)########################
(  72%)######################### (  75%)########################## ( 78%)###########################
(  81%)############################ (  84%)############################# ( 87%)##############################
(  90%)############################### (  93%)################################ (
96%)################################# (  99%)################################# [100%]
```

17. Once the Chef client is installed on the AWS instance, it will start its first Chef client execution.

18. Observe the run list and synchronizing cookbooks. It will converge and start installing packages:

```
[36mec2-52-23-215-193.compute-1.amazonaws.com[0m Thank you for installing Chef!

[36mec2-52-23-215-193.compute-1.amazonaws.com[0m Starting the first Chef Client run...

[36mec2-52-23-215-193.compute-1.amazonaws.com[0m Starting Chef Client, version 12.12.15

[36mec2-52-23-215-193.compute-1.amazonaws.com[0m resolving cookbooks for run list: ["tomcat"]

[36mec2-52-23-215-193.compute-1.amazonaws.com[0m Synchronizing Cookbooks:

[36mec2-52-23-215-193.compute-1.amazonaws.com[0m   - tomcat (0.17.0)

[36mec2-52-23-215-193.compute-1.amazonaws.com[0m   - java (1.39.0)

[36mec2-52-23-215-193.compute-1.amazonaws.com[0m   - apt (3.0.0)

[36mec2-52-23-215-193.compute-1.amazonaws.com[0m   - chef-sugar (3.3.0)

[36mec2-52-23-215-193.compute-1.amazonaws.com[0m   - openssl (4.4.0)

[36mec2-52-23-215-193.compute-1.amazonaws.com[0m Installing Cookbook Gems:

[36mec2-52-23-215-193.compute-1.amazonaws.com[0m Compiling Cookbooks...

[36mec2-52-23-215-193.compute-1.amazonaws.com[0m [2016-07-28T20:42:33+00:00] WARN: Chef::Provider::AptRepository already exists!  Cannot create deprecation class for LWRP provider apt_repository from cookbook apt

[36mec2-52-23-215-193.compute-1.amazonaws.com[0m [2016-07-28T20:42:33+00:00] WARN: AptRepository already exists! Deprecation class overwrites Custom resource apt_repository from cookbook apt

[36mec2-52-23-215-193.compute-1.amazonaws.com[0m Converging 3 resources

[36mec2-52-23-215-193.compute-1.amazonaws.com[0m Recipe: tomcat::default

[36mec2-52-23-215-193.compute-1.amazonaws.com[0m   * yum_package[tomcat6] action install
```

19. Verify the package installations:

```
[36mec2-52-23-215-193.compute-1.amazonaws.com[0m Recipe: tomcat::default

[36mec2-52-23-215-193.compute-1.amazonaws.com[0m  * yum_package[tomcat6] action install

[36mec2-52-23-215-193.compute-1.amazonaws.com[0m    - install version 6.0.45-1.5.amzn1 of package tomcat6

[36mec2-52-23-215-193.compute-1.amazonaws.com[0m  * yum_package[tomcat6-admin-webapps] action install

[36mec2-52-23-215-193.compute-1.amazonaws.com[0m    - install version 6.0.45-1.5.amzn1 of package tomcat6-admin-
webapps

[36mec2-52-23-215-193.compute-1.amazonaws.com[0m  * tomcat_instance[base] action configure (up to date)

[36mec2-52-23-215-193.compute-1.amazonaws.com[0m  * directory[/usr/share/tomcat6/lib/endorsed] action create

[36mec2-52-23-215-193.compute-1.amazonaws.com[0m    - create new directory /usr/share/tomcat6/lib/endorsed

[36mec2-52-23-215-193.compute-1.amazonaws.com[0m    - change mode from '' to '0755'

[36mec2-52-23-215-193.compute-1.amazonaws.com[0m  * template[/etc/sysconfig/tomcat6] action create

[36mec2-52-23-215-193.compute-1.amazonaws.com[0m    - update content in file /etc/sysconfig/tomcat6 from 32bba1 to
7eb379

[36mec2-52-23-215-193.compute-1.amazonaws.com[0m    --- /etc/sysconfig/tomcat6 2016-07-18 23:03:48.000000000 +0000

[36mec2-52-23-215-193.compute-1.amazonaws.com[0m    +++ /etc/sysconfig/.chef-tomcat620160728-2391-pszhdv        2016-
07-28 20:43:24.765025585 +0000

[36mec2-52-23-215-193.compute-1.amazonaws.com[0m    @@ -1,3 +1,9 @@

[36mec2-52-23-215-193.compute-1.amazonaws.com[0m    +#

[36mec2-52-23-215-193.compute-1.amazonaws.com[0m    +# Dynamically generated by Chef on ip-172-31-31-
133.ec2.internal
```

20. It will also display `conf.xml`, where port-related details can be verified based on the configuration:

```
[36mec2-52-23-215-193.compute-1.amazonaws.com[0m          <!-- A "Connector" using the shared thread pool-->

[36mec2-52-23-215-193.compute-1.amazonaws.com[0m          <!--

[36mec2-52-23-215-193.compute-1.amazonaws.com[0m          <Connector executor="tomcatThreadPool"

[36mec2-52-23-215-193.compute-1.amazonaws.com[0m    -                port="8080" protocol="HTTP/1.1"

[36mec2-52-23-215-193.compute-1.amazonaws.com[0m    -                connectionTimeout="20000"

[36mec2-52-23-215-193.compute-1.amazonaws.com[0m    +                port="8080" protocol="HTTP/1.1"

[36mec2-52-23-215-193.compute-1.amazonaws.com[0m    +                connectionTimeout="20000"

[36mec2-52-23-215-193.compute-1.amazonaws.com[0m                     redirectPort="8443" />

[36mec2-52-23-215-193.compute-1.amazonaws.com[0m    -    -->

[36mec2-52-23-215-193.compute-1.amazonaws.com[0m    +    -->

[36mec2-52-23-215-193.compute-1.amazonaws.com[0m          <!-- Define a SSL HTTP/1.1 Connector on port 8443

[36mec2-52-23-215-193.compute-1.amazonaws.com[0m    -         This connector uses the JSSE configuration, when using
APR, the

[36mec2-52-23-215-193.compute-1.amazonaws.com[0m    +         This connector uses the JSSE configuration, when using
APR, the

[36mec2-52-23-215-193.compute-1.amazonaws.com[0m              connector should be using the OpenSSL style
configuration

[36mec2-52-23-215-193.compute-1.amazonaws.com[0m              described in the APR documentation -->
```

21. Once the package installation is finished, it will start service management:

```
[36mec2-52-23-215-193.compute-1.amazonaws.com[0m   * service[tomcat6] action start

[36mec2-52-23-215-193.compute-1.amazonaws.com[0m     - start service service[tomcat6]

[36mec2-52-23-215-193.compute-1.amazonaws.com[0m   * execute[wait for tomcat6] action run

[36mec2-52-23-215-193.compute-1.amazonaws.com[0m     - execute sleep 5

[36mec2-52-23-215-193.compute-1.amazonaws.com[0m   * service[tomcat6] action enable

[36mec2-52-23-215-193.compute-1.amazonaws.com[0m     - enable service service[tomcat6]

[36mec2-52-23-215-193.compute-1.amazonaws.com[0m   * execute[wait for tomcat6] action run

[36mec2-52-23-215-193.compute-1.amazonaws.com[0m     - execute sleep 5

[36mec2-52-23-215-193.compute-1.amazonaws.com[0m   * execute[wait for tomcat6] action nothing
:nothing)

[36mec2-52-23-215-193.compute-1.amazonaws.com[0m   * service[tomcat6] action restart

[36mec2-52-23-215-193.compute-1.amazonaws.com[0m     - restart service service[tomcat6]

[36mec2-52-23-215-193.compute-1.amazonaws.com[0m   * execute[wait for tomcat6] action run

[36mec2-52-23-215-193.compute-1.amazonaws.com[0m     - execute sleep 5

[36mec2-52-23-215-193.compute-1.amazonaws.com[0m

[36mec2-52-23-215-193.compute-1.amazonaws.com[0m Running handlers:

[36mec2-52-23-215-193.compute-1.amazonaws.com[0m Running handlers complete
```

22. Now, the Chef client execution has finished, and it will display related information for the AWS instance we created:

```
[36mec2-52-23-215-193.compute-1.amazonaws.com[0m

[36mec2-52-23-215-193.compute-1.amazonaws.com[0m Chef Client finished, 13/15 resources
seconds


[36mInstance ID[0m: i-024d3bf83022b89e4
[36mFlavor[0m: t2.micro
[36mImage[0m: ami-1ecae776
[36mRegion[0m: us-east-1
[36mAvailability Zone[0m: us-east-1d
[36mSecurity Groups[0m: default
[36mSecurity Group Ids[0m: default
[36mTags[0m: Name: DevOpsVMonAWS
[36mSSH Key[0m: book
[36mRoot Device Type[0m: ebs
[36mRoot Volume ID[0m: vol-00aae3951d7ed88bb
[36mRoot Device Name[0m: /dev/xvda
[36mRoot Device Delete on Terminate[0m: true


[35mBlock devices[0m
[35m===========================[0m
[36mDevice Name[0m: /dev/xvda
[36mVolume ID[0m: vol-00aae3951d7ed88bb
[36mDelete on Terminate[0m: true


[35m===========================[0m
[36mPublic DNS Name[0m: ec2-52-23-215-193.compute-1.amazonaws.com
[36mPublic IP Address[0m: 52.23.215.193
[36mPrivate DNS Name[0m: ip-172-31-31-133.ec2.internal
[36mPrivate IP Address[0m: 172.31.31.133
[36mEnvironment[0m: _default
[36mRun List[0m: role[v-tomcat]
Connection to 192.168.0.103 closed.
Finished: SUCCESS
```

23. Check the AWS management console for the successful status.

24. We have used a different agent node for some build jobs. To keep it ready, make it active:

```
C:\Users\Mitesh\Downloads>java -jar slave.jar -jnlpUrl
http://192.168.1.35:8080/computer/TestServer/slave-agent.jnlp -secret
65464e02c58c85b192883f7848ad2758408220bed2f3af715c01c9b01cb72f9b
```

```
C:\Users\Mitesh\Downloads>java -jar slave.jar -jnlpUrl http://192.168.1.35:8080/compu
ter/TestServer/slave-agent.jnlp -secret 65464e02c58c85b192883f7848ad2758408220bed2f3a
f715c01c9b01cb72f9b
Jul 30, 2016 11:21:00 AM hudson.remoting.jnlp.Main createEngine
INFO: Setting up slave: TestServer
Jul 30, 2016 11:21:00 AM hudson.remoting.jnlp.Main$CuiListener <init>
INFO: Jenkins agent is running in headless mode.
Jul 30, 2016 11:21:00 AM hudson.remoting.jnlp.Main$CuiListener status
INFO: Locating server among [http://192.168.1.34:8080/, http://192.168.1.35:8080/]
Jul 30, 2016 11:21:01 AM hudson.remoting.jnlp.Main$CuiListener status
INFO: Handshaking
Jul 30, 2016 11:21:01 AM hudson.remoting.jnlp.Main$CuiListener status
INFO: Connecting to 192.168.1.35:33337
Jul 30, 2016 11:21:01 AM hudson.remoting.jnlp.Main$CuiListener status
INFO: Trying protocol: JNLP3-connect
Jul 30, 2016 11:21:02 AM hudson.remoting.jnlp.Main$CuiListener status
INFO: Server didn't accept the handshake: Unknown protocol:Protocol:JNLP3-connect
Jul 30, 2016 11:21:02 AM hudson.remoting.jnlp.Main$CuiListener status
INFO: Connecting to 192.168.1.35:33337
Jul 30, 2016 11:21:02 AM hudson.remoting.jnlp.Main$CuiListener status
INFO: Trying protocol: JNLP2-connect
Jul 30, 2016 11:21:02 AM hudson.remoting.jnlp.Main$CuiListener status
INFO: Connected
```

25. Go to the Jenkins dashboard, and click on **Manage Jenkins**. Navigate to **Manage Nodes** and verify the status of both the master and agent:

26. Verify hosted Chef for registered nodes:

Now, we have all the resources ready to configure the build pipeline.

Configuring the build pipeline for build job orchestration

Now, it is time to integrate all the work in a way that continuous integration, cloud provisioning, configuration management, and continuous delivery is orchestrated in a sequence:

1. In the Jenkins dashboard, go to **PetClinic-Build-Pipeline-View**:

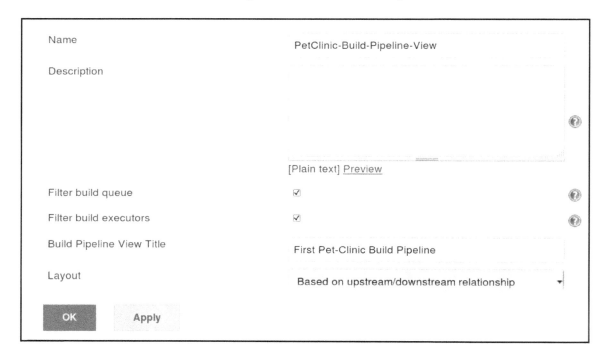

2. Click on **Configure** to view settings or modify them:

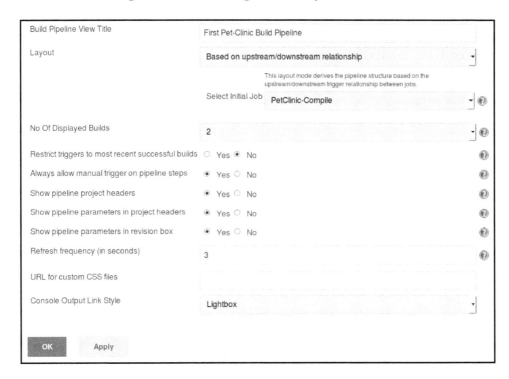

3. Once we click on **OK**, changes are saved and we see the configuration, as shown in the following screenshot. It is the output of the upstream and downstream job configuration:

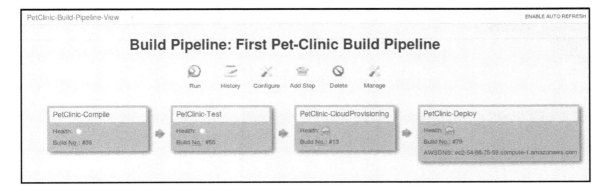

To create complete build pipeline mentioned in previous screenshot, we need to configure post build actions of each build job that we want to execute in specific sequence. We have different build job for continuous integration, configuration management and continuous delivery so we will configure them as upstream and downstream jobs to make pipeline. Let's look at each build job configuration step by step:

1. Click on **PetClinic-Compile** | **Configure**. Go to **Post-build Actions**. In the **Build other project** section, we have configured the build to be executed after **PetClinic-Compile** has been completed successfully:

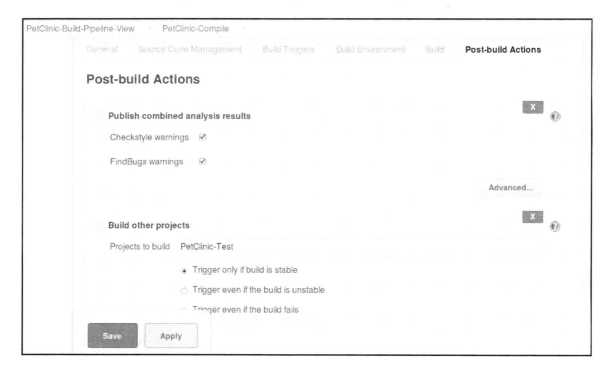

2. Save it and verify **Downstream Projects** on the Jenkins dashboard:

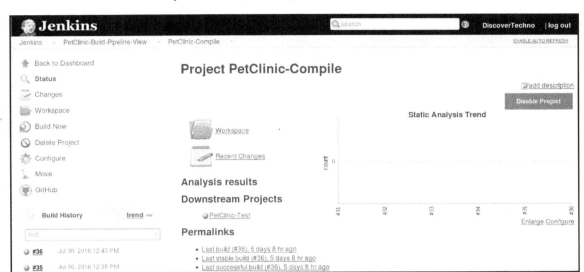

3. Click on **PetClinic-Test** | **Configure**. Go to **Post-build Actions**. In **Build other projects**, we have configured the build to be executed after **PetClinic-Test** has been completed successfully.

4. Configure the archive artifacts so we can copy it for deployment:

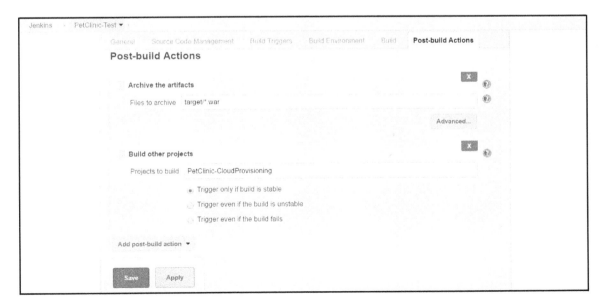

5. Verify **Upstream** and **Downstream** projects for the **PetClinic-Test** build job in the Jenkins dashboard:

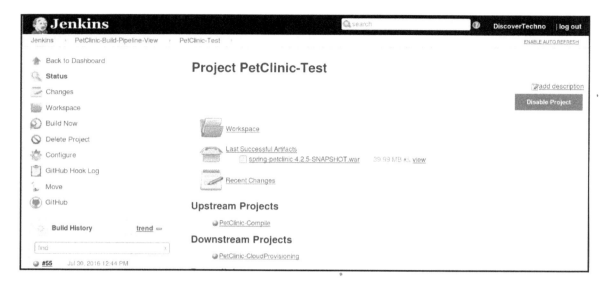

6. Execute the build independently to check whether the artifact or WAR file is archived:

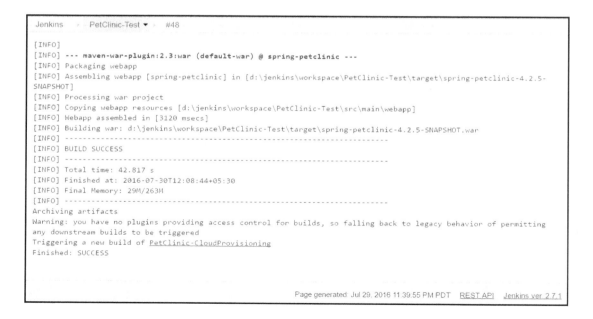

7. Verify the archived artifact in the Jenkins home directory:

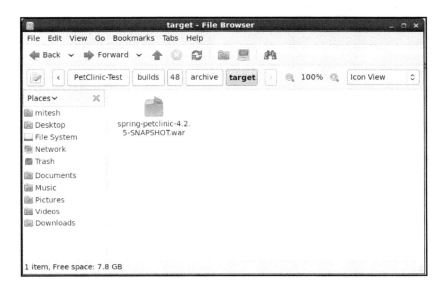

8. At this stage, the build pipeline will look like this:

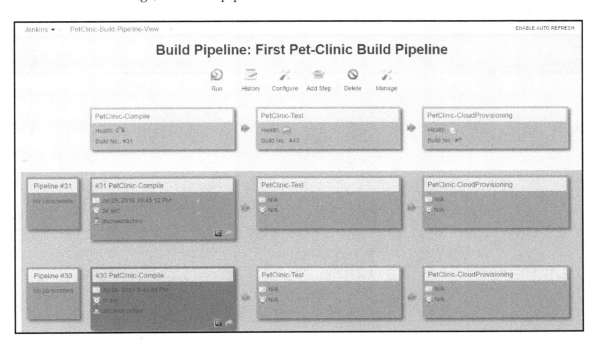

9. Click on **PetClinic-CloudProvisioning** | **Configure**. Go to **Post-build Actions**. In the **Build other projects** section, we have the configured the build to be executed after **PetClinic-CloudProvisioning** has been completed successfully:

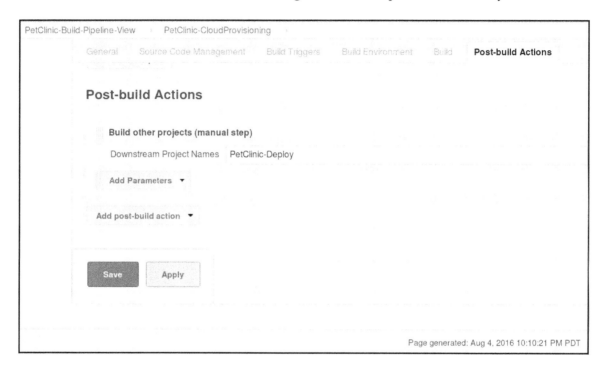

10. Verify **Upstream** and **Downstream** projects for the **PetClinic-CloudProvisioning** build job in the Jenkins dashboard:

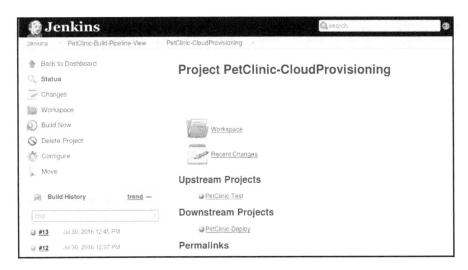

11. Click on **PetClinic-Deploy** | **Configure**. Our WAR file was ready in the **PetClinic-Test** build job, so let's copy it to a common location and configure it as a build step:

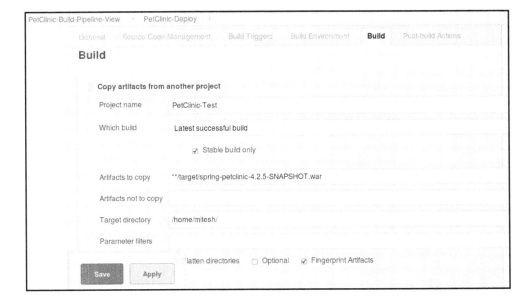

12. Configure the build step to copy the artifact and verify it by executing the build independently:

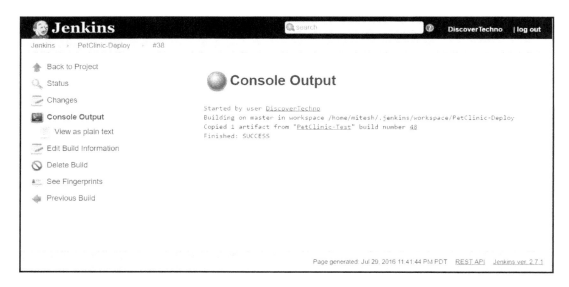

13. Once the artifact copy operation is verified, configure the build job so we can deploy it as a manual operation. We will create a job with the **String Parameter** of a newly created instance's domain name or IP address:

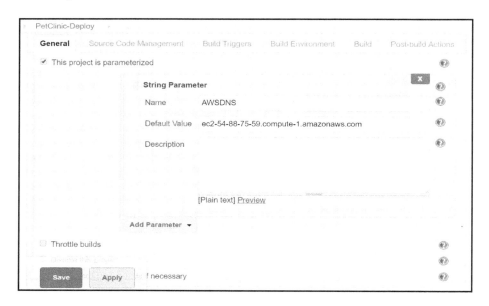

14. Go to the **PetClinic-CloudProvisioning** build job and check whether we have added **Build other projects (manual step)** for the **PetClinic-Deploy** build job:

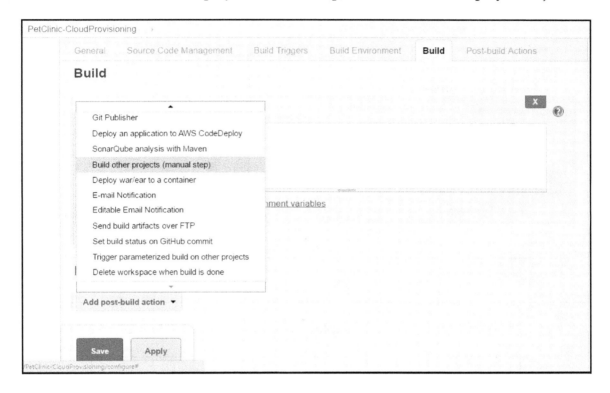

15. Once you've verified this, let's move to executing the build pipeline:

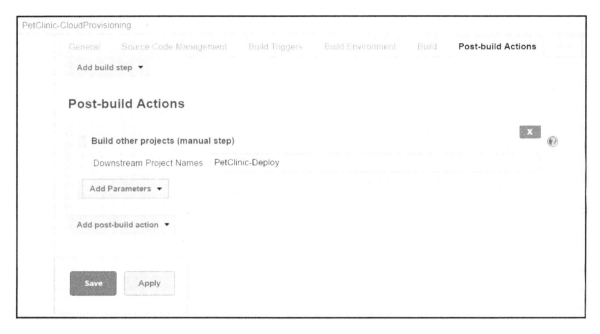

16. Once our artifact is ready to deploy, we need to perform following steps:

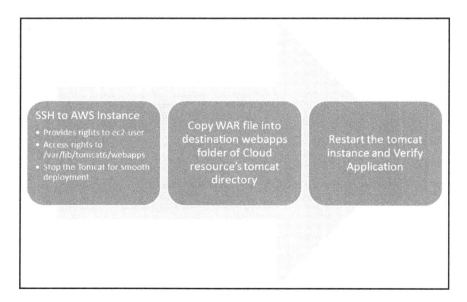

Let's configure the build job to execute deployment of WAR file in AWS instance by executing following command:

```
ssh  -i /home/mitesh/book.pem -o StrictHostKeyChecking=no -t -t ec2-
user@ec2-52-90-116-36.compute-1.amazonaws.com "sudo usermod -a -G tomcat
ec2-user; sudo chmod -R g+w /var/lib/tomcat6/webapps; sudo service tomcat6
stop;"
scp  -i /home/mitesh/book.pem /home/mitesh/target/*.war ec2-
user@ec2-52-90-116-36.compute-1.amazonaws.com:/var/lib/tomcat6/webapps
ssh  -i /home/mitesh/book.pem -o StrictHostKeyChecking=no -t -t ec2-
user@ec2-52-90-116-36.compute-1.amazonaws.com "sudo service tomcat6 start"
```

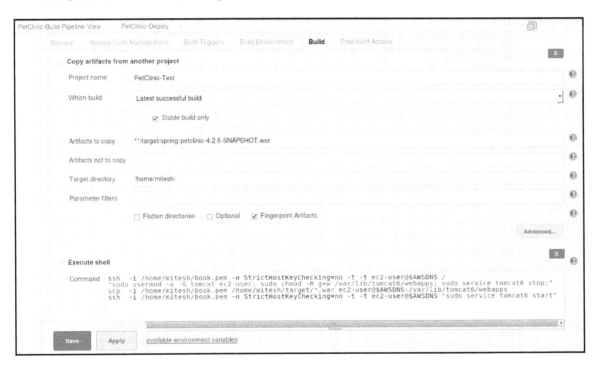

1. Save the build job configuration. Verify the **Upstream Projects**:

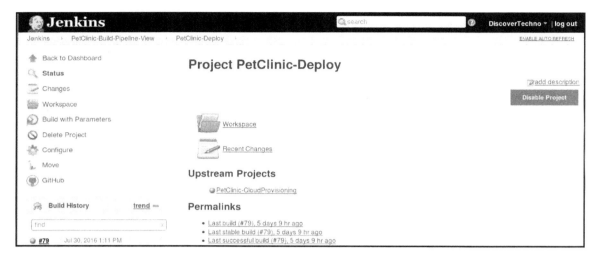

2. It says **PetClinic-CloudProvisioning**, so once instance provisioning in the cloud is completed, the deployment process will start:

3. Make sure to configure **Downstream Projects** in the **PetClinic-CloudProvisioning** build job.

4. The key downloaded from AWS must have proper permissions. If it doesn't, the shell command gives an error saying the permissions for the key are too open:

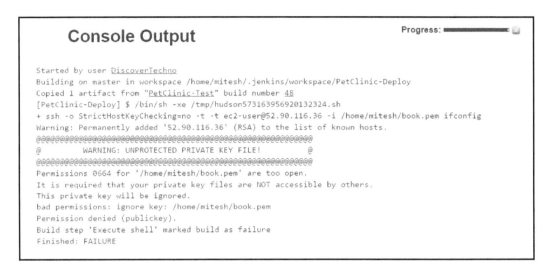

5. To fix it, use `chmod 600` to change the permission for the given file, and execute the command.

6. Once all build jobs have been verified as running individually, run the build pipeline:

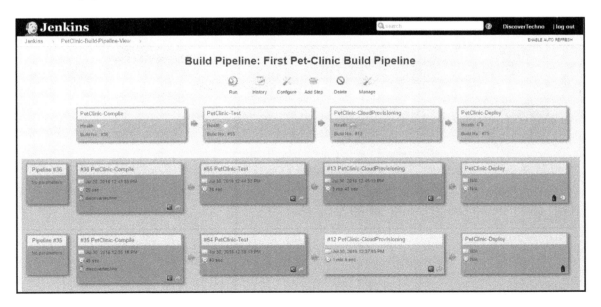

7. Once all three build jobs have been executed successfully, we need to manually execute the last build job for deployment:

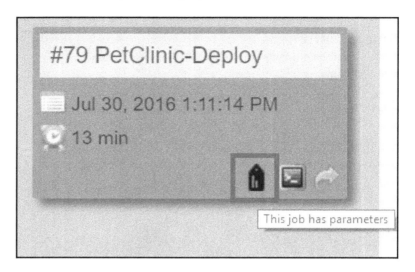

8. Wait for the build job's result:

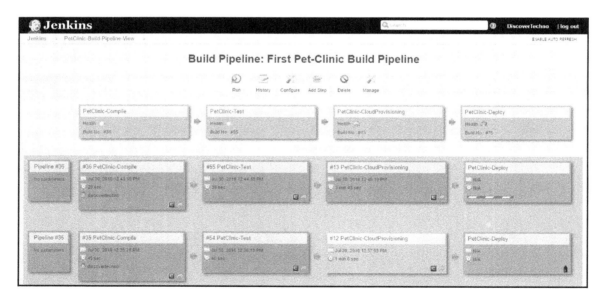

9. Once the application deployment is successful, we have all the successful build jobs in the build pipeline:

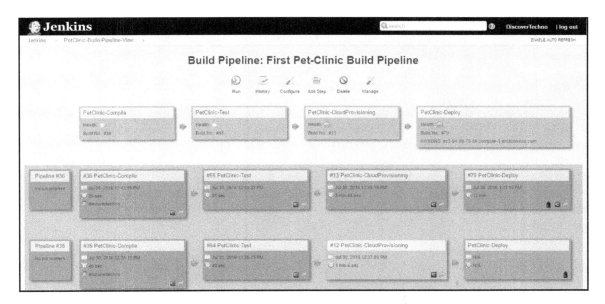

10. Check whether the application is running properly and whether it is configured in hosted Chef.

To deploy the PetClinic Spring application in Amazon Elastic Beanstalk (PaaS), we need the following flow:

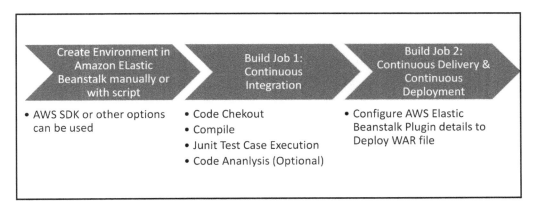

To deploy the PetClinic Spring application in Microsoft Azure web apps (PaaS), we need the following flow:

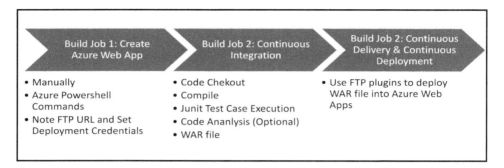

In Microsoft Azure's case, there is an alternative as well. We can use Visual Studio Team Server and TFS online for continuous integration, continuous delivery, and continuous deployment:

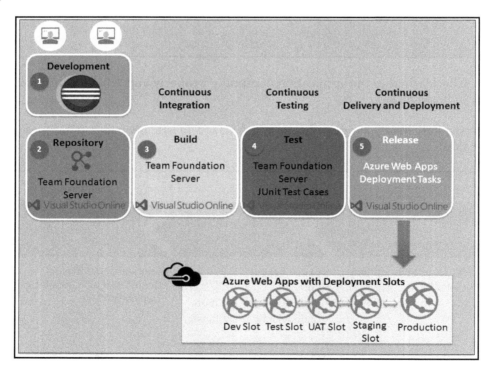

To deploy the PetClinic Spring application in a Docker container, we need the following flow:

Build Job 1: Continuous Integration

- Code Chekout
- Compile
- Junit Test Case Execution
- Code Ananlysis (Optional)
- WAR file

Build Job 2: Create Docker Container

- Create Docker Container from Community Tomcat Image
- Add tomcat-users.xml for Manager App

Build Job 3: Continuous Delivery & Continuous Deployment

- Use Manager App credential and Jenkins Deploy Plugin for Deployment in Docker Container

In the next section, we will see how to use the pipeline feature of Jenkins 2.0 in brief.

Executing the pipeline for application deployment automation

The pipeline feature in Jenkins 2.0 also provides features to orchestrate end-to-end automation for application deployment.

To give you an overview, here's a script that achieves checkout, continuous integration, cloud provisioning, and configuration management:

```
node('Master') {
    // Mark the code checkout 'stage'
    stage 'Checkout'

    // Get code for PetClinic Application from a GitHub repository
    git url: 'https://github.com/mitesh51/spring-petclinic.git'

    // Get the maven tool.
    // This ' Maven3.3.1' maven tool must be configuredin the global
configuration.
    def mvnHome = tool 'Maven3.3.1'

    // Mark the code Compile'stage'....
```

```
stage 'Compile'
// Run the maven build
sh "${mvnHome}/bin/mvn clean compile"

// Mark the code for Unit test execution and package 'stage'....
stage 'Test&Package'
sh "${mvnHome}/bin/mvn clean package"

// Mark the code Cloud provisioning 'stage' where instance is allocated
in Amazon EC2
// Once Instance is available, Chef will be used for Configuration
Management
// knife ec2 plugin will be used for instance provisioning in the AWS cloud
    stage 'Cloud Provisioning'
    sh "ssh -t -t root@192.168.1.39 'ifconfig; rvm use 2.1.0; knife ec2
server create -I ami-1ecae776 -f t2.micro -N DevOpsVMonAWS9 --aws-access-
key-id XXXXXXXXXXXXXXXXXXXX --aws-secret-access-key
XXXXXXXXXXXXXXXXXXXXXXXXXXXXXXXXXXXX -S book --identity-file book.pem --ssh-
user ec2-user -r role[v-tomcat]'"
}
```

1. Create a new item in the Jenkins dashboard, and select **Pipeline**:

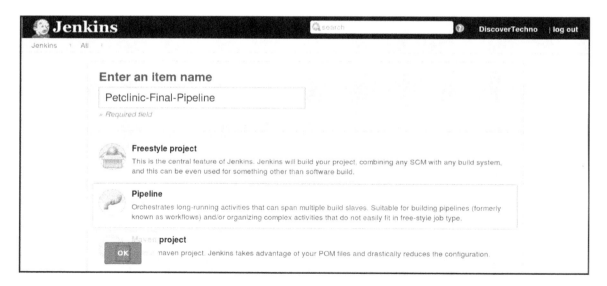

2. In the **Pipeline** section, write the previous script, and make necessary changes:

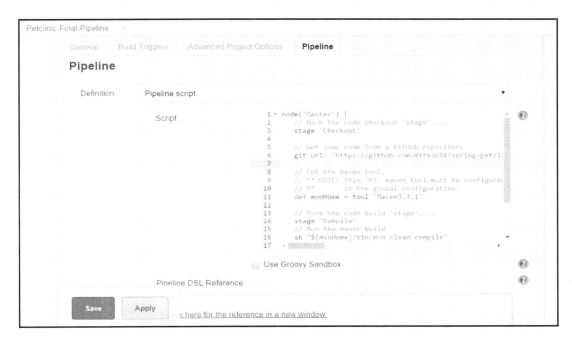

3. Once the script is modified and saved in the build job, click on the **Build Now** link and verify the execution:

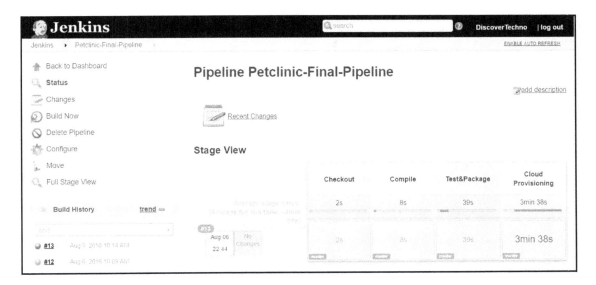

Check the DSL reference and use the script to perform all the operations. In the next section, we will get an overview of DevOps dashboards.

Hygieia – a DevOps dashboard

DevOps dashboards are also an emerging need. The point of having them is to have a view of all the tools in a single dashboard. **Hygieia** is an opensource initiative to provide a unified, configurable, and easy-to-use DevOps dashboard for an end-to-end application delivery pipeline:

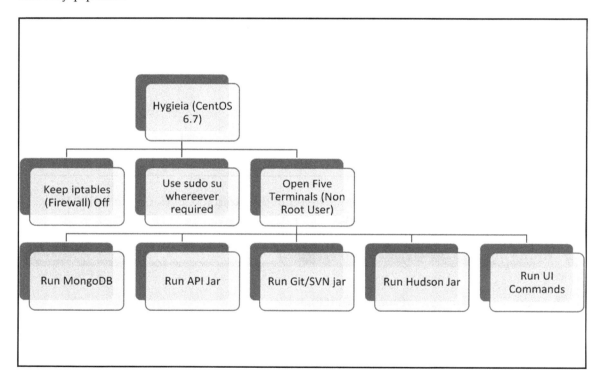

For the installation, visit `https://github.com/capitalone/Hygieia/blob/master/Setup.md`.

Once installation and configuration is successfully completed, we can create a DevOps dashboard that might look something like this:

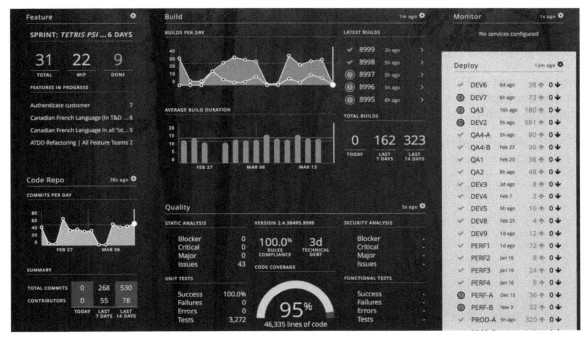

https://github.com/capitalone/Hygieia

We can configure SVN, Git, Sonar, Jenkins, and IBM UrbanCode Deploy in a Hygieia dashboard.

Self-test questions

State whether the following statements are true or false:

- AWS security groups need to have port 22 as an inbound rule to go further for configuration management
- A deployment build job is configured for manual execution with a parameterized job

Summary

In this chapter, we covered how to use a Jenkins build job to execute SSH commands to be executed on a Chef workstation for configuration management on an AWS instance, and we also covered setting up permissions for application deployment.

We used the build pipeline plugin as well as the pipeline feature of Jenkins 2.0 for end-to-end automation. This chapter provided a brief overview of all deployment methods covered in this book and how they are different from each other. It also provides a brief overview of deployment methods with respect to the build pipeline.

Finally, we covered the Hygieia DevOps dashboard as it provides an end-to-end unified view of tools used in the automation process.

> *"Every new beginning comes from some other beginning's end."*
> *– Seneca*

Index